Analysing
Social Policy

*Michael Hill
and Glen Bramley*

Basil Blackwell

Copyright © Michael Hill and Glen Bramley 1986

First published 1986
Reprinted 1987, 1988

Basil Blackwell Ltd
108 Cowley Road, Oxford OX4 1JF, UK

Basil Blackwell Inc.
432 Park Avenue South, Suite 1503
New York, NY 10016, USA

British Library Cataloguing in Publication Data

Hill, Michael, 1937-
    Analysing social policy.
    1. Great Britain – Social policy
I. Title   II. Bramley, Glen
    361.6'1'0941   HN385
ISBN 0-631-14691-1
ISBN 0-631-14692-X Pbk

Library of Congress Cataloging in Publication Data

Hill, Michael J. (Michael James), 1937—
    Analysing social policy.
    Bibliography: p.
    Includes index.
    1. Policy sciences.   2. Social policy.   3. Welfare
state.   4. Welfare economics.   5. Great Britain – Social
policy.   I. Bramley, Glen.   II. Title.
H97.H55   1986   361.6'1'0941   85-26682
ISBN 0-631-14691-1
ISBN 0-631-14692-X (pbk.)

Typeset by Columns of Reading
Printed in Great Britain by Billing & Sons Ltd, Worcester

Contents

Preface

Some years ago one of us, Michael Hill, was encouraged by Sue Corbett of Basil Blackwell to consider writing a book about social policy which would follow on from his basic textbook, *Understanding Social Policy*, by exploring in more depth some of the concepts and theories used in the study of the subject. His thinking on this subject was further stimulated by discussions with Gordan Chan, an academic from Taiwan, who was then engaged on trying to apply the often rather British preoccupations of social administration to the analysis of social welfare policy in the Far East. But Michael Hill felt unable to proceed with the idea of writing the book by his own lack of expertise on the application of ideas from economics to the study of social policy. Collaborative teaching of public policy studies with the other author of this book, Glen Bramley, then led to a solution to that problem.

Like all collaborating authors we run the risk that our styles contrast and that the 'joins' are very obvious. We have, of course, divided the responsibility for the different chapters, but have then worked extensively on each other's drafts. As we acknowledge in chapter 1, a book of this kind is bound to be in many respects a series of interrelated essays. Readers may wish to confine their attention only to specific chapters. However, for those who approach the book as a whole, and we hope most people will do so, we offer an exploration of most of the 'tool kit' of concepts and theories necessary for the study of social policy. We have tried to integrate a policy analysis perspective with the social policy and social administration tradition

Our intellectual debts to our colleagues, to students on the Public Policy Masters degree course at the School for Advanced Urban Studies, and to the many public servants we have met in the course of short-course teaching and research are too numerous for us to single out individuals for mention. We are grateful to Betty Hill and Alison Bramley for their encouragement, support, ideas and tolerance in the preparation of this book. Finally, we are grateful to Jean Harding and Pam Aldren for struggling with two of the more difficult handwritings they must ever have encountered, particularly in combination.

1

Social Policy Analysis

Introduction

This book is about the analysis of social policy in advanced western societies, written from a British perspective. As such it is an attempt to marry the relatively recent interest in policy analysis as a systematic intellectual endeavour with the rather longer-established tradition of enquiry into the nature of social policy, which in Britain has found a home in the academic discipline of social administration. We attempt to provide the reader with a framework for the analysis of social policy issues which is not bound exclusively to the institutions, traditions and intellectual assumptions of one particular context, the British welfare state. In doing so we draw on our own differing disciplinary backgrounds and on a wide range of theoretical and empirical research.

We are writing at a time when the economic climate for social policy has become significantly harsher, and when the political environment has moved away from the apparent consensus which supported the post-war growth of welfare states. The fundamental assumptions underlying the design of social policies are increasingly questioned, and any analysis must be explicit about the standpoint adopted. At the same time, in the world of practice policies must continue to be designed, or redesigned, and implemented. If there is a consistent theme running through this book it is that any practical proposals for the design and execution of social policy must be sensitive to the political and social environment in which they are launched if they are to be of value.

Most people have some idea about what is meant by 'social policy', often thinking of the 'social services' or 'the welfare state', and contrasting this with other aspects of public policy, 'economic policy' or 'defence policy' for example. It is not quite so obvious what social policy is when you try to define it and draw boundaries around it. The difficulties and disagreements here stem from differences in the kind of social theory which underlies any definition and the value judgements it embodies. As will become clear later in the book, such theory and value differences arise in any aspect of the analysis of social policy. Thus the discussion of the definition and categorization of policy which this chapter develops indicates some of the broad alternative frameworks within which analyses may be set.

The word 'analysis' suggests an approach to social policy which is rigorous, questioning, systematic and reliant on objective evidence. Beyond this somewhat idealized picture, however, it begs more questions than it solves. Is the analysis about what the policy is or what it should be? Is it about the execution as well as the determination of policy? Who or what is the analysis for? Is the analyst a detached observer or a partisan actor in the drama of policy development? In the latter part of this chapter we try to clarify the different ways in which social policy may be analysed, and relate the remainder of the book to these categories.

The idea of policy

What do we mean by 'policy'? First and foremost we would stress the point that in discussing social policy we are discussing an aspect of *public* policy, that is the actions and positions taken by the *state* as the overriding authoritative collective entity in society. The state comprises a range of institutions, and its policies can take many forms, but they share these essential characteristics of authority and collectiveness. In a sense this emphasis on the state as a collective, public entity is particularly important in relation to social policy, because the word 'social' in itself tends to imply the publicness or collectiveness of matters that relate to society as a whole, as opposed to the private concerns of individuals or small groups. Having said this, our analysis cannot ignore private individuals, agencies or behaviour. If social policy is predominantly about providing services, it has to be recognized that typically public services work in conjunction or in parallel with private, voluntary, informal, family and self-provided services. The implications of these interactions between the state as a service provider and other forms of social policy or social care provision are explored at various points in the book, and particularly in chapters 6 and 7.

Rather than offer our own particular definition of public policy we would initially draw attention to the following definition offered by Jenkins (1978, p. 15, attributed in part to Roberts, 1971): 'a set of interrelated decisions taken by a political actor or group of actors concerning the selection of goals and the means of achieving them within a specified situation where these decisions should, in principle, be within the power of these actors to achieve'. This definition is useful because it is carefully phrased to emphasize a number of features of public policy. Firstly, policy is virtually synonymous with *decisions*. However, an individual decision in isolation does not constitute a policy; rather, it is patterns of decisions over time, or decisions in the context of other decisions, which make a policy. Secondly, policy decisions are taken by *political* actors, whether or not the people in this role are formally designated as politicians (e.g. civil servants as well as ministers may make policy). We would interpret this as implying that the nature of the decisions makes them 'political', and this in turn is what defines the actors as political. Thirdly, policies are about *both means and ends*. Fourthly, policies are *contingent* in the sense that they refer to and depend upon a 'specified situation'. Exactly how the boundaries of this situation may be interpreted is one of the fine points around which policy debates may rage: for example, how far a commitment to maintain health service expenditure may be contingent upon economic and financial conditions.

Finally, the definition restricts policy to things which can in principle be achieved, in other words to matters over which the state has *authority*, and to actions/results which are *practically feasible*. This is a very significant restriction, which raises issues about the largely unwritten rules governing the proper role of the state, and also issues about policies which may be 'symbolic' (see Edelman, 1971) in the sense of not being seriously intended to be achieved in practice. We would not wish to interpret this restriction too strongly, since many of the most interesting issues in social policy raise precisely these questions. In chapter 8 we examine this and other definitions of policy more carefully. The preceding commentary on Jenkins's definition is intended to give a flavour for some of the key features and issues.

Classifying policies

How do we go about defining social policy? In asking what distinguishes social policy from, say, economic policy, we are looking for some criteria by which public policies in general might be distinguished and classified. Such criteria, if they can be found, may be useful in developing a further, more detailed breakdown of policies within the social sphere into sub-categories, and in suggesting certain inherent differences in the nature of policies which may be helpful in the subsequent analysis of policy. Let us start with the sort of everyday distinctions which spring most readily to mind.

Many people would begin by listing certain labels given to public policies or services, asserting that a particular group of these constitute social policy. The initial list would certainly include:

(1) social security (income maintenance, pensions, national insurance benefits, etc.);
(2) health services;
(3) welfare or personal social services.

Most people would include education, and many would mention housing. However, as the list was extended, there would be less and less unanimity on whether the policy or service in question was 'social'. Consider, for example, policies on job training and information, recreation, town planning or public transport. This illustrates the first difficulty with this 'conventional' approach to defining social policy – there is insufficient general agreement. We would also argue that this approach lacks any theoretical base. This hinders its general application, for example to other periods or countries, to other aspects of policy, or to the sub-classification of social policies. It tells us nothing other than what is commonly understood by the label in everyday usage in one particular culture. Despite these limitations, at certain stages in the book we find it helpful to illustrate theories under a number of these conventional headings.

A rather similar approach is that which defines social policy in terms of the *institutions* involved in the making and delivery of policy. Thus, in Britain social policy embraces:

(1) certain central government departments, notably the Department of Health and Social Security, together with associated ministers, parliamentary committees, etc.;
(2) certain local government departments, notably Social Services Departments, and associated committees;
(3) the National Health Service;
(4) other offshoots of government such as (perhaps) the Manpower Services Commission;
(5) (possibly) certain professional bodies whose members are

centrally involved in social services, e.g. medicine, nursing, social work, teaching, and associated teaching and research institutions.

This institutional approach, perhaps linked to the conventional one mentioned above, is often used to define social policy, particularly in British discussions of the 'welfare state'. It is still unsatisfactory for our present purposes, for the same sort of reasons as the conventional approach alone. It lacks generality, a theoretical base, and clear boundaries. In particular it is tied to a particular time and place, and not readily translatable to other countries where institutional arrangements differ markedly. It distracts attention from the role of other social institutions – commercial firms, voluntary organizations, the family – in dealing with very similar needs or concerns. To the extent that the 'mixed economy of welfare' may become more important, in policy terms and/or in reality, the institutional focus may be increasingly unhelpful.

An approach which suggests itself when social policies are contrasted with economic is to stress the *non-market* character of the processes and transactions involved in the former. This is a somewhat more helpful criterion, but taken on its own it is still inadequate. It reflects the *status quo* in terms of which services are in or out of the market, which is unhelpful if this division is subject to change (and change is the essence of policy debate). It is not difficult to show that there is in fact substantial interpenetration between market and non-market processes: for example, the resources used in social programmes (e.g. drugs, buildings) may be purchased on the market, whilst the operations of private firms are constrained by regulations imposed on 'social' grounds (e.g. health and safety at work). Heald (1983, pp. 18-22) contains a useful discussion of 'policy substitutes for public expenditure'. Again, the boundaries vary between countries (health is a good example); and the non-market sector is in fact far broader than what most people would regard as social policy: if defence is included, we seem to be dealing with a sector which is so broad as to be unwieldy and so heterogeneous as to require additional criteria to help sort it out.

The main conclusion we draw from this brief survey of 'instant' or everyday definitions is that they are inadequate because (a) they isolate particular attributes rather than bring together a combination of factors, and (b) they lack a coherent theoretical base which can be invoked to explain and justify any classification. In overcoming these shortcomings there are a number of theoretical traditions to choose from, and three of these seems to us to be important and helpful enough to spell out a little more fully at this stage. These traditions are:

(1) social administration;
(2) welfare economics;
(3) political economy.

Social administration

Although it seems, as the intellectual discipline which has grown up (if only in Britain) with the social welfare services, the natural place to start looking for coherent definitions, in fact it is difficult to find a single simple definition on which there is general agreement. Perhaps this reflects the practical nature of the discipline, where concerns with empirical evidence and policy development take precedence over theoretical debate. It also reflects the mixture of intellectual backgrounds which are represented in the field.

This discipline tends to equate the concept of social policy with a concern with welfare. Marshall, in an influential textbook, claims that 'the avowed objective of twentieth-century social policy is welfare' (Marshall, 1975, p. 12). More recently Weale (1983, p. 4) argues: 'that we should define social policy not in terms of a specific range of public policies or institutions but rather in terms of a specific set of dimensions of individual welfare'. The concept of welfare is then often brought together with the idea of a 'welfare state' which is seen as having a broad range of concerns which may include macroeconomic policy, regional and planning policies, taxation, the arts and recreation, but within which 'the provision of social services is its most characteristic aspect' (Sleeman, 1979). Weale sees his 'dimensions of welfare' as falling into three broad groups:

  (i) 'the distribution of the command of resources, particularly in connection with the contingencies of life' (e.g. sickness, invalidity, old age);
 (ii) 'some specific dimensions of consumption to which social importance is attached' (e.g. health, education, housing);
(iii) 'the individual's capacity to take part in the life of the community'. (Weale, 1983)

These suggestions are helpful in moving forward on to slightly more specific ground, by stressing the ultimate concern with people's welfare and the different components of this. The idea of 'contingencies of life' is introduced – essentially this is about groups of people who are in a situation of dependency. However, it is not made clear why certain specific dimensions of consumption have social importance. Although both the second and third categories have a 'social' dimension, the emphasis in Weale's work is on individuals, reflecting a liberal philosophy. We refer again to this approach in our discussion of needs in chapter 4.

Another liberal philosopher of social policy, Watson (1980, p. 10), stresses a somewhat different aspect when he quotes Boulding with approval: 'we can identify the "grant" or unilateral transfer – whether money, time, satisfaction, energy, or even life itself – as the distinguishing mark of the social just as exchange or bilateral transfer is the mark of the economic.' Thus, individual or social welfare will be affected by both economic and social inputs, with the latter being confined to the more limited case of one-way transfers. Another way of saying this is to say that social policy concerns redistribution, although the above quotation makes a particular point of stressing that this need not be in money, and Watson stresses the lack of this common 'measuring rod' in the social case. Equally important is the view that the unilateral transfer represents the 'fulfilment of an obligation' which helps to 'create a moral relationship between individuals'. The most influential writer within the post-war British social administration tradition, Richard Titmuss, gave most articulate expression to this view of social policy. He asserted that: 'all collectively provided services are deliberately designed to meet certain socially recognized "needs"; they are manifestations first, of society's will to survive as an organic whole and, second, of the expressed wish of all the people to assist the survival of some people' (Titmuss, 1963, p. 39). A number of points here are worth noting. Firstly, the statement covers all collective services, which implicitly includes things like defence. However, no neat divide into 'social' and other is possible on the basis of the two aspects of society's 'will' identified in the latter part of the sentence. Secondly, there is clearly a strongly collectivist (as opposed to liberal) philosophy at work here: society has a 'will', can recognize 'needs', and should 'survive as an organic whole'. This relates closely to the 'functionalist' tradition in sociology, to which we refer later on. Thirdly, and related, in so far as individual's wishes relate to selective assistance to other individuals, there is what seems to us a very strong assumption of consensus. However, if this is merely in terms of 'survival' (subsistence), without reference to the quality of life, perhaps it is not so contentious. Again, these issues are explored further in chapter 4.

A further quotation (from Titmuss, 1973, p. 283) underlines

the positive role perceived for social policy in influencing social values and relationships, and not just passively responding to them:

> In the last analysis, therefore, social policy is not simply about therapy for the dependent but about how people interact; and ought most of all to focus on processes, transactions and institutions which promote an individual's sense of identity, participation and community and allow him more freedom of choice for the expression of altruism and which, simultaneously, discourage a sense of individual alienation.

Very high value is placed here on a concept of community, or social solidarity, the intellectual roots of which can be traced to the sociology of Durkheim and particular emphasis is placed on acts of altruism. Social policy, then, is the embodiment of certain values and kinds of relationships which stand in stark contrast to the values and relationships characteristic of the economic market.

To summarize, the social administration tradition offers us the following criteria to help define and distinguish social policy:

(1) positive attempts to promote the well-being of individuals/ society, including compensation for 'diswelfares' imposed by the economic system;
(2) the diversion of resources to and promotion of the care of dependent groups subject to specific contingencies of life;
(3) more general redistribution of resources according to moral criteria;
(4) the promotion of altruism, through giving wider opportunities for its expression;
(5) similarly, the promotion of community.

This list provides us with some basis for distinguishing sub-categories within the social policy field. Firstly, policies concerned with (2), specific contingencies, can often be distinguished from policies concerned with the more general redistribution of resources (3) according to some principles of social justice or equity. Both these kinds of resources policies might in principle be distinguished from the promotion of altruism or community, at least in the sense that alternative means to the former ends might give a greater or lesser bonus in terms of the promotion of values.

The social administration tradition has come under increasing criticism on a number of fronts. This is not the place to review this critical literature in detail. We pick up some of the arguments in later chapters, and in particular in chapter 2 we initially examine the broad interpretations and explanations offered of the emergence of the welfare state. As an approach to defining social policy, or classifying policy in general, our main reservation concerns the emphasis placed on values. While recognizing that any recommendations one makes about policy rest on a set of values, it is making a rather strong assumption to assert that a large part of the policies administered and services provided by the modern state are founded on a generally shared sense of altruism. It is at least hard to demonstrate that this is so, and there are plenty of alternative explanations and rationalizations of the existence of these services. Much of the argument of Titmuss and his followers is based on the example of blood donorship, which is a relatively minor and arguably untypical case (for example, giving blood costs the donor little). The tradition seems sometimes to be concerned as much with the altruism there *should be* as the altruism there is (see, for example, Watson, 1980).

While the relationships between social policy, social values and social relationships are undoubtedly important areas for consideration in the analysis of policy, we find it difficult to utilize these ideas in a realistic classification of policies. However, the concepts of dependency and redistribution must be taken on board as central elements in social policy.

Welfare economics

The second tradition on which we can usefully draw is that aspect of the discipline of economics which has concerned itself with normative policy questions, conventionally known as 'welfare economics' ('welfare' here referring to a general concept of well-being, and not welfare in the narrow sense of certain social services). The classic statement within this tradition of the roles of the state is that of Musgrave (Musgrave and Musgrave, 1975) who identified three functions for the state in a predominantly market economy:

(1) allocation;
(2) distribution;
(3) stabilization.

These functions are seen here as relatively distinct; so much so that Musgrave postulated three 'branches' of government separately charged with responsibility for each.

Taking the *allocation* function first, with economics being the study of the allocation of scarce resources, it is not surprising to find the most fully worked out view of the state's role in this case. The primary mechanism for resource allocation in western mixed economies is of course the market. The overriding aim is taken to be efficiency in the broad sense (as discussed more fully in chapter 10).

A central theorem of microeconomics is that perfectly competitive markets generate an efficient allocation. The case for state intervention arises where particular assumptions underlying the perfect competition model fail to hold; cases of 'market failure'.

There are at least five distinct general sources of market failure, each of which implies a case for particular kinds of corrective action or intervention by the state.

(1) *monopoly* (or imperfect competition): the situation of one (or few) sellers in a particular market;
(2) *increasing returns to scale*: these raise issues of monopoly and subsidy;
(3) *uncertainty* about future contingencies or the requirement of specialist knowledge to take rational decisions;
(4) *externalities* arising where the actions of one economic unit affect another economic unit and thereby create a divergence between private and social costs/benefits;
(5) *public goods* are those providing benefits from which individuals cannot be excluded once provided.

Some of the literature also highlights *merit goods* as another category, where society deems the consumption of certain goods or services as being worth more than individuals are willing to pay. Although highly relevant to social services, this concept is difficult, at least for a liberal, to reconcile with the conceptual framework of economics, since it seems to require individual preferences to be overridden. Most cases can be interpreted as particular kinds of externality, as cases of redistribution based on conditional altruism or as cases where specialist knowledge is involved. Perhaps there remains a class of 'paternalistic' interventions which can be reconciled directly on the grounds that the recipients/beneficiaries are not, by common consent, judged to be autonomous agents, including children, the mentally ill and severely handicapped, and the confused elderly.

These categories (1) to (5) have some relevance to social policy. Obviously this is true by definition if by 'social' we mean non-market, but even on more stringent definitions they have some bearing. If certain social services such as health or education are characterized by economies of scale, then a subsidized, 'universal' supplier would be efficient so long as its monopoly power was publicly regulated or controlled. Insurance against uncertain future contingencies is clearly relevant to issues of dependency based on the contingencies of life mentioned earlier, although the case for comprehensive state social insurance rather than commercial insurance rests on wider grounds, not least distributional issues (Culyer, 1980, pp. 31-45). Some types of 'social policy' are clearly related to externalities, for example the neighbourhood and public health effects of bad housing. On the other hand, the major categories of pure public good – defence, law and order, roads, parks – are not in most conventional definitions of social services, whilst most social services are clearly not in this technical category of public goods.

Economics makes less detailed or confident prescriptions about the *distribution* function of the state. There are any number of efficient allocations which differ in how well off different individuals or groups are, and clearly choices between these involve losers as well as gainers and hence contain no basis for consensus. A market system will generate a distribution which reflects the endowments of participants in terms of property rights, wealth, aptitudes and skills; this may be termed *the primary* distribution of welfare. If the state is concerned about the final distribution of welfare, it can consider acting on this primary distribution, either by altering endowments (e.g. through altering property rights, or through education) or by interfering with certain markets (e.g. pay policy), or it can *redistribute* welfare through such mechanisms as progressive taxation, social security cash benefits, and social service benefits in kind. Economists have an efficiency orientation and a respect for markets as mechanisms for achieving efficiency, which tends to lead them to eschew direct interference with markets and rather to favour cash redistribution. This helps to separate the distribution function from the allocation function in the way Musgrave suggested.

On what basis should governments redistribute? Two distinct rationales are offered here. One treats distribution as part of the general problem of efficiency, by assuming that people derive welfare not just from their own consumption of goods and services but also from knowing that other people, particularly poor or dependent groups, have an adequate amount of these things. This approach invokes altruism (Collard, 1978; Culyer, 1980) and so raises some of the same difficulties and scepticism as we encountered in the social administration context. How widespread and substantial is altruism, beyond the immediate family?

The other rationale offered involves general principles of social justice or equity, claims which would be made regardless of their implications for efficiency or the state of individual preferences. There are a range of 'theories of justice' which seek to provide a philosophical basis for redistributive policies. Unfortunately these cover such a wide range of positions as to make any hope of consensus unrealistic (see chapter 4). Nevertheless, appeals to social justice are a powerful element in political debate.

As these comments indicate, in giving substance and normative justification to any stance on (re)distribution, it is necessary to step outside the economics tradition and appeal to writings in the field of political and social philosophy. The main contribution of economics has been to comment on the effectiveness of alternative forms of redistribution and to emphasize the point that equity and efficiency may be in conflict.

By *stabilization* Musgrave means what are generally referred to as 'macroeconomic' policies, which are attempts to influence the behaviour of economic aggregates such as the levels of investment, output and employment through rather broad policy instruments such as taxation, public spending and monetary policy. The view that governments have such a responsibility and capability is essentially a post-World War Two phenomenon, and there is less consensus now, in the era of the monetarist revival, about the scope and capability of macroeconomic policy than at the time of Musgrave's original formulation (see Brittan, 1977, for a sceptical view). Macroeconomic stabilization is typically seen as being concerned with trying to achieve acceptable levels of unemployment, inflation and the balance of payments, counteracting tendencies in the economy to booms or slumps. Its objectives tend to conflict and policy involves trade-offs between objectives, with governments assigning higher priority to one or another at particular times. Governments are also concerned about the longer-term growth performance of the economy, although there is even less consensus here about the appropriate degree and likely success of intervention (Smith, 1984; Blackaby, 1979). In Musgrave's scheme such policies would probably be seen as part of the 'allocation' branch (e.g. government backing long-term research and development to overcome uncertainty).

It is a moot point whether stabilization is in any sense social policy. Conventionally we label it 'economic policy' and, whether in terms of academic specialization, departmental responsibilities or the attention of the media, it tends to be analysed quite separately. However, the objects, outputs or outcomes of macroeconomic policy have important impacts on social welfare and the social services. Unemployment has been recognized as a central social problem since the era of Beveridge, with a clear link to poverty, and an impact upon health and other social problems (Showler and Sinfield, 1980). Inflation affects savings and financial assets, including pension rights, and affects the financing of housing in significant ways. Pay policy may affect the primary distribution of income. Most important of all, macro-economic policies are the main influence on public expenditure and thus on social policy programmes. We discuss this relationship more fully in chapter 5.

For these reasons it is unsatisfactory to exclude macroeconomic policy from the scope of social policy. It is understandable why it should be treated in this way, since clearly many wider issues and interests are involved. There is a temptation to treat 'the economy' and the imperatives of economic management as givens, part of the 'environment' of social policy. But it is precisely this very strong presumption in the political system to treat economic policy as an imperative, something prior to social policy, which is problematic for social policy analysts. To repeat the point made about distribution, policy objectives are probably best not reduced to a single higher goal (growth/efficiency) but recognized explicitly as distinct values to be weighed one against another.

How then would we define social policy in the welfare economics tradition? At the core of 'social' policy are the concerns of the 'distribution branch'. This can embrace redistribution in cash and in the form of services, policies (in so far as they exist) on the primary distribution of income, wealth and other endowments, and a recognition within policies that are primarily allocative or stabilizing of the distributional consequences of alternative options. This is still too restricted a definition. It should clearly be extended to include certain types of allocative interventions, namely:

(1) insurance against the uncertain contingencies of life which create dependency (unemployment, sickness, disability);
(2) the regulation of monopolies created by economies of scale or the key role of particular professions, particularly in the 'human' services;
(3) responding to certain kinds of externalities, particularly those which have potentially significant effects on individual welfares or which take the form of widely shared concern about the maintenance of certain values and relationships within society;
(4) merit goods, in the specific cases where paternalistic welfare judgements can be justified.

One of the main strengths of economics, its logical rigour, is also a weakness in that it exposes more clearly the underlying assumptions, which can easily be shown to be, in their pure form, either false or unduly restrictive. Clearly, much of the economy is not 'perfectly competitive'; this situation is not always matched by state intervention, and it makes it more difficult to give guidelines for how the state should intervene efficiently. The orthodox welfare economic approach is founded on the liberal precept that individual preferences should be the main basis for its recommendations, and has to be strained and stretched a little to incorporate the necessarily social phenomena which are significant in social policy. The approach is unashamedly normative, and does not pretend to offer an explanation of 'how we got where we are', a question which suggests more emphasis on the history of social policy and, of course, on its politics. This question forms the subject of chapter 2.

Political economy

The third tradition contrasts strongly with welfare economics in terms of the comments just offered. This is true at least of the main stream of writing which has made the running in intellectual reconsideration of social policy in the last decade, neo-marxist or critical social policy. The term 'political economy' need not refer to this perspective alone, and others use it; the essential element is perhaps the attempt to explain and interpret developments in policy as a political process strongly influenced and conditioned by economic processes and interests. We will concentrate here on the marxist/critical school.

Perhaps the best exposition of this perspective on social policy is provided by Gough (1979), who characterizes the welfare state as 'the use of state power to modify the reproduction of labour power and to maintain the non-working population in capitalist societies' (p. 44). Features which strike one immediately about this definition include the use of the word 'power', with its connotations of coercion, the technical marxist term 'reproduction of labour power', and the reappearance of a common element in all our definitions, the dependent population. We will come back to the idea of social policy as social control, but what first of 'reproduction'? Both aspects are best seen in the context of an overview of the functions of the state.

Gough offers a similar framework to one proposed initially by O'Connor (1973), and much referred to since. The state in capitalist societies is seen to have three broad functions:

(1) assisting the process of capital accumulation directly ('social investment');

(2) assisting the reproduction of labour power and hence indirectly assisting capital accumulation in the longer term ('social consumption');
(3) undertaking tasks necessary to secure the continuance of the system as a whole ('social expenses'), including legitimation and control through diversion or repression.

It is recognized that conventional policy categories do not correlate neatly with these functional categories, but this is implicitly a criticism of the conventional labels. Education, for example, is a mixed case; some aspects increase labour productivity and come in category (1); much is to do with general socialization, part of the qualitative aspect of (2). Gough sees social policy as being built around the idea of reproduction, and distinguishes a number of elements. There are quantitative contributions to the budgets of working households in the form of cash benefits (e.g. child benefit, national insurance benefits), regulation of the quality of key commodities, subsidizing their price and supply (e.g. housing), and direct provision of some services important to the continued availability of a productive labour force (e.g. health). There are also qualitative aspects, as mentioned in the case of education, and 'generational reproduction', i.e. the rearing of children. The latter highlights the key role of the family, which is recognized as sharing responsibility with the state, and we discuss this further in chapter 7.

The social expenses category is composed of a diversity of state functions which do not contribute to the economic system in its broad sense ('unreproductive') but which are necessary for the system to maintain itself politically. This function is generally seen as having two sides, the positive one of 'legitimation' – securing consent – and the negative one of 'control' – overcoming dissent. Particular policies may seem to have elements of both; for example policies towards inner cities and ethnic minorities. A radical view of social and community work is to see it in this kind of role (see Jones, 1983; Bailey and Brake, 1975). Other policies and services on the margins of conventional social policy – for example sports provision and training provision for young people – can be seen as having at least a diversionary, and hence indirectly controlling, function.

Social administration writers tend implicitly to take a special interest in 'human services', and Gough to some extent reflects this, referring (p. 4) to: 'human services involving interaction between consumer and provider with the aim of changing the physical, mental or emotional state of the consumer'. Although this kind of activity is implicit in our earlier definitions, and very important in much of social policy (medicine, social work,

16 *Social Policy Analysis*

therapy, counselling, rehabilitation, etc.), the radical school have put more emphasis on the potential this creates for control and compulsion which need not necessarily be in the true interests of the recipient. This creates something of a problem in our search for definitional clarity, since Gough's definition does not refer to legitimation and control. In other words, a strict marxist view of social policy might well exclude much of the activity conventionally seen as being at the heart of social policy. However, a definition broad enough to encompass these activities, and education, would then embrace the full range of state functions.

This is not the end of our boundary problems. Gough himself admits (p. 52) that state activities in relation to transport and public utilities (water, sewers, etc.) might act functionally to assist reproduction and thereby qualify within his definition of social policy. There is also a good deal of fuzziness about the boundary between labour power (actual and potential) and the non-working population. Children are seen as part of the future labour force, whilst the unemployed, some housewives and young elderly are regarded as the 'reserve army' of unemployed who serve to absorb economic fluctuations and keep wages down.

To summarise, the marxist political economy definition of social policy would comprise some or all of the following elements:

(1) policies, services and benefits which serve to secure the reproduction (adequate supply at low cost) of labour power over time;
(2) 'human' services, whether these serve the function of reproduction or control;
(3) support of the non-working population.

This approach represents a quite distinctive approach to the analysis of social policy, making different assumptions about the role and function of social services and policies. There are variants of the approach and some or all of these pose puzzles and difficulties. Some relate to the coherence of the initial definitions. For example, if social policy is primarily about reproduction, it is hard to see how control-oriented human services fit into this, or why some of the dependent population is maintained at all. Solving some of these puzzles involves theorizing about beliefs and values in society, rather in the way that the social administration tradition does. The political economy approach seems at its strongest in its attempts to offer explanations for the evolution of policies. Thus it features strongly in chapters 2 and 8. It also focuses on the interconnection of the economy, and economic interests, with social policy, for example through the phenomenon of 'fiscal crisis'. Here there is a strong parallel with our comments on the 'welfare economic' approach, where we argued that macroeconomic policy (and some allocational policies) raised social issues. This theme is addressed in chapter 5.

Before leaving the issue of definition and classification, and while under the general heading of 'political economy', it is worth mentioning some other policy typologies which exist. Lowi made an influential contribution to political science by suggesting that 'policies determine politics' (Jenkins, 1978, p. 95), or more specifically that policies vary in the way that government coerces and consequently in the types of political relationship this generates. We expand on this approach in chapter 8. It is difficult to relate the classificatory activity directly to our attempts at defining social policy, because it concentrates on political process rather than on substantive content of policy and its impact on the community.

A simple typology, developed primarily in the context of employment policy but possibly of wider relevance, is Davies and Mason's (1984) distinction between:

(1) restructuring;
(2) alleviation, or 'mopping up';
(3) redistribution.

The central thesis is that the status and resources devoted to policies is greatest in the case of restructuring and least in the case of policies to do with redistribution, and that this is most evident in the implementation stage of policy. Social policy is about both (2) and (3), whilst (1) constitutes economic policy. Restructuring generates a lot of casualties or transitional problems which require alleviation. Meanwhile, a basic structure of socioeconomic status and reward remains relatively unchanged by redistributive policies.

Defining social policy – conclusions

The definition of social policy in a theoretically coherent way is a more difficult task than might have been expected. Within any one theoretical tradition there are problems of unsatisfactory boundaries; choices between narrower core definitions and broader, more unwieldy ones; and unsatisfactory/unconvincing elements in the 'story' (e.g. altruism). Between the traditions there are few common elements, apart from support for dependent groups. Even redistribution, a key element in economic and social administration perspectives, is absent from the marxist political economy definition. This reflects in part the pessimistic conclusion drawn from evidence on actual redistributive patterns, which we review in chapter 3. Perhaps what this exercise in definition should remind us is that such definitions are always to a degree ideological, since they involve essentially contestable assertions about the causes, intentions and effects of policies.

Because of these difficulties of definition, in subsequent chapters of this book we adopt a pragmatic rather than a purist line in defining the boundaries of our topic. The bulk of the illustrative examples quoted come from the group of services or policies which are both conventionally labelled as 'social' and definable as social in terms of one or more of the frameworks outlined in this chapter: social security, health, personal social (or welfare) services, education, and housing. However, we also draw some illustrations from what seem to us to be interesting marginal cases, such as public transport and employment-related policies. More important, we try to highlight, wherever it seems relevant, the point that interpretations of the nature and function of particular policies or services are open to question and debate.

Policy analysis

Having started with the thought that we all know what social policy is, and effectively demonstrated that we should not be so confident, how are we to regard the other part of our title, the idea of analysing policy? What does 'policy analysis' mean? In the remaining part of this chapter we sketch out briefly what seem to us to be the range of ways in which policy may be analysed. We hope this is of some help to the reader in locating the kinds of analysis dealt with in subsequent chapters, and indeed in other work on social policy.

There are different ways of analysing policy, both in the sense of different questions that one wishes to answer and different methods one might employ to arrive at an answer. Firstly, there is the distinction between *process* and *substance* (or content). The systems model concentrates on the former, whilst our previous discussion of what is social policy dealt with the latter. Chapters 3 to 7 and 10 are mainly concerned with substantive issues, whilst 8, 9 and 11 are more about process. Chapter 2 is about both. Even this classification is superficial, in the sense that our own general stance is that policy analysis should always contain a lively awareness of both aspects. Within the process orientation, the concern may be more about the *determination* of policy or more about its *implementation*. Chapter 2 is mainly about the former, chapters 10 and 11 about aspects of the latter, whilst chapters 6, 7, 8 and 9 are concerned with both.

Another fundamental distinction is between *explanation*, an attempt to identify mechanisms of cause and effect, and *prescription*, where normative recommendations are made about what ought to happen. Values are clearly central to the latter, relevant social theory to the former, but accurate *description* involving the systematic examination of evidence clearly underlies both modes of analysis. Much prescriptive analysis suffers from a failure to take on board lessons about cause and effect and is consequently ineffective. On the other hand, we would reject a deterministic view of explanation which excluded the possibility of conscious choice and change based on a prescriptive mode of argument. Explanation tends to be associated with analysis of the policy process, but it has a role in the analysis of substantive policy choices in the sense that these involve judgements about the impact of policies on behaviour in the environment. Conversely, prescription tends to be associated with issues of substance but can also be directed to aspects of process, for example the design of organizations, the establishment of planning and budgeting procedures and so forth. We illustrate this in our discussion of efficiency innovations in chapter 10 and participation and judicial review in chapter 11.

Reviewing policy analysis in practice one observes a distinction, or at least a range of variation, between the relatively *detached* stance and the active, *committed* stance, whether on matters of process or substance (but particularly the latter). Some would identify *advocacy*, the selling of policy, as a distinct mode of policy analysis (Gordon et al., 1977). Whether or not this is seen as a distinct role, it reminds us that anyone engaged in policy analysis must ask themselves why they are doing it, what audience they are addressing and what effect (if any) they expect their work to have. We would regard the stance of this book as *relatively* detached, with a predominant concern about (a) explanation, and (b) the clarification of concepts, issues, arguments and evidence which are involved in any more prescriptive analysis of social policies.

Some further distinctions can be made about the methods available for answering questions about social policy. These are familiar issues throughout the social sciences (Ryan, 1970; Lessnoff, 1974; Pratt, 1978). Firstly there is the issue of how the relationship between theory and practice is approached. On the one hand, there is the *deductive* approach, where the starting point is some fairly general theory, or set of generalizations, from which one derives models which involve predictions about particular situations which may be tested empirically. Different levels of theory may be involved. For example, in the explanation of policy determination the emphasis may be on the 'macro' level of the structure of power and interests in society (as in chapter 2), or on 'middle-level' generalizations about mechanisms of demand articulation and regulation (see, for example, Hall et al., 1975). On the other hand, the approach may be *inductive*, or 'grounded', starting from the evidence observed in practice in particular cases or across a range of cases.

Secondly, there is the issue of *quantification*. Quantification is important in matters of explanation in so far as there are usually plenty of causal mechanisms which seem plausible in isolation but which may vary substantially in how significant they are in practice. It is perhaps even more important in prescription, since an awareness of how many people experience a particular need or how seriously it affects their lives must be important in influencing the priority which the issue is accorded and/or the resources that might be involved. The scope for quantification in social policy is substantial, although not so well developed as in the field of economic policy. Quantities are not answers to questions in themselves, since we are ultimately concerned with the meanings of the phenomena we count or measure. Quantitative approaches are less prominent in the explanation of policy processes, although there has developed a mini-tradition of utilizing statistical techniques to explain variations in policy outputs between local authorities or, more contentiously, different countries (see chapter 8). There has also been some interesting recent work on attitude survey evidence on social policy issues (Judge et al., 1983; Jowell and Airey, 1984).

The predominant 'technique' in studies of the policy process, however, is the *case study*, either of a single case or comparing a limited number of cases, and utilizing evidence mainly from interviews with key actors and the review of documentary records. There is now a substantial case study literature on social policy issues which deals with process and substance issues together, a good example of which is Hall et al.'s (1975) collection. To some extent this can provide comparative material for new case studies. There are issues and choices in the way case study evidence is gathered, which are not always clearly addressed in published work based on this method. These include the structuring of interviews, the reliance placed on key actors' own definitions of the situation, and the effect of the analyst's own role or intervention in the organization being studied.

Conclusion

This book is perhaps better viewed as a collection of essays rather than as the development of a particular line of argument through a logical sequence of steps. Certainly, the ordering of the chapters is to some extent arbitrary and the reader may find it most useful to pick and choose which to read, or in what order, according to the issues which interest him or her at the time. Taken as a whole, we see this book as providing a reasonably comprehensive coverage of the important issues in social policy, some of enduring interest and some of special contemporary relevance. Social policy in advanced western countries is in a phase of restructuring associated with a more profound questioning of received wisdom than was characteristic of most of the post-war era. The central theme of this book is that in such conditions there is a pressing need for bringing a policy analysis perspective to bear on social policy. Such a perspective involves a questioning of what social policy is, or can be argued to be, about. This chapter offers a number of alternative ways of interpreting the boundaries, roles and functions of social policy. It further involves an ability to link analysis of the substantive content and impact of policy with an understanding of the processes by which policy is determined and implemented; and it requires an ability to take realistic account of factual evidence about society alongside an awareness that values and preferences are also at stake and that political choices are always involved.

2

Explaining the Welfare State

Introduction

One concept which is, as we showed in chapter 1, very often linked with discussions of social policy is that of the welfare state. It is a concept of comparatively recent usage. According to Briggs (1967, p. 25) it was first used to describe Labour Britain after 1945. From there, he argues, it 'made its way round the world', being used to described 'diverse societies at diverse stages of development'. He goes on: 'attempts were made to rewrite nineteenth- and twentieth-century history, particularly British history, in terms of the "origins" and "development" of a "welfare state".'

There are problems about the usage of this expression. It embraces a variety of meanings, from a fairly basic minimalist one which sees a welfare state as one where the government has assumed responsibility for a variety of specific, and perhaps relatively narrowly defined, social policies. Hence any society where there are in operation statutorily guaranteed social security and health insurance policies, together with state education provision and perhaps some state intervention in the provision of housing, is likely to be described as a welfare state. But such a definition of a welfare state may be contrasted with much more all-embracing ones which suggest that the expression should only be applied to societies where the state has adopted a positive role in the management of the economy, so as to take steps to enhance social equality.

Given this spread of meanings it is possible to find, on the basis of broadly the same evidence about state intervention in social policy, some writers arguing that the welfare state has developed too much, undermining individual initiative and limiting personal freedom, while others deny that a welfare state exists at all. The former group see quite limited state intervention as the hallmark of the welfare state, the latter point out that state social policies have had little or no redistributive impact.

Furniss and Tilton (1977) have made an interesting attempt to tackle the underlying definitional issue about the welfare state. They point out that 'no modern, democratic state has failed to address the difficulties resulting from the operation of the "market" '. But they go on to acknowledge that:

> the major issue is not that all states have a policy of intervention, but that different states employ different policies for different purposes. Abstracting from the historical record, we can aggregate these different forms of intervention in three 'models': the *positive state*, the *social security state*, and the *social welfare state*. (Furniss and Tilton, 1977, pp. 14-15)

In this typology the *positive state* is characterized by the limitation of government intervention to what is necessary to enhance economic efficiency, 'to protect the holders of property from the difficulties of unregulated markets and from potential redistributive demands' (p. 15). The *social security state* has similar characteristics but endeavours to make a distinction between economic and social policy, providing through the latter a 'guaranteed national minimum' (p. 17). Hence Furniss and Tilton quote the Beveridge report as endorsing this approach in the following terms: 'the state in organizing security should not stifle initiative, opportunity, responsibility; in establishing a national minimum, it should leave room and encouragement for voluntary action by each individual to provide more for himself and his family' (Beveridge, 1942, p. 13). Furniss and Tilton then see the *social welfare state* as clearly going much further than this in placing social goals before economic goals. Such a state uses its power much more positively to ensure equality, seeing economic planning and wages policy as devices for this purpose alongside social security policies: 'public services remove important sectors of social life from the influence of the market' (Furniss and Tilton, 1977, p. 20).

In their book Furniss and Tilton go on to analyse the state's role in the United States, Britain and Sweden. They see the United States as a 'positive state', while Britain is a 'social security state' and Sweden a 'social welfare state'. Their analysis offers an approach to distinguishing the extent of welfare state development in a comparative way which gets away from approaches which examine aggregate expenditure on social policies and are unable to distinguish different forms of social expenditure or identify the extent to which they are truly redistributive (see Wilensky, 1975, for example, and the critique of this kind of approach in Higgins, 1981). In particular Furniss and Tilton recognize that really effective state intervention towards the enhancement of equality must rest just as much upon efforts to influence before-tax incomes as to redistribute through tax and social security measures. However, certainly many Swedish social observers would have reservations about Furniss and Tilton's tendency to idealize their society, and many radical students of social policy have suggested that the protection of the economic market system is just as much the hallmark of state policy in Britain and Sweden as in the United States.

Hence while Furniss and Tilton raise some important questions about the way we use the concept of the 'welfare state', and suggest an interesting approach to comparisons between states, the fact that they make their tripartite distinction in terms of the 'purposes' of state intervention begs an important question. It will be shown in the remainder of this chapter that the issue of 'purpose' is very much at the centre of dispute between writers who have sought to advance different explanations of the ways in which the social policies characteristic of the so-called welfare state have come to be developed in western societies.

The discussion below will not attempt to go further in exploring the definition of the welfare state, or in attempting to answer the question whether any particular state can lay just claim to calling itself a welfare state. It is regarded here as of more use to beg such questions by accepting the crude generalization that all the states of western Europe, North America and the White Commonwealth are to some extent welfare states, but then going on to examine the question, how do we explain the fact that all have experienced state interventions in social policy? When we have done that we can then return, in later parts of the book, particularly chapter 3, to those other questions set out above.

It should also be seen as very much an introductory presentation of issues which will be raised again in various parts of the book. In particular the link between theories explaining the welfare state and the notion of the 'crisis of the welfare state' will be explored in chapter 5, and the utility of various approaches to explaining how policy is made will be further examined in chapter 8. The idea here is to show the ways in which any attempt to explain how the complex of social policies characteristic of the advanced capitalist societies has developed requires attention to a range of social and political theories, which are the subject of intense controversy.

The influence of individuals

Let us take as our starting point for this discussion a view of the origins of social policy which was certainly encountered in school books not so very long ago, and still lives on implicitly, if not explicitly, in the way many historical accounts of social policy growth are written. This sees individual men and women coming to recognize the evidence of the incidence of poverty and on that basis seeking to persuade governments of the need for social policies. Hence accounts of the earlier developments in British social policy give considerable attention to the social investigations, philanthropic interventions and policy advocacy of, for example, Charles Booth, Seebohm Rowntree, William Beveridge, Beatrice Webb and Eleanor Rathbone. Key ingredients in this process have been seen to be the growth of empirical social science particularly devoted to the investigation of poverty, and the christian moral philosophy of T.H. Green teaching at Oxford in the late nineteenth century a concern for the whole community. An account of the life of Charles Booth, for example, portrays him as a successful businessman engaging in social research initially to try to prove socialist accounts of the extent of poverty to be exaggerated, but finding those accounts to be substantially correct, and accordingly becoming himself an advocate of new social policies and particularly a driving force in the campaign for the first state pension measure enacted in 1908 (Simey and Simey, 1960). But the individual most linked with British social policy development is William Beveridge, who is seen both as involved in the social security legislation of 1911 and subsequently the architect of the legislation of the 1940s (Harris, 1977). Beveridge was the son of an Indian civil servant who came under the influence of Green and his followers as a student at Oxford, and who moved into public service via the University Settlement movement in East London.

These patrician figures secure considerable attention in accounts of the development of British social policy. Yet, of course, such Whiggish 'great men' theories of history are viewed with great suspicion today. At the very best altruism supported by social investigation are seen as no more than ingredients in processes of social reform driven by wider social forces. An alternative formulation of the explanation of social change based upon the actions of individuals is one which sees commitments to social change underpinned by broader electoral forces. Then Beveridge and 'company' are seen as rather more backstage actors supplanted at centre stage by politicians – Lloyd George,

Attlee and Bevan in Britain, Roosevelt in the United States – whose commitments were underpinned by electoral mandates. Or perhaps such a formulation will have no place for the individuals, the British social policy reform of the 1940s being seen as neither Beveridge's not Attlee and Bevan's but the Labour Party's or even as the working class's.

What, then, we are beginning to contrast here are theories which see individuals as the architects of social reform with those which explain the emergence of social policies in terms of some form of democratic theory. Individuals are still likely to be involved in the latter kind of explanation as the people who help to establish, crystallize or implement the political agenda but the underlying forces are those of mass politics. But do such explanations of the growth of the welfare state move far enough away from the older individualistic ones? Should one move to explanations which turn away from methodogical individualism altogether? The next two sections look at explanations which do this, the first dealing with those which retain a connection with liberal democratic theory and are generally describable as within the traditions of 'pluralism', while the second looks at explanations developed from the marxist theory of the state.

Explaining the welfare state – liberal approaches

Reference has already been made to the extent to which some involvement of the state in social policy is a general characteristic of 'western' societies. Some studies of social policy have gone further than this rather weak generalization to suggest that there is some degree of correlation between economic development and social policy developments (see particularly, Wilensky, 1975). Studies of this kind have some difficulty in moving from demonstration of statistical association to development of a causal explanation (see Carrier and Kendall, 1977; Higgins, 1981). We will give further attention to the strength and weaknesses of this sort of comparative analysis in chapter 8. For our purpose here we wish to draw attention simply to its strength in indicating some very similar trends in welfare state development across societies, and its weakness in showing a general and very loose association between this and economic and political growth without providing a satisfactory approach to the explanation of the association.

Such studies do suggest weaknesses in other explanations. Quite clearly the demonstration that there is a considerable degree of similarity between social policy developments across a broad group of nations of similar economic development must give grounds for hesitation about explanations of social policy growth in specific countries which rest heavily upon the deeds of 'heroic' individuals or pressure from specific ideological political parties. These may explain the more subtle differences between nations, but the data suggest that something general has happened to the 'western' nations which lies outside these kinds of explanations. The developments these nations share, generally speaking, are, of course, industrialization and the growth of representative forms of government. These can be discussed separately to some extent but clearly relate to each other. To discuss very fully how they relate to each other would be beyond the brief of this book. In the rest of this section, however, we will examine how they together are related to the theme of the growth of the welfare state by theorists broadly in the liberal democratic tradition.

Room, in a valuable discussion of these themes, distinguishes between 'market liberals' and 'political liberals' (Room, 1979). The market liberals contribution has, however, been rather more normative than analytical. Their concern has been to develop ways of distinguishing the social effects of market processes in a way which will enable them to identify situations in which state intervention in society is necessary from those in which it will unnecessarily interfere with the working of market mechanisms. They recognize that the complex economies of industrial societies work in ways which produce dysfunctions which may either destabilize market systems or produce social effects which will lead to political opposition. They believe that most social allocation issues are best handled by market mechanisms and their concern is to delimit the exceptions to that rule. The particular way in which welfare economics has sought to assist with this was outlined in chapter 1. The 'market liberals' identify, therefore, a necessary role for the state to prevent individual economic actors operating in restraint of free trade, to maintain law and order, and to solve social problems which arise when individual actions produce undesired collective effects which the market mechanism cannot control. Their last category is essentially a small one; this is an essential difference between them and the marxists who regard the contradictions of capitalism as of massive significance. These themes will be explored further in chapter 6. The point here is that, while the general concern of this approach is to answer the question 'when is state intervention right', not 'when is it likely', the market liberals do recognize that advanced capitalism creates very many more situations where state intervention is likely to occur than do the simpler forms of economic development.

The body of theoretical work Room calls 'political liberalism' is perhaps more pertinent to this discussion than 'economic liberalism'. It has connections with the latter, however, for one of the questions some of those who have espoused this theory have sought to answer is: why does the state become so much more heavily involved in interfering with the economy for social ends than is appropriate (according to liberal economic theory) for the smooth working of the economy? Not surprisingly the answer they come to has something to do with democracy. The main plank of this argument has a long history. Those two leading nineteenth-century liberal theorists, Mill (1975) and de Tocqueville (1954), both recognized the threat posed to the liberal economic order by the growth of democracy. They foresaw that the propertyless, uneducated majority were, once enfranchised, likely to demand legislation which would interfere with free market processes.

But the 'political liberal' theory developed since that time takes this argument forward in a rather more elaborate way. Democracy is seen to work as a process in which competing elites leading political parties bid for mass support at election times (Schumpeter, 1947). This is the pluralist theory of the political process, one of the models for the analysis of political decision-making which we will explore further in chapter 8. This has been the necessary basis for the stable development of political institutions in a capitalist society, the 'democratic class struggle' (Lipset, 1960). In this sense the growth of political institutions has accompanied the growth of economic institutions, providing a mechanism for resolving conflicts arising out of the latter. However, the problematical aspect of this political process is that the political elites create a political market place in which they bid for power against each other (Downs, 1957). In the process they offer benefits, particularly social benefits. This leads to the rapid growth of state expenditure, which, since it is carried out in a context in which parties are equally reluctant to increase taxation, is likely to be inflationary and is likely to undermine the productive economy (Brittan, 1977). That contributes, then, to the development of a 'fiscal crisis', a topic we explore further in chapter 5.

So these variants of liberal theory see social policy growing out of some of the defects of the market process in a complex economy; but they tend then to see the baby (the state) produced by this process as growing rapidly, so that to some it threatens to become a monster. Of course, all the liberal theorists do not see the logic of the process as proceeding in this way. For some what has happened is that democracy has imposed upon the productive system a series of necessary constraints which stabilize both it and the political system. The masses have been granted a measure of political participation, essential if a complex industrial system is to work smoothly, which they operate responsibly without pushing their demands beyond the limits of the system's capacity. The management of the total system by the representative elites is of fundamental importance for future stability. This is the model of democracy in advanced capitalist society particularly cogently expounded by Galbraith, and very much associated with Keynesian management of the economy. It views the dysfunctions of market systems as very much more extensive than the market liberal suggest, but sees the growth of the welfare state as providing satisfactory solutions to these problems. We will return again in chapter 5 to examine further the case for this more optimistic view of the welfare state, against the views that it is in crisis which are outlined alike by many market liberals on the right and marxist-influenced writers on the left. In the meantime we must now turn for the purposes of this discussion to the latter group.

Explaining the welfare state – marxist approaches

The starting point for explanations of the growth of the welfare state rooted in marxist theory is the same set of issues about the smooth working of the capitalist economy which were the concerns of liberal theory. Marx himself developed, out of classical economic theory, an alternative view that market processes were bound to develop increasing dysfunctions. The principal victims of those dysfunctions would be the ordinary workers, the proletariat. They would experience increased 'immiserization' as they were forced to work for lower and lower wages or were forced into the reserve army of labour, the unemployed. The development of the capitalist economy, furthermore, far from providing increased benefits to people, would tend to destroy older pre-capitalist systems of family and community support. Ultimately Marx predicted the proletariat would rise up against their oppressors and replace capitalism by a socialist system.

A modern follower of Marx, who sees our productive system as still essentially capitalist, has therefore to explain why the chain of events predicted by Marx has not come about. He has to deal with the ways in which the character of capitalism has changed, explain why the immiserization process has not proceeded in the way outlined by Marx, and analyse the role the state plays today as a much more significant entity in society than it was when Marx wrote in the middle of the nineteenth century. He also has to decide how to characterize the self-proclaimed socialist societies of the Eastern bloc, determining whether they represent Marx's next stage in the transformation of society or some deformation of the predicted revolutionary process.

There are issues here which are, of course, beyond the brief of this book. Our concern is that clearly the development of a 'welfare state', in which individuals are protected from pure market forces and capitalism appears to have been brought under some form of control, does not appear as part of Marx's scenario.

One possibility here is that the welfare state represents the achievement by the proletariat of an accommodation with capitalism through the use of state power. Marx, while describing the immiserization process as historically inevitable, also urged the proletariat to develop class-consciousness through political and trade union action. For his immediate successors this political action generated a fierce controversy between those who saw it as merely a stepping stone towards revolution (above all Lenin) and those who saw themselves as democratic socialists transforming society by participating in the political institutions of the capitalist state. In this sense the welfare state may be perceived as the achievement of socialist movements, securing the partial trans-formation of capitalism. Amongst socialists or social democrats today, therefore, fierce controversy rages from time to time about the extent to which real social change has occurred in this way, and perhaps even more importantly about the extent to which this kind of action can be expected to continue to yield progress towards greater equality. It is for this group of people that the issues about what the welfare state really implies, particularly as far as its contribution to the reduction of inequality is concerned, are very important.

But many contemporary marxist theorists see the welfare state in a different way, not as concessions wrung from the capitalists but as the successful use of the state by capitalists to preserve capitalism. To them, as for Marx and Engels, 'the executive of the modern state is but a committee for managing the common affairs of the whole bourgeoisie' (Marx and Engels, 1848/1967). They argue that what has happened is that capitalists have effectively used the machinery of the state to help them solve the problems thrown up by capitalism. In part these problems are those which the 'economic liberals' also identify. There are some matters, like for example investment in and maintenance of human resources (education, health) which market processes do not deal with very effectively. But what the state also does is to help to legitimate the capitalist system (see Wolfe, 1977) by reducing the impact of some of its most unpopular consequences (unemployment) and by meeting needs that would otherwise cause dramatic discontent (pensions, housing).

Hence, much contemporary marxist theory about the role of the welfare state is based upon O'Connor's analysis (1973; see also Gough, 1979) of the functions of the capitalist state. Their treatment of this issue was outlined in chapter 1. To recapitulate, they identify three key functions: these are to provide *social investment*, *social consumption* and *social expenses*. It is, of course, the *social expenses* element in this theory that is particularly controversial. These are state expenditures designed to advance social harmony and legitimize the capitalist system of accumulation. A great deal of interesting historical evidence has been collected on this theme. Just as we can trace the growth of socialist and labour movements making demands, so too we can identify capitalist leaders and politicians warning their colleagues that they will have to make conciliatory gestures and concessions if they are to hold on to power. It was obviously particularly convenient to make those concessions by enhancing the role of the state, leaving labour politicians to perceive themselves as successfully entering the political arena, whilst leaving work-place prerogatives untouched. Of particular significance is the growth of what is sometimes called social imperialism – Bismarck in Germany, Chamberlain in Britain, Theodore Roosevelt in the United States – seeing a way of maintaining domestic harmony and capitalistic progress through social concessions at home and imperial adventures abroad (see Semmel, 1960). In the twenties and thirties, we see a different, more defensive, response as economic cycles became more marked and the working class became more militant, with concessions being advocated explicitly to prevent revolution (see the evidence in Gilbert, 1970).

Piven and Cloward have developed a more general analysis, using data from Britain and the United States for the period between the sixteenth century and the present day seeing: 'relief arrangements . . . initiated or expanded during the occasional outbreaks of civil disorder produced by mass unemployment and . . . then abolished or contracted when political stability is restored' (Piven and Cloward, 1972, p. xiii). Some of the examples in their analysis, however, seem to draw attention to what is the main problem about this kind of thesis. They cite amongst their evidence for increased unrest, which could lead to disorder, marked electoral swings to the left. The problem is, in general, in analysing the applicability of this thesis to the recent past; how is it possible to distinguish the social policy growth brought about by the increased demands from the working class, legitimately articulated through the political system, from the concessions granted by the 'wise' capitalist leader who perceives the threat posed to the system?

The title of Piven and Cloward's book, *Regulating the Poor*, reminds us of the underlying theme here which should be emphasized a little more. The older historical accounts of the welfare state, with which this discussion started, tended to emphasize the concern to legislate to provide a more satisfactory system of care for the poor. The very concept of the 'welfare state' implies such care. Yet a theme evident in radical accounts of the development of the welfare state emphasizes control – the concern to prevent revolution, the concern to legitimize the capitalist state.

This discussion has seen these issues in terms of class struggle. However, when we examine many of the measures characteristic of welfare states carefully we find, alongside those policies, that an analysis like O'Connor's could interpret in terms of their direct contribution to the support of capitalism, policies which are very much directed towards casualties of the social system. Many of these 'casualties' are individuals who would be very unlikely to pose threats to the capitalist system themselves. Indeed it is recognized in marxist theory that the 'lumpen-proletariat', the 'urban mob', are unlikely to become a class-conscious element in the struggle against capitalism. In this sense the notion of 'social control' has at least to imply a general concern for order regardless of the potential for class conflict. One difficulty with this is then that social control involves both measures to increase the legitimacy of the system and measures to increase control over dissidents. The characteristics of social policy, and the relative balance between ameliorative and repressive measures, will vary markedly according to which of these is given greater emphasis. The results may be very different in different kinds of 'welfare states'.

However, to return to our central theme, Marx was in agreement with Mill and de Tocqueville in seeing the potential conflict between capitalism and democracy. The same issue arises here that also arose earlier when we constrasted the views of those who, like Brittan, see democratic demands as threatening the market system with those like Galbraith who see an accommodation between the two as having been achieved. Hence in the analysis of the so-called crisis of the welfare state we find theorists from both the market-orientated right and the marxist left arguing that the ultimate conflict between democracy and capitalism is now beginning to emerge. As promised earlier, we will return to that in chapter 5.

Towards an integrated explanation

Can we put together an integrated explanation of the growth of the welfare state from these various separate approaches? It has been shown that the two interrelated issues of the inadequacies of markets and the impact of mass politics appear in a way which is not dissimilar in two approaches which initially appear to be very different. Of course they differ in their views as to where the driving force in the process comes from. For the right it is the excessive demands of the proletariat, while for the left it is the inadequacies of capitalism. Yet the basic idea of a clash between market processes and political demands is common to both theories.

However, it is perhaps misleading to lay excessive stress on the very broad general features which two relatively extreme theories have in common. More fundamental problems which concern both these two theoretical strands, and mark them out from other attempts to understand the growth of the welfare state, are (a) the extent to which they often seem to interpret the processes involved as relatively autonomous social forces rather than the results of conscious individual action; (b) the extent to which theories of this kind largely ignore the actors within the state; and (c) the extent to which they are unconcerned with the very different ways different social policy systems may develop. Let us explore each of these points a little more.

Much of the theoretical work, on either side, described above, treats the forces involved as relatively impersonal. The theories explain what has happened, rarely referring to the specific actions of individual actors. They represent the opposite extreme to the 'great men' explanations advanced earlier. In particular some of the marxist or neo-marxist interpretations of the role of the state see it as acting against the short-run interests of capitalism but in its long-run interests (Poulantzas, 1969). In this way they seek to explain the evidence of capitalist hostility to the development of the welfare state whilst arguing that the state is, in a functional sense, still the tool of capitalist interests.

But in a not dissimilar way we find non-marxist functionalist theories of the growth of the social policy in which the state is seen as developing to ensure social integration (see discussion in Mishra, 1977). This sort of theory, used to support the more optimistic views of the relationship between welfare state and capitalism, has been considerably discredited in recent years, and hence has not been fully discussed above. However, even the less functionalist theory, which was discussed, which sees state growth as a potentially uncontrollable destabilizing force for capitalism, tends to see electoral competition as a relatively mindless process. The evidence on the actual behaviour of political leaders only partially supports this thesis. It seems to have been particularly associated with pre-election expenditure growth during the period between the adoption of Keynesian economy-management in the 1940s and the shift to a concern with inflation and the need to restrain public expenditure in the 1970s (see Mosley, 1984).

Hence while, in the most general terms, it may make sense to interpret the history of the western welfare state as involving a series of uneasy trade-offs between capitalism and democracy, any more detailed discussion needs to look behind these general trends at the more detailed behaviour. One particular way in which this must be done involves analysing more closely the nature of the growth of the complex organizational system which provides the state policies, and asking whether it (or part of it) does not itself play a role in enhancing the development process.

This is a view that has been expounded by some of the theorists who see state growth as a threat to markets. Downs (1967), Niskanen (1971) and Tullock (1967) have each argued that once state organizations are set up the bureaucrats who run them will be driven by self-interest to expand their territories. Thus Tullock argues: 'As a general rule, a bureaucrat will find that his possibilities for promotion increase, his power, influence and public respect improve, and even the physical conditions of his office improve, if the bureaucracy in which he works expands' (Tullock, 1976, p. 29). The relevance of this kind of theory for contemporary developments in social policy is explored further in chapter 5; but there is also some interesting historical evidence available on the way in which the development of state activities was carried forward by committed groups of state officials – school inspectors (Roberts, 1968), medical officers of health (Lambert, 1962), alkali inspectors (Ashby and Anderson, 1981) and so on. The professionals became key policy advocates within the state system. Professional advancement and the public interest went hand in hand.

While Tullock and others have sought to add this dimension to the picture of welfare state growth provided by the right, theorists on the marxist side have seemed to be rather more reluctant to take it into account. However, in recent years an argument has developed about the extent of state autonomy. For the more functionalist marxist writers this often implies no more than an analysis of what they see as the tendency for the state to operate in the long-run rather than short-run interests of capital. Others have sought to widen out this to take into account the possibility of greater freedom of action (see the discussions of this theme in Offe's work (1984), where his earlier essays take the narrower quasi-functionalist stance but some of the later ones suggest a more flexible position). This argument has been taken very much further by some theorists influenced by marxism but perhaps more appropriately described as 'corporatist' (see the further discussion in chapter 8). Hence Cawson argues:

> the expansion of the activity of the state, as measured by the growth of the public sector, has created a 'vertical' grouping of state employees – or a sectoral location – with an interest in the maintenance or expansion of the level of state spending. The public sector has spawned a number of powerful working-class (trade union) and middle-class (professional) organisations which cannot be fitted easily into the class categories of marxist analysis. It is not at all clear whether to speak of, for example, doctors or town planners as members of a capitalist class or bourgeoisie makes any sense at all, let alone provides an explanation of the political determinents of policy-making within the public sector. (Cawson, 1982, pp. 52-3)

Cawson, developing an argument which also finds support in the work of Saunders (1981) and Dunleavy (1980), suggests that this public official influence is particularly significant in areas of consumption rather than production policy. This is a significant distinction. Some marxist writers (Offe, 1984; Leys, 1983) suggest that it is in the consumption sphere that relative autonomy occurs up to the point where the growth of consumption begins to have an impact upon the production process. This is then, as for some very different theorists on the right, the point at which a crisis is created for the welfare state by the conflict between the two (see our further discussion in chapter 5).

Another feature of Cawson's argument is the particularly dominant position he attributes within the welfare state to certain professional interests. This particularly fits with arguments which have developed on the key role of doctors in developing, and giving a particular shape to, the development of state-supported health care (Alford, 1972). Gould has taken this point further, seeing the new middle class as the main beneficiaries of the development of the welfare state both as workers within the system and as consumer beneficiaries from it (Gould, 1981). This view fits well with the evidence (Le Grand, 1982; Townsend, 1979) on the extent to which middle-class groups are the prime gainers from the development of the British welfare state. Room's critique of theories of the sociology of welfare reaches a similar conclusion on these points (Room, 1979).

Our last point about general explanations of welfare state growth follows in part from these observations. If, in fact, the major beneficiaries of that growth are either specific professional and administrative elites, who run the system, or middle- and upper-income groups, who derive substantial benefits from it, then explanations which attribute it to the solution of legitimation problems are to some considerable degree beside the point. This theme of 'who benefits' is explored further in respect of recipients in chapter 3 and in respect of functionaries in chapter 9.

However, in practice we probably need to develop an approach to explaining welfare state growth which combines the use of 'macro' theories, like those provided by both marxists and 'political liberals', with forms of explanation which give attention to more 'micro' factors: the special concerns of interest groups, the influence of professional and administrative elites, and even, exceptionally, the roles played by key individuals. If we do this we are likely to be better able to deal with some of the more detailed questions about welfare states. Once we have established that social policy growth has occurred in all types of developed western society, and that this seems to be correlated with the growth of industrialism and democracy, a development which may be explained in some way in relation both to the developing needs of capitalism and the impact of emerging popular participation in politics, we have still said nothing at all which explains the different forms that growth takes from country to country. Hence we have in no way addressed the issues raised by Furniss and Tilton, with their underlying suggestions that relatively similar systems may differ substantially in their redistributive impacts.

There are here a series of questions which comparative analysis of welfare state growth has not really started to answer. In addition to Furniss and Tilton's general issues, we may want to explain why, for example, state health policy has developed more effectively in Britain or family social security policy has developed better in France or public higher education policy has developed further in the United States. Any analysis of social policy development in any single country will want to explore the factors which have given it some features and not others, and may want to go on to the longer-run questions raised by Furniss and Tilton to see what further development is feasible. When the analysis of policy development moves to this level attention inevitably shifts back from the major factors which have been the main concern of this chapter to the more minor ones (as Heclo's (1974) interesting comparative analysis of social policy development in Britain and Sweden demonstrates). Throughout the rest of this book we will move to and fro between macro-level and micro-level factors to try to provide an understanding of the range of factors which need to underpin macro-analyses of the development of social policies.

3

Poverty, Inequality and Social Policy

Introduction

In much that is written about social policy an assumption is made that somehow it has as its fundamental goal the elimination of poverty, or to put it slightly differently, to attack inequality. This is an assumption which we will examine critically in this chapter. Its centrality to the analysis of social policy has led us to put it at this early stage in this book. However, the things we have to say about this issue need to be related very closely to our discussion of the use of the concept of need in social policy, which is the subject of the next chapter.

Many writers on social policy seem to us to take for granted its concerns with poverty and inequality. We have already made clear our scepticism on this point. Our scepticism is clearly shared by many modern radical analysts of social policy. However it is interesting to note how often these writers cast their analyses in terms of a challenge to that dominant assumption. Perhaps one day books on social policy will cease to do this, but meanwhile we, in an exploration of the concepts used in social policy, clearly cannot ignore the role the debate about the nature of poverty and the impact of social policy upon it has played in discussions of our subject.

In chapter 1 we identified redistribution, implicitly in favour of the poor, as a central element in definitions of social policy employed in social administration or welfare economics. However, we also showed that this element was absent from definitions in the marxist political economy tradition. We showed that social policy was also about things other than redistribution, for example the promotion of certain kinds of relationships, dealing with certain market failures, or social control. A key feature in all definitions, however, was provision for dependent groups in the population, involving redistribution of a predominantly 'horizontal' kind in favour of, for example, certain demographic groups. The importance of this aspect of social policy emerges strongly in this chapter.

We consider first issues about the definition of poverty, and its relationship both to income inequality and to other forms of inequality. From that we will be able to go on to the exploration of some of the questions raised about the actual relationship between social policy and poverty or inequality.

Defining and measuring poverty

Poverty is one of those words which seems at first sight to be easy to define. On looking for help to a dictionary we found, of course, that it was defined as 'the state of being poor'. The relevant definitions of poor were 'possessing little or nothing; without means; needy; deficient'. We see here then a mixture of ideas, nicely illustrated by the notion of 'little or nothing'. At the worst extremes there is no ambiguity about poverty, but how far away from those extremes do people have to be to still be regarded as poor? At the time of writing there are pictures nightly on television of starving people in Ethiopia. Clearly they are poor. But if they are fed regularly so that the danger of death from malnutrition is lifted will they still be poor? Most people will answer that question in the affirmative. But then if they continue to prosper so that needs for good food are fully satisfied and other needs begin to be met, gradually some observers might begin to conclude that they are no longer 'in poverty', or that they have been brought 'above the poverty line'. Such remarks suggest that those who make them have, in their heads, some absolute standard, some concept of a 'line'. Yet the Ethiopians would probably still be, relatively speaking, deprived people.

At this stage some readers may begin to object that we are describing a silly and empty semantic argument. They may say: 'of course we nearly all have needs which we lack the financial resources to meet, we nearly all feel "poor" relative to some people.' Hence they may want to argue: 'what is so special about distinguishing between poverty and relative inequality or relative deprivation?' One answer may be that statements about poverty have a moral and political force which statements about relative inequality lack. Furthermore political goals and policy objectives have been formulated with reference to definitions of poverty, and concepts like 'the poverty line' have been used to determine scales of benefit to be used in relief and social security policies.

In the earlier years of this century quantifiable definitions of the poverty line were used in political controversy to seek to persuade governments there was a problem of poverty, and those definitions were taken into account in the determination of policies. In Britain studies of poverty by Rowntree (1901, 1941) and Rowntree and Lavers (1951) using such an approach were very influential. Townsend describes Rowntree's approach as follows:

> In 1899 he collected detailed information about families in York. He defined families whose 'total earnings are insufficient to obtain the minimum necessaries for the maintenance of merely physical efficiency as being in primary poverty'. Making shrewd use of the work of W.O. Atwater, an American nutritionist, reinforced by the findings of Dr. Dunlap, who had experimented with the diets of prisoners in Scotland to find how nutritional intakes were related to the maintenance of body weight, he estimated the average nutritional needs of adults and children, translated these needs into quantities of different foods and hence into the cash equivalent of these foods. To these costs for food he added minimum sums for clothing, fuel and household sundries according to size of family. . . .
> Rent was treated as an unavoidable addition to this sum, and was counted in full. A family was therefore regarded as being in poverty if its income minus rent fell short of the poverty line. (Townsend, 1979, p. 33)

Rowntree influenced numerous other studies of poverty and replicated his own study of York in 1936 (Rowntree, 1941) and 1950 (Rowntree and Lavers, 1951). Even more importantly his approach influenced definitions of minimum levels for relief payments in Britain and many other countries.

Rowntree's approach is not unassailable even on its own terms. His assumptions about minimum nutritional needs have been challenged, and the addition of minimum assumptions about other domestic costs leaves him open to a variety of challenges. We do not propose to go into those arguments in detail. What instead we want to emphasize is that Rowntree has been seen as providing an 'objective', 'scientific' definition of poverty; one that enables people to argue that while there is manifestly poverty in Ethiopia there is little in Britain today. That was indeed how Rowntree argued, presenting in his 1950 study 'evidence' that the welfare state had largely eliminated 'primary poverty'. 'Secondary poverty' remained a problem. That was, in Rowntree's terms, poverty arising because many low-income people did not follow the kind of 'rational' principles of domestic budgeting assumed in Rowntree's definition of primary poverty. They spent money on convenience foods or Christmas presents or, worse, tobacco and drink!

These comments on Rowntree's distinction between primary and secondary poverty highlight the two fundamental problems about his approach. First, that embedded in his concept of minimum standards are assumptions about how low-income people *ought* to behave. It is a very rigid and harsh approach to offer an objective definition of poverty which assumes that there is no longer an income distribution problem but only a behavioural problem when incomes are still so low that any departure from 'rational budgeting' (as, of course, defined by a non-poor student of poverty) causes hardship (in terms of the original 'objective' definition). Second, despite Rowntree's concern to provide a firm objective yardstick applicable at any time and in any place, his concept of minimum necessities contains what can be described as cultural assumptions. The additions for clothing, fuel and household sundries would undoubtedly have been lower if he had made similar estimates a hundred years earlier, and probably therefore needed substantial revisions between 1899 and 1950. His approach to the issue of housing costs ducked a similar issue as far as that element in budgets was concerned. These reservations suggest severe limitations in the extent to which Rowntree's approach can be used cross-culturally. But, most fundamentally of all, does not this flaw in the so-called objective approach suggest that whether people are so seriously disadvantaged as to be judged as in poverty is something we can only say by making a comparison between the life styles their incomes provide and the life styles of other people in their society?

Do these reservations about the attempt to define absolute poverty in Rowntree's work drive us back to an *essentially* relative definition? Peter Townsend, perhaps the most important British student of poverty, believes that it need not. We are not so sure. Let us have a look at how Townsend tackles this issue, before we express our reservations. According to Townsend:

> poverty is insufficient resources (i.e. widening the idea of income to include assets and goods and services in kind) to obtain the conditions of life, i.e. the diets, amenities, standards and services to allow people to play the roles, participate in the relationships and follow the customs which are expected of them as citizens. . . . Poverty is more

than inequality. It is a state of demonstrable deprivation (as measured by premature death, disability or ill health, lack of the common facilities of membership of society and withdrawal from or denial of participation in common social roles and relationships. (Townsend, 1984, pp. 12-13)

Because Townsend described his approach to the definition of poverty as a 'relative deprivation' approach he has been attacked as not offering, as his observation above acknowledges, a way of distinguishing poverty from inequality. However, in his large empirical study of poverty in the United Kingdom he set out to show that it is possible to ascertain income levels below which individuals are unlikely to enjoy material goods, amenities and patterns of social life generally available to the rest of the population. He developed a 'deprivation standard of poverty' using a set of indicators of benefits the poor were unlikely to be able to enjoy. Such an index was based, of course, upon correlational analysis – he does not suggest that individuals in the group below the poverty line never enjoy any of these benefits; that depends on how they choose to spend their money. By approaching his subject in this way he naturally avoids the Rowntree 'primary'/'secondary' poverty distinction. He is saying that below his 'deprivation standard' poverty line poor people are unlikely to enjoy these benefits – if they choose nevertheless to enjoy some they do so at the expense of other things (perhaps those things Rowntree would have defined as necessities).

In some of his more recent work Townsend has given particular attention to the relationship between poverty and ill-health in Britain (Townsend and Davidson, 1982). The strong evidence here of a correlation between income and health offers, perhaps more strongly than Townsend's earlier emphasis upon social behaviour indices, a good argument for regarding low income as a cause for concern – a concern which can be expressed with more force if it is described as poverty. There are good grounds for saying that poverty does not only kill people in Ethiopia it also does so, albeit in a less obvious way, in Britain. There is, in this approach, therefore an attempt to give the concept of poverty a moral force, comparable to the similar approach adopted by some social philosophers (particularly Plant et al., 1980) to the concept of need. This is explored further in the next chapter.

We accept that Townsend's approach to the definition of poverty has a firmer basis than those who would dismiss it as 'merely relative'. He has demonstrated most effectively the flaws in Rowntree's claim to offer a 'scientific' definition of poverty.

Yet he seems at times to be too strongly wedded to an alternative definition similarly rooted in the positivist canons of traditional social science. He sees as his goal the need to put theory and methodology 'on to a respectable scientific footing' (Townsend, 1979, p. 60). In doing this he lays himself open to the criticism that he makes normative assumptions about the social and cultural considerations which are used to help him define his poverty line (Piachaud, 1981). Townsend has made an enormous contribution to the careful study of the correlates and consequences of low income in Britain and in other societies. We agree that there is ample moral justification for using the strong term, poverty, to describe the condition of large numbers of low-income people in Britain; but the description of his approach as scientific implies that his particular selection of definition points for the poverty line has somehow greater objectivity than the alternative definitions chosen by other researchers. In our view, since we think there is no case for going back to so-called 'absolute' definitions of poverty, it is important to recognize that poverty means an unacceptable level of deprivation, and that any view of what is unacceptable will be coloured by the degree of inequality, particularly observable inequality reflected in different patterns of social behaviour. Moreover such observations will typically be made within societies as well as between them. Social policies are after all largely created *within* societies.

In outlining the so-called 'absolute' approach to the issue of poverty, and in contrasting the way in which Townsend has been able to develop a more relative approach which offers more than merely a way of measuring income inequality, we have by no means exhausted the possible approaches to the subject of poverty and inequality. A recent study by Mack and Lansley (1985), for example, has developed a variant on Townsend's approach which relates what poor people can afford to a list of 'necessities' established by means of an opinion survey. There are, in particular, two other approaches, one of which does indeed rest very firmly on the inequality criterion alone whilst the other tries to use another clear yardstick for the definition of poverty.

The approach which avoids the problem of the definition of poverty altogether looks at income relativities, examining relationships within the income distribution. Hence much of the work done in Britain for the Royal Commission on the Distribution of Income and Wealth highlighted (see particularly its 6th Report, 1978) the evidence on the relationship between the lowest quartile or the lowest 10 per cent in the income distribution and the income distribution as a whole. This was clearly important for the examination of the correlates of low income, and for the consideration of the relationship between low income from social security benefits and low income from wages and other sources.

The other approach, which features to a considerable extent in Townsend's work alongside his other measures, involves using the state's definition of the poverty line, enshrined in the minimum-income scales set for social assistance purposes. Studies have looked at the evidence on the numbers falling below that level and on the numbers only a small amount above. For example, Abel-Smith and Townsend's study published in 1965, *The Poor and the Poorest*, which played an important role in the shaking of British complacency about poverty, related incomes to the social assistance (then called national assistance) scale and also looked at people falling in the various income bands up to 40 per cent above that scale level. What was particularly important about that study was the evidence it provided on the large number of people below national assistance level not getting help from that source, and on the numbers of people only barely above that level.

Clearly there is nothing particularly 'objective' about a state-determined minimum level. In the British case the original setting of that level was influenced by Rowntree's studies, but the subsequent history of the uprating of the scale has been an erratic one depending upon incremental political decisions (see Barr, 1981). Nevertheless studies which relate data on poverty to an official 'poverty line' can have some political force. Such a line, developed by Orshansky (1969) secures considerable attention in political debate in the United States. It uses a figure, like Rowntree's, which is based on the cost of a minimum diet but is then multiplied by three on the basis of evidence that the average American family spends one-third of its income on food. Even if they can say nothing about the actual adequacy of that line it is likely to be important to show how the incomes of those who do not receive social assistance relate to the line.

There are, however, ways in which studies which focus on officially set 'poverty lines' can develop significant arguments about low incomes. The official 'lines' may be related to other data on, for example, average earnings. Perhaps even more important are studies which monitor the movement of the official lines over time in relation to movements in general incomes and earnings (Barr, 1981). In Britain the pressure groups have monitored those movements very carefully in the recent past, armed by the academic studies which initially made such an exercise possible.

Poverty and inequality: a wider perspective

In the previous section considerable attention was given to Peter Townsend's work because of the important role it has played in moving the terms of discussion of poverty away from an emphasis upon a narrow income-based absolute definition. You will notice how in his 1984 definition he emphasized the importance of considering poverty in terms of insufficient resources, including assets and goods and services in kind. That emphasis is very important if poverty is to be considered in the context of wider questions about inequality in society. Its examination must then include issues about the distribution of wealth, including assets in non-cash forms such as houses and possessions. It must include services in kind, both those provided by the state and those provided by others (employers, neighbours, family, etc.). Finally it needs to take into account assets in forms which, whilst not necessarily realizable at the time, will eventually contribute to enhancing the well-being of the individual, that is rights to pension, assistance when sick and so on.

An essay of great importance for its discussion of the need to take a wide view of the distribution of social advantages was Richard Titmuss' 'Social Divisions of Welfare' (in Titmuss, 1963). Titmuss' work has been followed up not only by Townsend but also in a subsequent essay on the same theme by Sinfield (1978). These contributions show how, alongside the public welfare sector, there is a private welfare sector which is, even in Britain's so-called welfare state, probably larger. Within this private sector employees secure extensive benefits in cash and kind – pensions, sick pay schemes, subsidized meals, subsidized cars and transport, leisure facilities and so on. The distribution of these benefits additional to basic pay is considerably skewed towards those in the higher income brackets. Hence Titmuss sought to show, when it was being argued that the poor gained extensive benefits from the welfare state (a proposition which we shall want to examine critically below), that those were likely to be more than counterbalanced by private systems of 'welfare', whose benefits went disproportionately to the non-poor.

Townsend examined this issue quantitatiely in his study of poverty in the United Kingdom. He asked questions about 'meals subsidies and vouchers, subsidized and free travel, . . . use of a firm's car . . . for personal purposes, free goods, medical expenses received or covered, shares or options to purchase shares, life insurances, educational expenses, free and subsidized accommodation' (Townsend, 1979, p. 216), as well as rights to pensions and sick pay. His conclusions were that 'The total value of employer welfare benefits correlates highly with income' and that 'Welfare benefits are distributed more unequally than earnings' (pp. 217-18).

In this discussion private rights to pensions and sick pay have featured as significant elements. Leaving on one side for the time being the question of public rights of this kind, an important related question about poverty is its distribution over individual life cycles. To what extent are the poor always poor, or are there specific points in individual life cycles when poverty is particularly likely to occur, separated by periods when most of those people are likely to enjoy a reasonable degree of prosperity. Certainly this was how Rowntree portrayed the incidence of poverty in the first of his studies (Rowntree, 1901, p. 171).

This picture of a life cycle of incidence of poverty has been influential in Britain. It has fuelled arguments for particular social security interventions – in the provision of family allowances or child benefits, and in the provision of pensions. Despite these interventions it remains the case that poverty is widespread at times of high commitments to the care of young children and during old age. Pressure groups concerned with family poverty and poverty amongst the elderly continue to accumulate substantial evidence on these two 'peaks' in the life cycle, and sometimes find it difficult to avoid being perceived by politicians as competing lobbies for scarce resources.

Yet Rowntree's is a generalization about the British working-class family at a particular point in time. We should beware giving that generalization universal validity. First, his example is of a relatively low wage earner sufficiently close to the poverty line to be driven below it at various points in his life. It is not self-evident that wage levels will necessarily always be above the poverty line for single people. Clearly, taking an overall view about inequality, differentials play a central part in determining differential life chances. Second, Rowntree's assumption is that work is available. The incidence of unemployment, however, may be of considerable importance in adding other spells in poverty during the life cycle. Furthermore, as Townsend (1979) and Sinfield (1981) have shown, the burden of unemployment is very often 'unequal'. The experience of unemployment, certainly in Britain and the United States, is not shared evenly across the labour force. That section of the population who tend to be least well paid when in work are also more likely than others to experience long-term and/or frequent unemployment. As Liebow puts it: 'Unemployment does not, like air pollution or God's gentle rain, fall uniformly upon everyone . . . it strikes from underneath, and it strikes particularly at those at the bottom of our society' (Liebow, 1970, p. 28). Third, Rowntree makes some significant assumptions about the roles of post-school-age children, that they will be earners and that they will remain in the household until they marry. Neither of these assumptions can be made in Britain today. A new phenomenon has emerged, of unemployment amongst young people. Furthermore, Rowntree takes this form of inter-generational support for granted; something which many will want to question. Finally Rowntree's observations on the family cycle of poverty implied family and sex role assumptions which modern readers will want to challenge. In Rowntree's time, as in contemporary Britain, women who went to work received, in general, much lower wages than men. Most women caring for families on their own did not, and generally still do not, experience a life cycle in and out of poverty; they experienced continuous poverty; and the question that all propositions about poverty which treat families as single units do not ask is: what income transfers occur within those families? When Rowntree's working men were in the relatively prosperous part of the cycle, to what extent did their wives share in that prosperity?

Notwithstanding reservations of this kind Townsend sees the life cycle pattern of poverty as still important in Britain, indeed in some respects more important (Townsend, 1984, p. 19). Townsend goes on to refer to the way in which, in modern Britain, women's earnings have made a crucial contribution to this pattern. Yet they are still on the whole low earnings, likely to provide below-poverty-line incomes for households where women are the sole breadwinners.

We referred above to the way in which the evidence on the life cycle of poverty has been used in discussions of the case for the development or enhancement of social security policies. In our next section we will therefore look at the role of social security in the relief of poverty.

Social security and poverty

The most important policies in the relief of poverty come under the heading of 'social security', by which we mean all forms of public income maintenance. It is a common feature in all western countries to observe a major division between social *insurance* and social *assistance*, the former involving entitlements earned through contributions while the latter involves means-tested assistance for the very poor. In practice, this distinction is an oversimplification of schemes which vary widely and overlap. There is also a third alternative of some significance; namely transfers without means tests to particular categories of people funded from general taxation (e.g. child/family benefits).

The idea of social insurance developed in late nineteenth-century Europe, out of the experience of both commercial insurance and trade union or friendly society schemes which aimed to provide individuals with protection against income fluctuations arising out of unemployment or sickness (Heclo, 1974; Harris, 1977). Modern social insurance schemes can be seen as the result of evolutionary developments from this base, involving the growing intervention of the state, widening and universalizing the scope and coverage of schemes. Inevitably, evolution towards more comprehensive coverage of groups and problems which would be commercially uninsurable (i.e. wider risk-pooling) has taken social insurance further from its commercial or self-help model (Gilbert, 1970); so has the unavoidable reliance on a 'pay-as-you-go' approach (present contributors paying for present recipients rather than funding their own future entitlements). Social insurance contributions are increasingly resembling a tax rather than payments closely related to future entitlements; elaborate contribution records continue to feature in insurance schemes, but arguably these represent an unnecessary administrative overhead. Governments themselves implicitly recognize the move away from insurance when, as in Britain in the early 1980s, they summarily abolish entitlements to earnings-related unemployment benefit.

While social insurance may be an increasingly fictional concept, it probably retains an enduring political appeal. By conferring 'rights' which people could claim to have 'earned' it was much more attractive, in the period around the Second World War, than traditional forms of poor relief. Social insurance was an innovation strongly associated with the trade union movement, representing the 'respectable working class'. It provides for systematic redistribution of a horizontal kind in favour of many if not all 'dependent groups', essentially those with a 'normal' employment pattern (and their immediate families) experiencing temporary interruption of earnings or in retirement. To the extent that the schemes have been universalized in their coverage, and emphasize flat rate benefits and possibly graduated contributions, then they can be seen as more redistributive in a vertical sense, reducing inequality. In practice, social insurance schemes are only modestly redistributive in this sense, because coverage is partial, because contributions are often flat rate and because some benefits are earnings-related.

Social insurance arrangements have never provided adequate coverage for all groups in poverty (e.g. the disabled, long-term unemployed, single-parent families) and thus some form of means-tested poor relief or social assistance exists in all western countries. The origins of such schemes in harsh, moralistic systems, designed to deter claims from any but the most absolutely deprived, still show through in negative public attitudes towards social assistance. In Britain the 'Beveridge' reforms of the 1940s were intended to reduce social assistance to a 'safety-net' role for a very small group not covered by the comprehensive insurance arrangement. In practice, the group reliant on social assistance has never been small, because governments have not set standard insurance benefit levels high enough to cover all combinations of family circumstances plus housing costs. Without politically unpopular and deterrent means-testing of insurance benefits, the cost of higher insurance benefits paid indiscriminately to many families not needing the full amount would have been fiscally unacceptable. Insurance benefits do not cover longer-term unemployment, and in the 1970s and 1980s rapidly rising unemployment has further increased numbers reliant on social assistance. Similarly, single-parent families (other than in cases of widowhood) are another large and growing group dependent on social assistance.

There is no shortage of proposals for reform of social security in Britain (Atkinson, 1971; Lister, 1975; National Consumer Council, 1984). Although often talking in terms of going 'back to Beveridge', their recommendations are better seen as seeking to move 'on from Beveridge', because they seek further moves away from insurance principles towards benefit rights which are universally available with fewer excluded groups and funded out of general taxation. Child benefit and universal housing allowances are partial models of the kind of provision argued for. Another strand of reform, best epitomized by Donnison (1979, 1982), is the attempt to make social assistance simpler, more comprehensible, less discretionary and more based on rights. There is a recognition here that means tests are inescapable in social security and that these should be humanized and rationalized as far as possible. Existing systems of multiple benefits and tests suffer the twin problems of deterrence of take-up and the creation of 'poverty traps' (where the combined marginal rates of taxation plus benefit withdrawal approach or exceed 100 per cent). A third set of proposals involve the idea of 'negative income tax', probably with a minimum income guarantee. The beauty of such a scheme is that a single, universal means test is applied for the purposes of both taxation and benefit assessment. The fundamental difficulty, however, is that to provide an adequate floor for all groups at the bottom of the income range requires a high marginal tax rate above the threshold (Deacon and Bradshaw, 1983; Meacher Committee, 1983; SDP, 1982; Dilnot et al., 1984). The effects of taxation on incentives and the economy are discussed in chapter 5. There are also formidable practical problems with schemes of this kind, for example changing the tax system from operation on a yearly basis to the weekly basis required to meet the needs of the poor.

So we find ourselves coming back in the consideration of reverse income tax schemes to similar issues to those discussed above in relation to social insurance. Once state social security schemes move outside a fairly narrow range of redistributive activity – where they are principally (a) meeting extreme poverty and (b) shifting income within the life and work cycles of individuals – they encounter increasing political difficulties. They begin to raise issues about the role of the state in relation to the overall distribution of incomes of a kind which governments have on the whole been disinclined to address. Social security policy is seldom as redistributive as it appears to be at a superficial glance, or in much political rhetoric.

At the time of writing the British government has just produced a new set of proposals for dealing with some of these issues. It proposes that the state role in pensions should revert to the provision of a basic flat rate benefit, leaving private pensions to add an earnings-related element. As far as means-tested benefits are concerned it plans radical simplification, with a safety net of highly discretionary social aid. The latter scheme involves abandoning its own endorsement, in 1980, of the idea of rights to special additional benefits. It is also proposing a way of reducing the poverty trap problem by relating specific means-tested benefits in a more logical way to the net incomes achieved after the assessment of other benefits.

Other social services, poverty and inequality

This chapter has given considerable attention to social security policy as the area of public policy most obviously likely to make a contribution to the relief of poverty and the reduction of inequality. But what about other social policies; do they not make some contributions to these ends? We suggested in our introduction that this is certainly how the welfare state has been perceived and justified. Le Grand (1982), in his review of the evidence on this theme, quotes a number of examples of radical and egalitarian theorists and ideologues who have seen the welfare state in this way. However he goes on to analyse British social policy in some detail and arrives at some forthright conclusions:

> Public expenditure on the social services has not achieved equality in any of its interpretations. Public expenditure on health care, education, housing and transport systematically favours the better off, and thereby contributes to inequality in final income. It has not created equality of cost (or equality of 'access'), and indeed in some cases has made cost differences worse; there persist substantial inequalities in outcomes. For several of the services there has not been even a reduction in the relevant inequalities over time. (Le Grand, 1982, p. 137)

Townsend arrives at similar conclusions by way of his social survey approach to the issue. In his major study of poverty he sought to quantify the public benefits in kind accruing to his sample, as well as the private benefits discussed above. Whilst acknowledging some methodological difficulties about doing this he was nevertheless able to arrive at some pretty clear conclusions:

> Contrary to common belief, fewer individuals in households with low than with high incomes received social services in kind of substantial value. Fifteen per cent of individuals had no benefits or benefits of less value than £25. Yet 46 per cent had benefits worth £150 per year or more. The proportion was, however, significantly larger among middle- and higher-income groups than among those in households under £1,000 a year.

> The relationship between income and value of social services in kind varied with type of service. More households with low than with high incomes had no health or welfare benefits, but more also had substantial benefits. Fewer had educational benefits, and fewer who had educational benefits had benefits of substantial value. (Townsend, 1979, pp. 222-3)

These are, of course, specific pieces of evidence on the British social policy system. In this discussion rather than simply explaining these findings we want to explore how they arise in ways which raise wider questions about the analysis of the impact of social policy upon poverty and inequality. We will do this by looking at the issues service by service.

Education stands out as an area of heavy public expenditure from which the main beneficiaries are manifestly not the poor, and generally not those in the lower half of the income distribution (Halsey et al., 1980). State provision of education offers a minimum level for all children, but it is children from higher-income families who (a) consume more education, inasmuch as they are more likely to take advantage of the education available beyond the minimum school-leaving age; and (b), more controversially, tend to benefit because better educational facilities are available to or secured by them even in the compulsory part of the system. If there were substantial opting out of the state system into the private system by the parents of higher-income children this would redress the balance, but in Britain it is not substantial and is, in particular, very low indeed as far as the very costly higher education system is concerned. Finally so-called free schooling is not necessarily entirely free – transport and clothing costs may be involved, the provision of extra books and equipment cost money, and many 'fringe' activities (music, outings, sports, etc.) may entail costs. Once beyond school-age the choices of continuing education may need to be made in the light of loss of earning opportunities. In Britain some benefits exist to offset some of these costs, they tend to be available only to the very poor, and are often little known and are thus subject to low 'take-up' (Bull, 1980).

The contribution of the health service has been given particular attention in Britain, perhaps because of the way it is seen as the 'jewel in the crown' of the British welfare state. The evidence on health is very disturbing as far as aspirations towards reduction of inequality are concerned. An important part of the case for a free health service was the presence of social class or income-related inequalities in mortality and morbidity. The years since the introduction of the service have seen general improvements in the nation's health, but the differentials between the classes have *not* changed for the better; indeed they have in some respects worsened (Townsend and Davidson, 1982). Of course, the problem about this finding is that it is far from clear to what extent the health service can, on its own, combat inequalities in health. However, there is in fact extensive evidence of social differentials in access to and use of the health service. This evidence is complex, and cannot be described in any detail here, but the evidence includes (a) inequalities in the geographical distribution of services, (b) underuse of services by deprived groups and (c) differences in the services health professionals extend to their lower-class patients (for example, shorter consultations by doctors). Overall on these issues Le Grand concludes 'that the top socio-economic group receives 40 per cent more NHS expenditure per person reporting illness than the bottom one' (Le Grand, 1982, p. 46).

The role of social policy in the field of housing in Britain has been to provide subsidized public housing; to subsidize housing expenditure by individuals by means of tax relief, social security and rebates; and to effect some controls over the private rented market. The balance between these various interventions has varied substantially over the past 70 years (such interventions largely began during and just after the First World War). They have been much affected both by changes in policies, particularly associated with shifts in power between the political parties, and by changes in the housing and money markets. In 1984 the main forms of subsidy are (a) tax relief for mortgage payers, a system of subsidy clearly biased towards people with higher incomes and larger houses; (b) direct subsidies for local authority tenants in general, now of a low and rapidly diminishing importance; and (c) social security and housing benefits providing means-tested support for low-income householders. The first of these subsidies is by far the most important. It therefore contributes to an increase of inequality in two senses: by redistributing towards high-income mortgage payers, and by making it easier for those people to be able to 'consume' better and larger houses than they might in an unsubsidized situation.

Le Grand includes transport policy in his survey of the distributional effects of social policies. This is interesting because it is a policy area rarely perceived as social policy. Nevertheless where there are state interventions in the provision of transport or in the pricing systems used for roads, buses, railways and so on they are likely to have redistributionary effects. The subsidization of public transport has been seen as a social service inasmuch as it aids the mobility of persons who lack cars. Le Grand attacks that argument on the grounds that low-income people are low users of many transport facilities, particularly the heavily subsidized railways. Hence the subsidy largely goes to higher-income people. His concern is, here, to suggest that transport subsidy is an inherently less efficient way of benefiting low-income people than direct income transfers. His examination of transport is interesting in raising general doubts about the efficiency of general subsidies in kind as opposed to specific subsidies in cash. There is, of course, also a middle alternative: specific subsidies in kind as provided where the transport system provides lower fares for groups of lower-income people (the elderly and students, for example).

Le Grand's survey of social policies does not examine the

personal social services. Townsend's tabulation does include them. These services, being much smaller in scale than, for example, health services, and explicitly targeted upon seriously deprived groups, are much harder to study in terms of their distributional impact. Significantly, George and Wilding (1984), like Le Grand, leave them out of their survey on 'social policy and inequality'. In Britain the personal social services took over from the poor law responsibility for residential care for the deprived and neglected. Since that time they have sought to develop a general approach to community care, through the use of social work and domiciliary services, which takes them away from the legacy of the poor law. Yet they have not found it easy to do this. Public residential care tends to be regarded, often quite inappropriately, as inferior to private care. Both residential and domiciliary services are generally rationed by the use of means tests. Social workers have had difficulty in establishing a view of their functions which identifies them with the treatment of problems of emotional disturbance, child neglect and so on regardless of the resources of the families concerned. The 'social' problems of well-to-do families are largely kept from their scrutiny. Hence, overall, the impact of the personal social services is likely to be largely distributive towards the poor, albeit on a small scale. It is important to note in this context that Britain is unusual in having a personal social services system which is not formally linked with its social assistance scheme. Such linking is likely to ensure personal social services are redistributive downwards, but with consequences for the civil liberties of the poor because of the linking of social security concerns about income with social work concerns about social behaviour (Jordan, 1974).

Social policy and inequality: conclusions

Le Grand's discussion of the way the distributional consequences of the social services tend to be away from rather than towards equality led him on to argue: 'if greater equality of whatever kind is desired, it is necessary to reduce economic inequality' (Le Grand, 1982, p. 150). In this chapter we have given much more emphasis to the policy which directly deals with this, social security, than to the other social services. Yet we have suggested that there are strong reasons why governments are reluctant to use social security as a strong equalizing device.

All the policies conventionally regarded as social policies tackle redistributional questions as issues about the post-tax distribution of earnings. Here we are brought back, therefore, to that distinction between social and economic policy which we considered in the first two chapters. In the last analysis all issues about government intervention in the economy have social implications. If poverty and inequality are problems for a society they are just as appropriately tackled through government intervention to affect the primary distribution of incomes and wealth as by secondary, social policy, interventions to attempt to redistribute at a later stage.

In practice in capitalist societies governments often operate in a contrary way. They see the problems of economy management, of the stimulation of economic enterprise and so on as issues to be tackled even if the social consequences are inegalitarian. Unemployment is created as a product of economic management, and social policy is left to deal with the alleviation of its consequences. Policies are developed for energy, for the construction industry, for food production, and so on, which may have particular cost consequences for low-income people; but these are seldom evaluated in terms of their redistributive consequences – instead there is a tendency to leave social policy to 'mop up' afterwards.

Hence we end reiterating our concern, expressed at the beginning of the chapter, about the tendency for discussions of social policy and discussions of inequality and poverty to be linked together; as if the latter was the only concern of social policy and the former the only device for tackling problems of inequality and poverty. It is hoped that in the course of this chapter we have made clear some of the reasons for wanting to see that link severed in discussions of these issues.

4

Need and Demand

According to Soper (1981, p. 1) 'There can be few concepts so frequently invoked and yet so little analysed as that of human needs.' 'Need' is a concept at the very heart of social policy, a touchstone for academics, politicians, administrators and professionals. In the social administration tradition as outlined in chapter 1, need is the rationale and the principal guide for policy, and this orientation is seen as distancing social policy quite markedly from the economic market place with its notions like demand. In political debate, assertions about need are frequently used in a manner which suggests inherent persuasiveness and perhaps even unchallengeability. Administrators and practitioners in the social services bid for resources with arguments or evidence about needs, or conversely reject requests for resources by arguing that other needs are greater. Radical critiques of western societies in the marxist tradition lay great emphasis on the failure of capitalism to meet human needs (Deacon, 1983; Marcuse, 1964; Leiss, 1976). Yet the concept of need itself remained relatively unexplored until recently. Doyal and Gough (1984) provide a useful review and synthesis of recent work from a radical perspective. In practice, it is not clear that the word has any coherent meanings, let alone that its many users share a definition. In this situation we regard some clarification of the concept of need as a priority for social policy analyses.

The *Concise Oxford Dictionary* offers us a choice of four definitions of 'need' which it may be helpful to review.

(1) Circumstance requiring some course of action.
(2) Necessity for presence or possession of ——.
(3) Emergency, crisis, time of difficulty; destitution, lack of necessaries, poverty.

(4) Thing wanted, in respect of which want is felt.

The first of these suggests that most uses of the term could be tautologous: a course of action is recommended because circumstances require it. The second is more useful in so far as it stresses the instrumental character of need, that need arises where there is some objective to be fulfilled (Barry, 1965, ch. 3; Williams, 1974). It is the nature of this objective, including *whose* objective, which must be explored further, as we do below. In the social policy context the implicit objective is typically the continuance of life at some given standard of health, comfort, independence or whatever. The third definition, particularly in its second part, indicates the more specific social connotation of need in some uses, where it is taken to mean 'poverty'. The final definition equates need with 'want', placing the individual's own preferences at the centre of the stage and taking us remarkably close to the economic concept of demand.

While it may seem pedantic to start from a dictionary definition, in our view the range of alternative interpretations this reveals is reflected in the ambiguity which characterizes use of the term in the world of social policy. There is a further point. The first two definitions in particular highlight the strong link between 'need' and necessity; the idea that some condition *must* be fulfilled. There is an air of the imperative about needs in this sense, which helps to explain the term's supposed persuasiveness; you cannot argue with necessity.

The first question we wish to pose is: how far is there a *consensus* about needs? Is there agreement about what we mean by needs, and when, in principle, action is called for? We examine the extent and limits of consensus firstly in terms of the more conceptual literature and secondly in terms of some practical examples.

Our second concern also grows out of these definitions, particularly the fourth, and out of our general unease with the traditional separation of the 'social' and 'economic' spheres. What is the difference between demand and need? In order to address this question, and pose some more, we consider how far the concept of need can be interpreted within, and reconciled with, conventional *economic demand theory*. The answer depends heavily on the role ascribed to individual, as opposed to collective or professional, preferences and judgements. Economic analysis highlights the importance of income, or lack of it, in accounting for need as unmet demand. But, as we saw in chapter 3, the role of social services in relation to inequality remains politically constrained so that 'inequality' cannot be simply substituted for 'need', in an immediate, practical policy context.

Consensus?

The attractions of consensus are obvious if you are in the business of making policy prescriptions. There is a solid foundation of agreement about ends, the political heat is taken out of the debate, and attention can focus on the technical, professional and administrative tasks of selecting the best means. It seems that need is a concept which has been seen as consensual, a basis for agreement and action, whether because of the idea of objective necessity or because of some shared values born of common humanity. In fact, as we attempt to illustrate, even something approaching consensus tends to be confined to more limited conceptions or applications of the concept, whilst in other cases there is clearly no consensus about need.

This situation in some ways parallels that in normative economics. In that discipline, the idea of 'efficiency' in the sense of 'Pareto-optimality' has been a key to much policy prescription. A Pareto-optimum, as we saw in chapter 1, is a situation where no-one can be made better off without someone else being made worse off, whilst a Pareto-improvement involves some people being made better off and no-one losing (see Culyer, 1980, for further discussion). Pareto improvements hurt no-one; therefore we should expect consensus support for them; therefore policy prescriptions based on Pareto efficiency criteria carry special force. As Sugden (1981) cogently argued, economists for many years operated under these assumptions without realizing that they, and some of the supporting assumptions and value judgements involved, were not universally accepted. This example suggests that a reliance on consensus may ultimately prove unfounded, and also that striving to meet a consensus criterion like Pareto may emasculate the policy content. Strict interpretation of the Pareto criterion implies that no recommendation can be made about the bulk of policy changes where some people lose from the change and are not compensated.

A rather similar picture emerges from a review of some key philosophical works on social justice. Barry (1965) and Rawls (1972) both stress the importance of 'procedural justice' (i.e. 'fair play') as a set of concepts which commands near-universal support. In itself, procedural justice does not say anything about substantive needs or distributive principles, but it is one of the few areas where consensus can be found, because such principles are necessary to the maintenance of peace in any community. According to Barry, to derive more substantial concepts, such as 'equality of opportunity', additional conditions of 'background fairness' must be invoked and these are less likely to command universal support. Rawls' particular contribution is to postulate a notional social contract, agreed unanimously by the prospective members of society prior, as it were, to the nature of that society, and each individual's position in it, being revealed. A generally agreed, fair procedure would generate agreement on substantive distributional principles. Other writers have also invoked this idea of a contract (Weale, 1978; Sugden, 1981). However, many objections are raised to this approach (see for example Daniels, 1978; Wolff, 1977). For example, many dispute the particular distributional principles which Rawls argues would emerge. More fundamentally, in the real world of established interests and power structures, there is no necessity or likelihood of going through these hoops and establishing agreed principles (Reidy, 1984). Even in the realm of philosophical discourse, different writers, while agreeing about some core concepts of procedural justice, can come to quite different conclusions about substantive distributional questions (contrast Nozick, 1974, with Rawls and Weale). Indeed, Weale (1983) appears to have changed his position significantly on this over time; and as Miller (1976) showed, philosophers differ in whether they regard 'need' as an aspect of 'justice' at all, or whether it should better be regarded as an aspect of 'right' or 'desert'.

Within philosophy one particular focus of attention has been Taylor's (1959) categorization of 'need' statements (discussed in Springborg, 1981) into four basic types:

(1) something needed to satisfy a rule of law;
(2) means to an end (the latter perhaps being implicit);
(3) motivations, e.g. wants, drives, desires;
(4) recommendations, or normative evaluations.

While in some ways paralleling our dictionary definitions, this highlights certain features more clearly. It includes possible use of the term to cover voluntaristic 'wants', indeed potentially the whole gamut of human motivations, in (3), but this is not a sense which implies necessity in the way (1) or (2) do. Secondly, it clearly distinguishes normative uses of the term, in (4). There seems to be some acceptance of the usefulness of these distinctions (see Springborg, 1981, Appendix, for a review), and to that extent we could say that, while we may have a high-level consensus about definitions, these actually imply quite distinct meanings which will be employed in different ways by different people in different contexts. Some writers have sought to treat 'need' as a bridging concept between 'is' and 'ought', arguing from some theory/facts about human nature that certain basic human needs must be met, but Springborg (1981) argues that this attempt inevitably fails and that need recommendations should be seen as explicitly normative.

Springborg's main theme, tracing the need concept through from ancient philosophy to the late 1970s, is the doctrine of 'true and false needs' and its role in radical, especially 'revisionist' modern critiques of civilization (e.g. Marcuse, 1964; Illich, 1978; Leiss, 1976). This asserts that human needs are increasingly distorted by a culture dominated by particular classes and relations of production, and that only in some radically transformed society will the recognition and meeting of true needs be possible. Springborg regards this doctrine as internally contradictory, untestable (i.e. metaphysical), and denying of the ethical character of social and political problems. Her view seems broadly consistent with Soper (1981), who seeks to argue that needs should be the subject of open political debate, and criticizes market liberals and marxists alike for adopting theories which suppress the politics of consumption and need. To say that needs are, and would be even under socialism, political questions is to recognize that they will not dissolve in instant consensus.

If 'needs' are those goods and services required if individuals are to live at a certain standard, then clearly it is differences in the definition of this standard which will threaten consensus. Weale (1983) defined need as:

> a certain minimum quantity of goods that are valued not necessarily for their own sake, but because they provide the conditions necessary to a wide variety of different projects. Food, shelter, clothing and a source of warmth comprise the obvious components of this basket of instrumental wants . . .

Miller (1976) follows a similar path, though rejecting the view that needs are solely instrumental. It is not at all clear that either the general or the particular components of this definition would command universal support. Plant et al. (1980) pursue a somewhat stronger line, both in terms of the justificatory argument and the specific conditions covered:

> If there are necessary conditions of moral action, irrespective of particular moral codes, there will be some things that must be classed as needs whatever one's moral position. These conditions include physical survival and autonomy, i.e. freedom from arbitrary interference, ill-health and ignorance.

This is perhaps the most sophisticated attempt to posit a

consensus basis for a relatively broad conception of needs, with its emphasis on autonomy as well as survival, implying the inclusion of civil rights, health care and education in the list of need goods. To the extent that people in practice appear not to accept such a definition, then implicitly they have not thought through the logic of their moral position.

Like earlier writers (e.g. Marshall, 1973) we would expect to find lower levels of agreement in respect of 'higher levels' of need, thinking for example of Maslow's (1943) distinction between five levels of human need – physiological, safety, belonging and love, esteem, self-actualization. Firstly, it seems inequitable to provide resources for higher-level needs for some when lower-level needs, for others, remain unmet. Yet redistribution to fulfil lower-level needs may interfere with the ability of the donors to realize their higher-order needs. It is also worth noting that there are strong social/cultural elements in Maslow's fourth level, while the fifth level seems very individualistic. Again, this suggests that agreement on what these goals require will be hard to achieve.

Moving from philosophy towards practice, it is quite clear that there are important differences which undermine, at least to some extent, the consensual image of needs. Bradshaw (1972) distinguished four types of need: felt, expressed, normative and comparative. The very fact that one can demonstrate the plausibility and practical employment of each of these concepts, and the different coverage and implications of each, is indicative of a situation where consensus is unlikely, at least in the many cases where people are 'in need' on one criterion but not on all. In particular, Bradshaw highlights the major distinction between professionally defined normative needs and individually defined felt needs. Smith (1980) develops a fuller typology, involving variation in three dimensions:

(1) the unit of need (e.g. individual-family-community);
(2) the cause of need (e.g. material circumstance vs. personal inadequacy);
(3) the assessor of need (particularly individual vs. professional).

Grounding his observations in empirical study, Smith argues that definitions in practice vary on all these dimensions according to ideology. In reviewing other need studies he observes both a lack of theoretical clarity in the definition of need and frequent inconsistency in the concepts actually employed.

Even within the paradigm of normative, professionally defined needs, in the case of medicine where this seems to be most strongly founded, it is clear from studies cited by Cooper (1975) and Lind and Wiseman (1978) that professional assessments vary very widely.

The general direction of our argument is that needs should be defined in the political arena. The evidence relating to political stances or attitudes towards need does not suggest complete consensus here either. Firstly, the platforms of the major political parties vary significantly in their implicit treatment of needs, particularly in relation to certain services like housing which are on the boundary of the market system. Secondly, there has been considerable interest recently in opinion evidence on attitudes to welfare (Whiteley, 1981; Webb and Wybrow, 1981; Jowell and Airey, 1984; Judge et al., 1983). This suggests systematic variations in attitudes between services, between social classes and different party affiliations, and between countries within Europe. Thirdly, with many social services controlled at the local government level it is possible to cite local variations in service outputs as indications of differing attitudes to the definition of need (Davies, 1968; Boaden, 1971; Sharpe and Newton, 1984).

Finally, referring back to our discussion of the definition and nature of social policy in chapters 1 and 2, it will be recalled that one interpretation of a good deal of social service activity, particularly in the 'human services', was of 'social control' in the sense of behaviour modification (Gough, 1979). On the face of it, this would seem to involve a lack of consensus, since what is involved is an attempt to change the behaviour of clients from what they would have freely chosen. Such intervention might be justified by an appeal to arguments about true and false needs, but the controversial nature of interventions in such fields as mental illness and deviancy remains all too apparent.

From this cursory review we are led to the conclusion that need is a concept which, at best, evokes limited and uneven degrees of consensus according to the circumstances, or at worst evokes a general lack of consensus. This unevenness can be illustrated by reference to a number of specific examples.

The extent of consensus in practice

Firstly, there are needs and services which seem to evoke fairly high levels of consensus. These include care for the elderly and disabled (Bebbington and Davies, 1980; Challis, 1981) and health care more generally (Cooper, 1975; Culyer, 1976). Salient features accounting for this consensus include the direct impact of these services on life itself, the potential universality of the problems giving rise to need, and the belief that most of these problems are beyond the control of the individuals affected. The concept of dependency, which was a common theme in chapter 1, recurs here (Marshall, 1973).

Secondly, we have the basic problem of poverty and income maintenance. As we showed in the previous chapter, while there is undoubtedly a consensus about the need for a subsistence income, this is arguably irrelevant to contemporary questions about the level of the poverty line enshrined in benefit scales. Townsend's (1979) attempt to define a contemporary poverty line is closely related to the ideas about need of Weale, Miller and Plant et al. reviewed above, emphasizing as it does the criterion of participation in normal social life. However, as we indicated in chapter 3, this attempt is not found convincing, empirically or theoretically, by many other commentators (e.g. Piachaud, 1981). This is not in any way to deny the political centrality of poverty/inequality, nor to belittle attempts to demonstrate effects of poverty (e.g. social isolation, ill-health) which can be argued, in the political arena, to be unacceptable.

Thirdly, we have cases where legal rights to assistance are confounded to some extent by concerns about client behaviour and desert. Homelessness and the right to public housing is a good example. The British legislation itself is criticized for excepting cases of 'intentional homelessness' from the right to rehousing, and local authorities are criticized for interpreting this clause in different ways. Yet this situation clearly reflects the possibilities which exist for individual households to put themselves into the potential homeless category by their own behaviour, for example by forming a separate household or engaging in domestic disputes, against a background of scarcity of available rented housing and long waiting lists for public housing. Whether one approves of restrictive interpretations of this clause or not, it is clear that there is no general consensus on its interpretation. The same kind of situation exists in relation to unemployment benefit levels in cases where jobs are available and have perhaps been voluntarily relinquished. The low levels of short-term supplementary benefits in Britain have been heavily criticized, and clearly they do function to sharpen up the work ethic to some extent, yet it would seem that such reinforcement is widely approved of. In case anyone believes that such considerations are simply a product of capitalism, it is instructive to quote Deacon (1983, p. 39): 'Under socialism, however, the work-income connection would not yet be broken. The allocation of benefits in cash and kind would therefore continue to be affected by the necessity of motivating people to work. The care of those who are not willing to work is likely to be less desirable than the care of those who are.'

We have already mentioned cases of social control and behaviour modification as involving inherently non-consensual relations between the service providers and the clients. Child care and supervision are examples. Interventions are made in the interests of the needs of children which may cut across the perceived needs or interests of parents. With older children and offenders the interventions may be concerned with protecting the needs and interests of other citizens as potential victims of crime or anti-social behaviour. Even within the narrower field of prevention of child abuse, the 'policy paradigm' in terms of perceived causes of the problem may vary (see Whitmore, 1984, discussed in chapter 8), an example of non-consensus within the social work profession of the kind identified by Smith (1980).

Another type of case where consensus about needs may be low is where minority interests or preferences are involved. Leisure services, including sports and cultural facilities, illustrate this phenomenon. Need-type arguments can be advanced for public provision of these services (Bramley, 1985), yet it is doubtful whether these would command general consent, especially at the level of provision for specific sporting or artistic endeavours. In Weale's terminology these are simply part of the 'wide variety of different projects'; in Barry's terms they are not part of the 'core' concept of needs; in Maslow's typology they represent higher-level needs.

Our last example illustrates the problem of need agruments becoming confounded with other powerful interests. Systems of territorial resource distribution, for example the British Rate Support Grant, represent attempts to operationalize what in Bradshaw's terminology would be called 'comparative need' (see Bennett, 1980 and 1982, and Bramley and Evans, 1981, for descriptions). In practice these systems have been very controversial, and it has been unusual for any positive changes in methodology to be agreed between even the very limited number of parties to the negotiations (central departments and the local authority associations). Underlying need criteria are ambiguous, inconsistent and hotly debated (Bramley et al., 1983). Judgements about need arguments *per se* are heavily clouded by considerations of how they would advantage/disadvantage particular geographical regions, political parties, government's expenditure control objectives, and so forth. The main dimension of dispute has been over how far grant distribution should reflect patterns of actual expenditure. This may be interpreted as a conflict between criteria of expressed need, or demand, and criteria of comparative need.

Economic demand theory

The question we want to address now is: how far can the concept of need be expressed through conventional microeconomic analysis of demand? This is an unconventional way of looking at need but we believe it may be helpful in illuminating some of the interactions between need and demand in particular situations where services have to be rationed. In a context where traditional assumptions about the boundaries between social services and the market are being questioned or overturned, such a perspective may be particularly helpful. We start by making some general observations about the economic concept of demand.

The demand for a good or service is the amount of the good or service consumers are willing and able to pay for, given the price charged, their incomes, the price and availability of other goods and services, and so on. It is assumed that the good/service can be defined and measured in some way, and (normally) that the quantity consumed can be varied. The dependence of demand on *both* willingness *and* ability to pay is crucial. The concept applies in principle whether the good/service is marketed or not, but if it is not marketed we cannot directly observe demand. Demand depends on other variables, such as price or income; it is normally expressed not as a single value but as a relationship with another variable (most often, price), holding other factors constant. Figure 4.1 shows a 'demand curve' as conventionally drawn, a graphical expression of the normal inverse (downward-

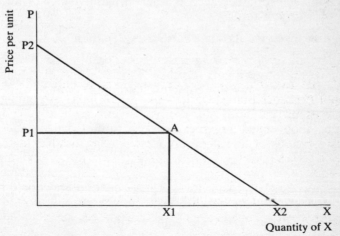

Figure 4.1   The demand curve

sloping from left to right) relationship between price and quantity. The line drawn from P2 through A to X2 connects points like A which represent particular combinations of price and quantity (such as P1 and X1) which consumers would choose. The 'curve' is drawn as a straight line for convenience.

One other general point about demand curves is worth making at this juncture. It is possible to interpret the vertical axis of figure 4.1, not as price but as the *marginal value* (MV) of a given amount of X. This means the value placed on one more unit of X, in terms of the amount of money (and thereby, other goods given up) the consumer is willing and able to pay for one more unit of X. Marginal values decline the more of X is consumed: the law of 'diminishing marginal utility' sets in; but the first few units of X are valued highly; typically more highly than the price charged in the market. This difference is known as 'consumers' surplus', and is measured by the area of the triangle P2 A P1 in figure 4.1.

This is an exceptionally abbreviated introduction to demand theory. For a fuller treatment in a social policy context see Culyer (1980), Gordon (1982), or Judge (1978).

With this limited toolkit we can now confront the question: what does 'need' mean in a demand theory context? We suggest that there are at least four distinct answers to this:

(1) client preference-based: need is inelastic or invariant demand;
(2) client income-based: need is inability to pay;
(3) others' preference-based: need is an externality;
(4) supply/cost-based: need is where treatment is worthwhile in cost-benefit terms.

Each of these merits some further explanation.

(1) *Inelastic or invariant demand.* This concept of need represents such an obvious bringing-together of the concepts of demand and need that it is really surprising to find little reference to it in the literature. 'Inelastic' demand means demand which does not vary much, in proportional terms, when either price or income varies. It is a property of people's preference structures. Figure 4.2(a) and 4.2(b) illustrate elastic and inelastic demand respectively. Inelastic demand is associated with basic necessities, as perceived by consumers; the things you are reluctant to do without. Elastic demand is associated with inessentials or luxuries, which you buy when they are cheap or when you have extra income. High price elasticity is also associated with specific goods or services for which there are close substitutes, i.e. alternatives which provide a similar kind of service.

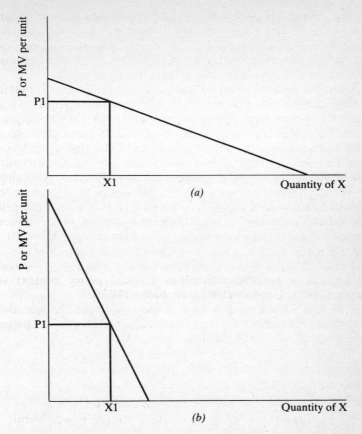

Figure 4.2   (a) Elastic and (b) inelastic demand

It is possible to estimate elasticities for marketed goods given suitable statistical data. Does this mean we can resolve debate about what constitutes need from empirical studies of behaviour? Quite apart from fundamental objections to relying solely on individual preferences (see below), there are many practical difficulties involved. Many social services are not marketed. Expenditure data may be aggregated into broad classes of consumption that include both necessities and non-necessities. The quality of the good/service can often vary in a way which the data do not pick up. Where estimates are available they do not necessarily conform to expectations; for example, some American estimates of the income elasticity of demand for housing show values in excess of 1.0 (de Leeuw, 1971), and similarly studies have shown high price and income elasticities of demand for health care (Cooper, 1979) and education (Feldstein, 1975). It is somewhat paradoxical that the class of goods most unambiguously in the need category on this criterion, food, is normally provided through the market (see Coates and Boddington's introduction to Heller, 1976).

Elasticities have implications for the benefits associated with services and the effects of different approaches to rationing. 'Benefits' in the economic sense, as used in cost-benefit analysis, refer to consumers' surplus, the area under the demand or MV curve. As figure 4.2 indicates, benefits will be high relative to marginal values in the case of price-inelastic services, and low for the elastic services. With inelastic demand, demand will tend to be finite if prices are low or even zero, whilst raising prices will not easily reduce demand. It is worth stressing at this point that one should interpret price to include not just charges but also any costs incurred in using the service, including time costs, which may well be more significant in the social welfare field. Where demand is price-elastic, zero or low prices may generate apparently infinite demands. Where it is income-elastic, usage and benefits will tend to be much greater by high-income groups, who will benefit more from any subsidies, a source of concern in respect of a number of social services, especially health and education (Le Grand, 1982).

Weale's (1983) definition of needs as instrumental wants, quoted earlier, suggests a slightly different approach to the identification of need goods in terms of demand characteristics. It suggests that 'needs' are those goods or services for which demand is relatively *invariant* across individuals (at a given income level); whilst varying preferences affect the demand for goods or services required to undertake 'a wide variety of projects', this does not apply to the basic essentials. We know of no systematic investigation of this interesting hypothesis. A potential difficulty with this approach arises where individuals have particular disabilities which require a high input of either basic necessities or specialized resources (e.g. domestic care) to bring them up to the same level of autonomy as other people.

(2) *Inability to pay.* This interpretation of need is much more familiar, but it immediately begs the question: pay for what? Need in this sense divides into the general question of income poverty and specific services where particular arguments are advanced for detaching consumption levels from ability to pay. In relation to the general poverty case, the choice of approach boils down to treating poverty as an aspect of inequality, or developing detailed checklists of deprivations related to general notions of

subsistence, autonomy and participation along the lines of Townsend's work. Demand theory does not really help us further in these tasks.

The idea that the consumption of specific services should not relate to ability to pay is quite widely held, at least in relation to minimum standards of service (George and Wilding, 1984; Sleeman, 1979) in such cases as education, health and housing. It has acquired the labels of 'categorical equity', 'specific egalitarianism' (Tobin, 1970) or 'wealth neutrality' (Feldstein, 1975). Again, however, demand theory as such does not tell us why such services should be treated in this way. Rather there is an appeal to arguments about the instrumental role of these goods or services in meeting such criteria as survival, autonomy and participation or to arguments about background fairness and equality of opportunity (Barry, 1965). The implementation of the principle of categorical equity raises interesting issues concerning the forms of subsidy and rationing to be adopted. For example, while superficially a 'universalist' mode of provision might seem appropriate, in practice if subsidies are not strongly differentiated by income the equity objective may not be achieved; housing and further education are examples.

(3) *Externalities*. An economic externality arises when the activity (production or consumption) of one economic unit (e.g. a household) impinges on another economic unit (e.g. the welfare of another household), other than through the normal working of the market. Externalities create a divergence between the 'private' costs and benefits, which guide the decisions of individual economic units, and the overall 'social' costs and benefits. They frequently justify some form of intervention in the market (taxes, subsidies, regulations) on Pareto-efficiency grounds. Ideas about externalities were originally developed primarily in the environmental field (e.g. pollution, congestion). The traditional concern of social analysts such as Titmuss (1963, 1968) with the 'diswelfares' imposed by industrial society can be interpreted as a concern with negative externalities of this kind (Reisman, 1977). Some of the effects alluded to by Titmuss, for example the effects of working conditions on health or of economic fluctuations on employment, might be better regarded as problems of uncertainty and insurance, or the results of other kinds of 'market failure', not least in the labour market, rather than as externalities in the normal sense. More recently interest has arisen in the fuller application of this concept to social phenomena. It is not unreasonable to argue that people's preferences are not wholly selfish and self-regarding but also

contain a degree of concern for the welfare of others, which can be labelled altruistic (Collard, 1978; Culyer, 1980, 1983). Such altruism is an externality which market processes neglect and which spontaneous acts of charity are unlikely to adequately reflect owing to problems of 'collective action' or 'free riding' (Olson, 1965; Laver, 1979). Some proponents stress a generalized concern with the overall income or welfare level of others (Hochman and Rogers, 1969; Collard, 1978), whilst others (notably Culyer) argue strongly that altruism or caring is specific to certain forms of consumption such as health and housing. This is perhaps the modern interpretation of the economists' concept of the 'merit good' (Musgrave and Musgrave, 1975; Head, 1974), where society's marginal value or demand exceeds that of some or all individuals. It also provides an underpinning in demand theory for 'categorical equity'.

Of course, such externalities need not all be positive. 'Envy' is the inverse of altruism, and some would see this as the source of 'demand' for equality. There are also concerns about the activities of disadvantaged groups which cannot be labelled as 'caring': concerns for example about crime, vandalism, 'antisocial behaviour', 'bad neighbours', and, in the limit, riots and social unrest. The 'need' for services to reduce these negative externalities is not necessarily a need of the client, and the services may justifiably be labelled as social control.

Externalities of this predominantly psychological kind are difficult to measure because there are limited opportunities for people to reveal their preferences in behaviour. It is not unlikely that such externalities are an inverse function of 'distance' from the people affected, both socially and geographically. This may account for the evidence cited by Culyer (1983) that the poor are more generous than the rich, since demand theory alone would suggest the reverse.

Figure 4.3 illustrates the effect of externalities of this kind associated with particular services, with again the service output level X on the horizontal axis and marginal values on the vertical. Figure 4.3(a) shows the case of a service which is valued significantly by the consumer, but where other members of society only value consumption up to a minimum level; housing might be a good example. These two sets of preferences are summarized by the 'marginal private value' (MPV) line and the 'marginal external value' (MEV) line. Adding these together vertically gives the 'marginal social value' (MSV) line for any given consumption level. This line is kinked at X2, but in general it has the appearance of the inelastic demand curve in figure 4.2(a). Thus, there is a certain convergence between these two

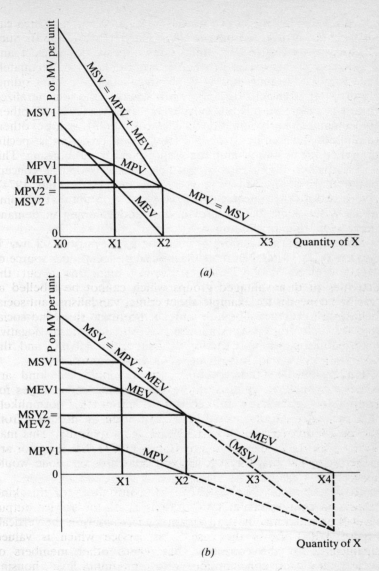

Figure 4.3 External benefits and need: (a) significant private (client) benefits; (b) external social benefits predominating

concepts of need. If X1 is consumed, there are both private and external marginal values. If more than X2 is consumed, only private marginal values are generated, although the external 'benefits' generated between X0 and X2 (the consumers' surplus) are not lost. The point X2 could be regarded as the level of absolute need, or at least its maximum level. Providing this level to all cases would give horizontal equity, but would be inefficient if marginal costs exceeded MPV2. A more relative concept of need would be to focus on MEV. On this basis one could allocate resources so as to equalize MEV or to equalize the ratio of MEV to cost or, more strictly, subsidy. Both these approaches neglect the consumer's own valuation; therefore it could be argued that policy should be guided by MSV (relative to costs).

Figure 4.3(b) brings out the importance of this issue more starkly, by considering a service which the consumer places little value on whilst the wider community values it more highly and over a wider range of output. Social work with young offenders might be an example. The broken lines show the implications of negative marginal valuations by the consumer: without coercion or compensation the service will not be used beyond X2. MEV appears to be a more dominant element in social decisions; but note that at X3 MSV falls to zero, even though this is less than 'absolute need' as defined in the previous paragraph (i.e. X4).

If 'need' is defined in externality terms, 'expressed demand' may have no relationship with it. If the service is free, expressed demand in figure 4.3(a) would be X3, well in excess of either need definition, whilst it would be X2 in figure 4.3(b), less than 'absolute' need and either more or less than relative need, depending on the standard set.

We are only sketching out the bare bones of 'need as an externality' here. Any full treatment must take account of differences in income, costs, and the forms of rationing and financing employed (see Culyer, 1980).

(4) *Cost–benefit judgement.* One recurring theme in economists' (and others') critiques of 'needology' is the frequent neglect of cost considerations (Nevitt, 1977). In health care, for example, need is often defined as a deleterious condition for which an effective treatment exists (Matthew, 1971). Williams (1974) suggests that this makes need, as a technical/professional judgement, a 'supply' concept. Many professionals believe in this, essentially absolute, need concept, that any such case should be offered treatment. The problem is that such potentially effective treatments exist for far more cases than we have resources to treat (Cooper, 1975). Some treatments are more costly than others, and some are more effective than others; need as a 'cost-effectiveness' judgement selects out priorities on this basis: however, it does not take account of the benefits of overcoming different circumstances. In principle, need as a cost–

benefit judgement would do that: it would combine judgements of effectiveness with information about costs *and* information about benefits, ideally in the kind of 'marginal value' form sketched in the previous section where wider social external benefits are counted. A number of writers in this field have concluded that need is best regarded as a cost–benefit judgement (Culyer et al., 1972; Bebbington and Davies, 1980; Knapp, 1984).

The attraction of this approach is that it not only brings in the cost and technical effectiveness aspects of the problem but that it provides a framework which can incorporate some of the other issues raised in this section. Firstly, cost–benefit analysis (CBA) is potentially sensitive to the link between need and demand elasticity, in the sense that CBA utilizes consumer surplus measures and, as we saw in figure 4.1, high consumer surplus is a feature of inelastic demand. Secondly, CBA is intended to capture both private and external benefits as well as costs. Thirdly, CBA can to some extent handle issues of risk and uncertainty. The main area of potential weakness, at the conceptual level, is in the handling of inequalities of income distribution. These affect the usage and benefits of services, including external benefits: higher-income groups use services more (if they can) and, more to the point, they derive greater benefit. Unless this is fully matched by the tax system, there is a danger of CBA need criteria infringing the principles of categorical equity. Furthermore, the rationale for CBA in welfare economics is, following Pareto, that gainers should be able to compensate losers and still be better off. This is alright, so long as (a) the compensation actually takes place, or (b) the income distribution is broadly satisfactory and the effects of these decisions are small and unsystematic, or possibly (c) any systematic redistributions favour the less well off (Layard, 1972; Sugden and Williams, 1978). However, if, as here, the effects may be large and systematically in favour of the better off, the CBA approach may be criticized on ethical grounds. It may be retrieved to some extent by weighting costs and benefits inversely with the incomes of the groups affected. In other words, a fully fledged economic approach to need assessment would have to discount for differences in ability to pay.

The discussion so far has been on a conceptual level. We have tried to show that there are a number of distinct economic interpretations of 'need', but that these can to some extent be brought together in a cost–benefit framework. In the practical world the difficulties of operationalizing this approach should not be underestimated. In particular the measurement of external valuations, and the ability to link these to particular income groups, is very problematic.

We have not exhausted the content of the economic tool kit by any means. For example, we have not discussed need in the context of production, employment and the labour market. Neither have we discussed matters of risk and uncertainty, where the role of social services in providing information and insurance is important. Thirdly, we have not discussed 'public goods' in the economic sense, although this is a topic which overlaps with externalities (Head, 1974). Public goods are the economic equivalent of needs which are seen as inherently collective or shared, such as the need for law and order (see the discussion of them in chapter 1).

An economic approach to need is unconventional and likely to encounter resistance on a number of grounds, which merit some comment at this point. Three broad grounds of criticism are (a) the failure to recognize any moral priority for needs; (b) neglect of non-material dimensions of welfare; (c) reliance on individual preferences. The idea that need has some moral priority over other wants, that there is a 'lexical' ordering of social goals (in the sense used by Rawls, 1972), is superficially attractive. It draws attention back to the goals underlying needs – survival, autonomy, participation. The first difficulty with this proposition lies in the lack of consensus about these goals and about particular instrumental needs which we have, we hope, fairly clearly demonstrated. It is hard to see why society should assign absolute moral priority to something for which there is not consensus support. The second difficulty is, as Culyer et al. (1972) convincingly argue, reality in the social services is all about trade-offs between different kinds of needs and priorities.

The economic approach is also vulnerable to the charge of focusing undue attention on the more material contributors to welfare, particularly the consumption of tangible goods and services, to the neglect of other factors which may contribute as much or more, for example the quality of personal relationships. Certainly the idea of distinct dimensions to welfare is a valuable one, as for example in Challis's (1981) work on the elderly. An emphasis on 'states' or 'outcomes' is not, however, incompatible with an economic perspective (Culyer, 1976, 1980); and if it is argued that money cannot buy caring relationships or a sense of community, it would seem that this poses a more general challenge to large-scale institutional social services.

Much the most serious challenge to the economic paradigm comes from those who do not accept the presumption that individual preferences and valuations are what should count (Sugden, 1981). It is possible to hold this view in the context of a liberal overall stance, by appealing to the distorting effects of consumerist propaganda (Galbraith, 1958), stigma (Spicker, 1984), ignorance, inadequate foresight and so on. Marxists and other radical critics of western capitalist societies hold that an emphasis on individual preferences is both misguided and futile in the present context; misguided because there is a wholesale false consciousness concealing from people's awareness their true needs or interests (Marcuse, 1964; Lukes, 1974), and futile because the power of the state is overwhelmingly biased towards the interests of capital and the ruling class.

Until recently, remarkably little discussion of the concept of need had emerged from the marxist school, despite its centrality both to the critique of capitalism and the foundations of an alternative society. Some of the literature in this tradition (e.g. Heller, 1976) is unhelpful both in the sense of the inaccessibility of its language to the uninitiated lay reader and in the sense of not dealing with concrete issues about need. There are helpful if short summaries of recent thinking in Deacon (1983) and Doyal and Gough (1984) which highlight the divergence of views about whether, in a different sort of society (non-alienated, socialist), there would be differences, choices, perhaps even conflicts, over issues of need. The emphasis in this literature seems to be more on the process than the substantive content of decisions, stressing that these issues should be resolved democratically at a (local?) community level. Thus, it could be argued, individual preferences are not, in a more ideal world, to be rejected out of hand. If anything it is the role of professional judgements, in our present system the main practical alternative, which is more seriously challenged.

What we have shown in this chapter is that 'need' is not a single concept which embodies a kind of imperative, objective necessity which social policy must respond to. Rather, the word is used in different ways in different contexts. Recent literature has pointed to certain general goals which 'needs' are instrumental in meeting: survival, autonomy and participation. However, while there are 'core' needs to do with survival which command near-consensus support, consensus diminishes as the scope of the need concept is broadened. In our view, need should be seen as a subject for political debate, not simply as a matter of objective necessity interpreted by technical specialists. We also believe that it is possible to reconcile the concept of need with the economic analysis of demand. Doing this highlights certain issues about the nature of different kinds of services, the key role of income distribution, the significance of externalities (including psychological factors) and the relevance of cost-effectiveness considerations to need judgements. Need concepts in practice are closely bound up with the rationing of resources and services. Although we do not pursue rationing issues further here (see Foster, 1983, for a useful review) it is clear that the insights offered by the economic analysis of demand are a valuable element in the analysis of rationing, alongside ideas about need *per se*.

5

A Fiscal Crisis?

Introduction

As we have indicated in some of the preceding chapters, the welfare state has been widely seen as in a period of crisis since the mid-1970s, both in Britain and other western countries (OECD, 1981). Marxists see this as part of a wider crisis of advanced capitalist/welfare states (O'Connor, 1973; Offe, 1984), adopting the traditional marxist view that capitalist societies have an inherent tendency to crisis, but taking on board the possibility that the welfare state has served to postpone the day of reckoning. In this chapter we want to look at this crisis in the terms in which it has most commonly manifested itself, a crisis of public expenditure and the means of financing it or, in short, a fiscal crisis. In doing so we bring out the point that it is not just marxists who predict fiscal problems for welfare states.

Firstly, we consider the definition of 'fiscal crisis'; what constitutes a crisis and what elements go to make a specifically fiscal one? Secondly, in the light of these definitions we pose the empirical question: has there been a fiscal crisis? The answer does not seem as straightforward as is commonly supposed. We consider mainly the case of Britain but also review more briefly some international comparisons. Thirdly, we show that it is possible to provide explanations for fiscal crisis in different ways, not just from a marxist perspective but also from a 'public choice' point of view. While the short-run responses can already be discerned, it is considerably more difficult to make predictions as to how the fiscal crisis of the welfare state might resolve itself in the longer run.

What is a crisis?

The idea of 'crisis' is best exemplified by the case of someone who is ill: the 'crisis' is a turning point in the course of the illness, but also a period of heightened danger and uncertainty. The person may recover, or may die. A preceding state, or set of trends, reaches a point where smooth continuance becomes impossible because of the contradictory pressures involved; some change of direction is required.

There are different levels of analysis at which one could talk about a crisis of the welfare state. Some work (notably Offe, 1984) seems to focus on 'the welfare state' as a term for the whole society/economy/government; the crisis is a feature of the system as a whole. Alternatively, the focus may be more narrowly upon 'the social services', the argument being that there is a crisis within these which may or may not parallel or relate to events in other sectors. The focus in this chapter is somewhere between these two positions, looking at social services in relation to the wider budgetary activities of government.

A broad distinction can also perhaps be made, as a first approximation, between a crisis in the realm of ideas and politics and a crisis in the realm of economics and finance. There is a difference between saying, for example, that belief in the legitimacy and efficacy of social services has declined and saying that finance for extra social services cannot be raised or that the cost of social services has risen in real terms. Apart from anything else, questions of the latter kind may be more susceptible to quantitative analysis. We do not for one moment pretend that economics and finance represent a separate realm of objective necessity, untainted by politics or ideology. All we suggest is that for the purposes of analysis it may often be useful to keep these aspects distinct in our minds.

Elements of a fiscal crisis

The essence of a fiscal crisis is straightforward – the government finds it cannot finance its planned/committed/actual expenditures. Such a situation can arise for one or more of the following immediate reasons:

(1) Public expenditure is *'out of control'*; bureaus, local authorities, legislatures, claimants, etc. are spending more and central government lacks the means to control this, including the means of monitoring and forecasting.

(2) Public policies involve substantial, probably unacknow-ledged, *growth in costs*, e.g. due to demography, productivity patterns, expectations, and take-up.
(3) Tax revenue, the main source of finance for public spending, is threatened by a declining or eroding *tax base*. This could be due to simple economic decline, international mobility of factors of production, tax avoidance or evasion, the 'black' and informal economies, or legislative creation of greater tax exemptions.
(4) There may be a *tax revolt*, which is essentially a political movement to limit particular taxes, or all taxes, as for example with property taxes in some American states.
(5) The 'excess burden' of taxation may become so severe as to threaten seriously economic growth; this refers to the adverse *incentive effects* of taxation, e.g. income taxes and work effort.
(6) *Borrowing* to close the gap between expenditure and tax revenue may be impossible; lenders may withhold funds until policies are changed.
(7) Any combination of taxation and borrowing to finance expenditure policies may generate accelerating *inflation*, which would be seen as unacceptably destabilizing, politically and economically.
(8) Similarly, borrowing in particular may generate *balance of payments* deficits which would either trigger exchange rate falls and inflation (hence (7) above) or international borrow-ing difficulties ((6) above).

These elements of possible fiscal crisis provide a convenient set of sub-headings under which we can consider the evidence on how far Britain and other western countries have been experiencing a fiscal crisis in the past decade. One word of caution is appropriate when dealing with this and related questions. The headings above suggest a model in which social welfare services are provided solely by incurring public expenditure, whilst the financing issues (3)-(8) relate essentially to the rest of the (non-welfare) economy. There is growing recognition that this is a misleading view, which is usefully corrected by Heald (1983) in his discussion of 'policy substitutes for public expenditure'. He identifies three alternative general means of securing policy aims (which may be 'social' in character), all of which involve a greater use of the resource of *laws* relative to the use of money and staff resources: confiscation without full compensation; coerced private expendi-tures; tax reliefs (alias 'tax expenditures'). Such methods are common and important. Their use changes over time and differs between countries, making international comparisons of policy 'outputs' quite difficult. We make some reference again to this issue under the tax-base subheading, but develop it more fully in the next chapter.

Has there been a crisis? The British experience

(1) *Public expenditure control.* It is generally believed that the British public expenditure system experienced a 'crisis of control' in the early and middle 1970s (House of Commons, 1976; Wright, 1977; Heclo and Wildavsky, 1981). A particular focus of attention was a sum of £5bn (over 10 per cent of public expenditure) argued by Godley (in House of Commons, 1976) to have been overspent without adequate acknowledgement in 1974/5. It should be recognized that this was a somewhat exceptional period, following the first oil crisis, the 1974 change of government, and a time of unprecedented inflation. However, a number of deficiencies in the techniques of public expenditure management were highlighted: inadequate discipline on ministerial decisions, which were often unannounced, and not charged against a limited contingency reserve; unrealistic economic growth projections; a failure to link expenditure explicitly to taxation and borrowing (House of Commons, 1982); planning expenditure in 'volume' terms without regard to the cash required to fulfil those plans. Reforms followed, notably the institution of annual 'cash limits' for the bulk of public expenditure (Barnett, 1982; Pliatzky, 1982). Although there was a difficult period in 1980-1, associated mainly with the preceding breakdown in public sector pay policy and the rapid onset of recession, it can be argued that these essentially managerial changes have successfully neutralized this particular source of 'crisis'.

It could also be argued that there was an over-reaction to the perceived crisis of the 1974-5 period. The period 1977-9 was characterized by substantial underspendings, arguably as much of a distortion of government policies as the preceding overspendings. Over this period the apparent ability of the governmental machine to deliver a pattern of public spending changes which corresponded with political decisions remained low, cash limits did not seem to increase the precision of expenditure control, and central government seemed less able to control closely some of the programmes it was supposed to have direct control over than it was to influence the formally autonomous local government sector (Bramley and Stewart, 1981). As far as the welfare state component of expenditure was concerned, there was a mixed picture in this period, some services being closely predictable and controllable (health), some being volatile upwards and downwards (housing) and some being treated as open-ended commitments (social security, especially with the adoption of inflation-indexation).

(2) *Growing costs.* There are three main factors in the tendency for the cost of any given set of welfare state policies to grow progressively: (a) demographic change, increasing the size of dependent or target groups in the population; (b) rising take-up of established services; (c) the labour-intensive, low-productivity character of public services, causing costs to rise faster than prices of other goods and services. The first of these is well recognized in the planning of parts of social spending in Britain, but its significance should not be exaggerated. For example, the demographic change component of health and personal social service spending is about plus 0.5-0.7 per cent per annum in the period 1975-85 (HM Treasury, 1982, p. 44), considerably less than the actual growth in real expenditure of around 3 per cent (HM Treasury, 1983, p. 17). Demographic effects are partially offsetting in any case: the demographic effect on schools expenditure was −1.0 per cent in the late 1970s and −2.8 per cent in the early 1980s (HM Treasury, 1982, p. 39). Demographic factors can interact with other factors, for example the state of the economy, as in the case of unemployment where the late 1970s witnessed a substantial expansion of the potential labour force not matched by economic expansion, thus leading to growing costs of unemployment benefit, job creation and training measures, and greater participation in further education. The last point is an example of the 'take-up' phenomenon (b); other examples arise in the social security field, where levels of take-up of certain existing benefits appear to have grown whilst new benefits (e.g. for the disabled) have a period of build-up. Take-up can be affected by policy directly, promotion on the one hand versus stricter rationing and the deterrence of 'abuse' on the other, as well as by wider economic and social trends.

Social services are typically characterized as labour-intensive services within which the scope for technical innovation to raise productivity is severely limited, although some would challenge this view. If this is true, then a given output will cost more if social service wages and salaries rise in line with levels in the rest of the economy. This phenomenon, associated with Baumol (Baumol and Oates, 1979, pp. 147-56) has been institutionalized by the practices of (a) setting public service output equal to input in the national accounts, and (b) explicitly allowing for this 'relative price affect' (RPE) in public expenditure plans. With indexation to average incomes, social security expenditure behaves in the same way. There are difficulties with this perhaps oversimplified view of social services, which we take up in chapter 10. There is also considerable uncertainty about the scale of the relative price effect; for example, Heald (1983, pp. 177-9) suggests that the long-run effect for government consumption has been +1.5 per cent p.a., whilst the Treasury figures have typically been around +0.6 per cent p.a. (HM Treasury, 1972). The logic of the argument quite clearly says that the effect will be greater the higher the rate of economic growth – it is a sort of fiscal 'disease of affluence'. The corollary is that low growth or decline relieves this source of pressure, and this indeed seems to have been happening to some extent since the mid-1970s, since measured RPEs have often been negative. Heald argues, however, that with high inflation the effect becomes volatile and that, implicitly as a result of temporary pay policies, the effect has merely been suppressed and not eliminated.

(3) *Tax base*. The basic measure of a country's tax base, or more generally its ability to afford social programmes, is its national output or income, most often measured by gross domestic product (GDP). Thus it could be argued that the most important proximate cause of fiscal crisis is economic decline, or a cessation of growth. Table 5.1 shows Britain's growth rate over the period 1961-82. The maximum rate ever sustained for any period was the 2½-3 per cent per annum of the early 1960s, much lower than the growth achieved by certain other economies. The growth rate faltered at the end of the 1960s, recovered slightly with North Sea oil in the late 1970s, and then went into an unprecedented negative phase between 1979 and 1982. Superficially, then, here is some explanation for two phases of fiscal crisis, the mid-1970s and the early 1980s. The argument becomes more difficult, however, when we discuss causality more fully below, since some would argue that cutting public expenditure has been partly to blame for the recent slump (Blake and Ormerod, 1980).

The 'black', or informal, economy is a more specific argument about tax base erosion which can occur whether the economy is growing or declining. Everyone has anecdotal evidence of economic activity (especially in the construction trade) outside the net of income and value added taxes. What is much less clear is how big this sector is as a whole, whether it is growing significantly, and if so why this is happening and whether it is reversible. If it is a large-scale phenomenon, highly sensitive to

Table 5.1   Trends in UK economic aggregates, 1961-1982

Economic category	1961-6	1966-71	1971-5	1975-9	1979-82
Output					
Gross domestic product	2.9	2.6	1.9	2.6	−0.5
Expenditure					
Consumption	2.4	2.0	1.8	2.2	−0.5
Investment	4.1	2.8	3.4	0.7	−5.5
General government	2.2	1.7	3.8	0.9	1.0
Income					
From employment	2.8	2.2	4.5	0.3	−2.0
Profits	0.9	1.5	−5.8	12.8	−0.6
Rent, dividends, interest	4.5	−0.3	1.5	4.9	0.5
Government grants and benefits	6.5	5.0	6.1	5.2	6.4
Taxation					
Personal income + NI	6.8	5.1	8.4	−2.3	1.9
Corporate taxes	−3.3	5.2	−2.3	6.4	13.5
Other indicators					
Inflation	3.6	5.6	14.0	13.5	12.8
Employment	0.7	−0.7	0.5	0.3	−2.1
Unemployment	−0.4	20.8	3.7	10.2	30.9

Average annual percentage changes in real terms
Source: Central Statistical Office: *Economic Trends, Annual Supplement 1983.*
London: HMSO

tax rates, then it effectively puts a limit on tax revenue, the so-called 'Laffer curve' (Laffer and Seymour, 1979). Estimates of its size in Britain are unreliable but range from 3 to 15 per cent of GDP (Blades, 1982; Dilnot and Morris, 1981).

The scale of the black economy would seem to depend strongly on cultural norms and the climate of (dis)approval surrounding tax evasion, and on the efforts incurred by government to control it. A factor which now works against trying to marginalize the black economy is the growing interest in the 'informal sector' (a broader but overlapping category) as a 'solution' to the growing problem of unemployment (Shankland, 1980; Gershuny and Pahl, 1980; Heinze and Olk, 1982).

Table 5.2   Estimated value of UK tax reliefs by broad category

	Percentage p.a. change, 1979-83	Amount, 1983/4 (£m)
'Social'/demographic reliefs (including Capital Transfer Tax; excluding basic tax structure)	2.6	1003
Pensions/personal savings	10.4	2650
Housing	−0.4	5720
Charities	1.3	290
Public social security and employment-related benefits	−8.9	792
Business-oriented reliefs	0.1	16,812
Financing inducements	4.3	2831

Average annual percentage change in real terms, 1979-1983, and absolute amount, 1983/1984
Sources: Public Expenditure White Papers.

Tax reliefs constitute, as already noted, an alternative means of pursuing social and other policies, a point long ago recognized by Titmuss (1963, ch. 2). There is some official recognition, if rather partial, of the need to look at tax reliefs alongside public expenditure as in the case of housing (Department of the Environment, 1977), although the theoretical problems involved in costing 'tax expenditures' are considerable (Kay and King, 1983). To precipitate a fiscal crisis one would need to postulate a rapid growth in tax exemptions for some reason. Table 5.2 summarizes the limited information available on tax reliefs in Britain, suggesting that the bulk of tax relief is business-oriented and that, in the recent period for which data are available (1979-83) there has been modest rather than explosive growth.

(4) *Tax revolt.* This element overlaps the previous one, in the sense that a tax revolt may take the form of illegal tax evasion or legal tax avoidance, exploiting exemptions and loopholes in the system. These are private, behavioural forms of tax revolt, whereas this heading refers mainly to collective political action to limit taxation. This phenomenon cannot be said to have yet become a major feature of the British scene. The 'new right' argue for quasi-constitutional limits on taxation and borrowing (Buchanan and Wagner, 1977). Although electoral success for a Conservative Party committed to tax reduction in the longer term

could be taken to be indicative of a political shift in this direction, the fact is that so far this government has been unable to reduce taxation in aggregate to any noticeable extent (see Table 5.1). Perhaps the most significant example of tax limitation in Britain is the rate-capping legislation of 1984, where central government is legislating in part on behalf of local ratepayer interests in selected urban areas. Interestingly it earlier considered and then rejected the development of provisions for local referenda to give such control directly to ratepayers.

(5) *Taxation and incentives.* The main economic argument for tax limitation, subscribed to by the present Conservative government, is that taxes reduce the incentive to work, invest and engage in entrepreneurial activities. Thus, it is argued that tax reductions now will encourage greater economic growth providing future benefits, including a larger tax base to support social programmes. It is difficult to see such adjustments in 'crisis' terms, unless there is a critical threshold tax rate beyond which this effect operates strongly. While superficially plausible, this argument is not theoretically clear-cut, since higher taxes tend to have opposing effects, a 'substitution' effect making leisure more attractive than work and an 'income' effect encouraging people to work more to make up the loss of income (Brown, 1983; Kay and King, 1983). Different taxes have different effects, and affect people at different levels of income or in different household circumstances in different ways. The main targets of criticism are high marginal rates of income tax associated with progressive, redistributional tax and benefits schemes, illustrating the fundamental conflict between goals of efficiency and equity. There have been a number of empirical studies of tax incentive effects, reviewed by Brown (1983), which confirm the complexity of the subject and provide mixed findings. The 1979 British tax changes, involving a shift from direct to indirect taxation, were found not to have a positive incentive effect for most groups (Brown, 1983, pp. 172-6).

(6) *Public borrowing.* Governments borrow to finance deficits, the difference between expenditure and tax revenues, and the level of the public sector borrowing requirement (PSBR) can be taken as indicative of fiscal stress. In this sense the rapid escalation of the PSBR in the mid-1970s was a potent symbol of fiscal crisis. It can be misleading to regard a high PSBR as unsound financial practice, however, since it is invariably more than matched by public sector investment and also, generally, by the excess of private saving over private investment. Since the mid-1970s the PSBR has been a key target variable for

macroeconomic management purposes. Depending on how it is funded, the PSBR can either contribute to monetary expansion, which monetarist doctrine sees as central to the generation of inflation, or to high interest rates, which are argued to inhibit investment and thereby economic growth. This current orthodoxy reflects assumptions about the behaviour of the economy which are highly contested (House of Commons, 1976, 1980; Heald, 1983, ch. 3; Cuthbertson, 1979). Some economists would argue that the government should use as its target a PSBR adjusted for the effects of inflation and recession (e.g. Ward and Neild, 1978). On the other hand, the widespread acceptance of monetarist ideas in the financial community leads to behaviour by the financial markets which turns this belief into a self-fulfilling prophecy in the short run, with 'bad' money supply or PSBR figures causing a reluctance to lend to the government, which forces up interest rates. This kind of effect reinforces the atmosphere of 'fiscal crisis' in particular periods, such as 1976 and 1980-1, when the government is considering public expenditure cuts, even though in the longer term there is no reason to expect funds not to continue to be available, since the financial institutions are constantly seeking outlets for their funds.

(7) *Inflation.* It is true that inflation in Britain showed sharp accelerations in the two recent periods of apparent fiscal crisis, 1974-5 and 1979-81 (see Table 5.1), and that the control of inflation has been a priority in economic policy. However, there are two quite major question marks over the view that inflation is central to the fiscal problems of British or other governments. Firstly, the question of what causes inflation is a highly contested issue in economics. Monetarists stress the connections between public borrowing, the money supply and inflation, yet these links are not particularly well supported by empirical data (see House of Commons, 1981; and especially Hendry and Ericsson, 1983; Kaldor, 1982). Keynesians stress cost-push factors, such as the price of oil and the process of pay bargaining, and many support incomes policies as the appropriate solution. A common element here is a concern with public sector pay (Heald, 1983, ch. 9), and if it is not possible to control this by other means then the blunt instrument of controlling cash expenditure may be forced on governments, causing cuts in services as a sort of by-product.

Secondly, we may question whether inflation need be regarded as a major, overriding problem economically or socially, unlike problems involving real resources like unemployment. If financial arrangements are adequately indexed (Liesner and King, 1975) inflation need not have serious disruptive effects. Unstable rates of inflation increase uncertainty and inflation is clearly politically unpopular. We are inclined to the view that inflation is best regarded, both in relation to its causes and its consequences, more as a problem of politics than of economy (Hirsch and Goldthorpe, 1978).

(8) *The balance of payments.* The balance of trade and overseas payments was a persistent constraint on British economic management in the 1960s and played a major part in the 1975-6 post-OPEC crisis. One notable round of public expenditure cuts was forced by the need to secure an international loan from the IMF in 1976. At the time of writing, the advent of North Sea oil has relaxed this constraint, but this relaxation is unlikely to continue indefinitely. It is unclear whether this long-term process of declining competitive performance can be blamed on fiscal factors (Blackaby, 1979). The argument of Bacon and Eltis (1976), that over-expansion of public services in the 1960s and 1970s undermined the performance of the trading sector of the economy, is considered further below. In our view there is a serious danger in the longer run, as North Sea oil declines, of the weak position of British manufacturing undermining the economic base for social policies in Britain. If so, this will be a fiscal crisis growing out of a more deeply rooted crisis of production in an economy having difficulty in adapting to international competition (Smith, 1984).

Conclusions on the British case

What conclusions can we draw from this review of the elements, or 'proximate causes', of fiscal crisis in Britain during the 1970s and 1980s. In general we draw the conclusion that fiscal crisis has been more apparent than real. There has not been a dramatic about-turn in all the economic indicators, or indeed in public expenditure, although as Table 5.1 shows growth trends were dented in the mid-1970s and early 1980s. Government's control over expenditure has been shown at times to be inadequate, but has been to some extent reformed. There are built-in growth factors in public spending, but the scale of these should not be exaggerated. The main threat to the tax base remains a decline in overall economic activity, but the main instance of decline so far (1979-81) has been, arguably, a product of government policies. There does not seem to be a tax revolt of major proportions, and the incentive arguments for tax reduction are not strongly supported by theory or evidence. Public borrowing symbolizes fiscal stress and is used as a control target, but the levels actually incurred can easily be rationalized. Inflation is more a political than an economic problem, and the balance of payments, Britain's long term 'Achilles heel', has receded from the agenda thanks to North Sea oil.

What emerges from this discussion is a feeling that fiscal crisis is more of a political phenomenon than an economic one. There has been an atmosphere of crisis at particular times (1976 and 1980-1), fuelled by such phenomena as inflation, the PSBR, and control failures within the public sector, but not really warranted by a broader economic assessment. At such moments it has been possible to make certain cuts in social programmes, and to shift the agenda of discussion towards a more critical stance toward the welfare state (Pliatzky, 1982; Ham, 1981). That such a shift has occurred, however, probably owes more to a general disillusion with aspects of the welfare state, shared by some of its former protagonists and based as much on doubts about its effectiveness in social terms (Le Grand, 1982; George and Wilding, 1984; Le Grand and Robinson, 1984) as on its financing.

International comparisons

The discussion so far has concentrated solely on the British experience. There are several reasons for wishing to look at evidence from other countries, as well. We may wish to see whether the patterns observed in the British economy and government spending are similar to those occurring elsewhere. Similarities may help to establish that statements made about processes of 'fiscal crisis' or whatever are reasonable generalizations about advanced western societies. In so far as there are differences between countries, we may also wish to see whether there are systematic patterns in these differences, which we can interpret as evidence in support of particular explanations of the processes involved. We are fortunate in that the recent work of the OECD has produced a range of statistics on a comparable basis for its member countries running back over more than two decades. The material in this section is wholly derived from this source. While this material is helpful for the two general tasks identified above, it does not provide the degree of detail needed to comment on all the more specific issues involved in the fiscal crisis notion in the way that we did for the British case.

How typical is the British case? Table 5.3 summarizes the main economic and governmental expenditure trends over the period 1960 to 1982, broken down into four phases. Britain (UK) is compared with the seven largest OECD economies as a group

Table 5.3   *Economic trends in OECD countries, 1960-1982*

	1960-8	*1968-73*	*1973-9*	*1979-82*
Gross domestic product				
UK	3.1	3.1	1.4	−0.5
Big 7[a]	5.1	4.7	2.7	0.9
Smaller European	5.1	5.4	2.5	1.1
Investment				
UK	6.0	1.8	−0.1	−3.3
Big 7[a]	6.4	6.0	1.3	−1.3
Smaller European	6.9	6.0	n.a.	−1.4
Government consumption				
UK	2.7	2.3	1.8	1.0
Big 7[a]	4.6	2.1	2.7	2.3
Smaller European	4.7	4.6	4.2	2.3
Social security transfers[b]				
UK	5.8	6.2	5.4	4.1
Big 7[a]	8.5	9.1	6.6	3.3
Smaller European	11.7	11.8	7.3	4.5

Average annual percentage growth rates in real terms
[a] The Big 7 are: UK, USA, Japan, W. Germany, France, Italy, Canada.
[b] Indirectly estimated.
Source: OECD (1984) *Economic Outlook: Historical Statistics 1960-82*, Paris, OECD.

and with another group of 'smaller European' economies. Common features include: (a) relatively good growth up to 1973; (b) a faltering of growth after 1973; (c) a further deterioration after 1979; (d) a growth of government consumption of goods and services below or in line with general economic growth; (e) a growth of social security transfers in excess of general economic growth. So there is a shared experience here of growth followed by recent periods of recession, and of a growth of state activity with particular reference to social security. Clearly, however, Britain differs systematically and across the board from these others groups in one respect: the British growth rates are typically lower. It should be noted that this applies to government and social security spending as well as other economic aggregates. There is clearly a distinctive British dimension of economic failure which distinguishes us. We shall see in a moment that there is a similar but opposite dimension of success in almost all the indicators for Japan. Both these cases are discussed in an interesting and accessible way by Smith (1984).

The other feature which emerges from Table 5.3 is that neither government consumption nor social transfers are the first casualty of economic recession. Growth rates in these categories are dented a little, at least after 1979, but they are not generally eliminated or reversed. Something else in the economy has to give, in a situation where economic growth comes to a halt. To some extent this is private consumption, or real disposable income; but much more striking is the impact on investment, as shown in Table 5.3. Investment is sensitively related to growth rates and prospects (in Keynesian terms this is called the 'accelerator' effect); but investment is also the engine of growth, both in the short run (Keynesian 'multiplier' effects) and in the long run, through increasing the capacity and the technological level of an economy. Japan invested 32.3 per cent of its GDP on average over 1960-82, compared with 21.4 per cent in OECD economies as a whole. Thus the initial impact of recession is on the seedcorn for future growth rather than on the welfare state; this may naturally tend to generate a debate about economic versus social priorities, such that in a subsequent phase welfare spending is indeed reduced. In marxian terms the initial problem is a failure of capital accumulation. Another expression of this may be a dip in profits. There is evidence for Britain in Table 5.1 of temporary dips in recessions. Without quoting detailed data, the OECD evidence suggests that profits are fairly resilient in the medium term.

We are not attempting to answer here the question of why the advanced western economies as a group have experienced more economic difficulty since the early 1970s, whether this is a temporary phase, and whether it can be accounted for in terms of some kind of 'trade cycle' or 'long wave' theory (Schumpeter, 1964; Coombs, 1981; Delbeke, 1981; Freeman et al., 1982). Clearly there are powerful transmission mechanisms of trade, finance and technology linking the performances of these economies together. Neither should we underrate the significance of government policies and the ideas underlying these in determining the course of events; for example, similarities in the reaction of governments to oil price rises in 1973 and 1979 may have had a good deal to do with recessions that followed those episodes.

We are, however, interested in whether we can infer anything from the *differences* in the experiences of these economies. Can we adduce evidence of this essentially correlational kind to support or refute particular hypotheses about the processes of economic change? We are particularly interested here in the kind of hypotheses advanced by Bacon and Eltis (1976) and of course by the present British government, namely that public expenditure was a direct cause of economic difficulty. Table 5.4 summarizes the OECD data on government spending in 11 countries, ranked in descending order of public spending's share of GDP. Four points stand out. First, Britain (the worst performer economically) is not a particularly high spender. Second, Japan (the best performer) is a consistently lower spender. Thirdly, some relatively prosperous and successful economies are quite high spenders. Fourthly, the rankings are not entirely the same if we look at components of spending, since some countries (e.g. France) emphasize social security much more highly than others (e.g. UK).

Figure 5.1 plots growth performance against government spending. The correlation at first sight appears weakly negative, which gives some support to the critics of government spending. However, this is solely a product of two extreme outlier cases, Japan and Britain. The same comment applies to figure 5.2, which relates growth to social security transfers. It could be

Table 5.4   *Government expenditure shares in 11 OECD countries*

	Total government expenditure		Government consumption		Social security transfers	
	1960-82	*1979-82*	*1960-82*	*1979-82*	*1960-82*	*1979-82*
Netherlands	47.8	(55.0)	15.9	(17.0)	22.2	(25.0)
Sweden	46.5	(54.0)	22.3	(23.5)	12.6	(16.5)
W. Germany	41.6	49.0	17.3	20.4	14.5	17.1
Norway	41.4	(49.0)	17.2	(18.5)	12.3	(16.3)
France	40.9	48.8	13.9	15.7	18.6	24.7
UK	40.2	47.0	18.7	21.8	9.3	13.0
Italy	38.2	50.3	15.1	17.7	13.5	17.2
Canada	35.5	42.8	17.8	20.1	8.5	10.7
USA	31.8	35.9	18.3	18.5	8.2	11.5
Australia	27.9	(35.5)	13.3	17.0	6.9	(9.5)
Japan	23.8	33.8	8.6	10.1	6.3	10.8

Percentage of GDP, averaged over relevant period, countries ranked by total public expenditure share, 1979-82
Figures in parentheses are estimated.
Source: OECD (1984), *Economic Outlook: Historical Statistics 1960-82*. Paris, OECD.

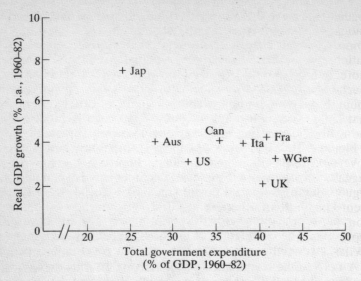

Figure 5.1   Growth performance and government expenditure in eight major OECD countries, 1960-1982

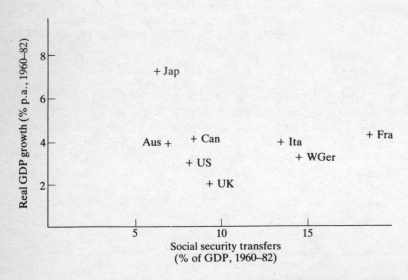

Figure 5.2   Growth performance and social security transfers in eight major OECD countries, 1960-1982

argued that Japanese society is so different, and so little understood in the west, that it should be excluded from such comparisons. Clearly, Japan is a more recently industrialized nation and as such has not developed its welfare state so far as more 'mature' industrial societies (Wilensky, 1975). It also has a much more advanced occupational welfare system which does not count as government expenditure; and one certainly cannot infer that Japanese governments intervene less in their economy; quite the reverse is the case (Smith, 1984).

Figure 5.3 relates growth performance to the growth rate in government consumption of goods and services. This evidence suggests the opposite from what the critics of state spending argue, and supports traditional Keynesian thinking, that government spending generates faster growth. An alternative interpretation, and probably the main point, is that more successful economies can afford and choose greater state spending (Wilensky, 1975), reversing the causality implied by this diagram.

A more subtle formulation of the Bacon and Eltis thesis would be that over-rapid government growth damages growth prospects, and that this would be seen in a greater downturn in growth following a period of high government growth. Figure 5.5 tests this hypothesis: again, the evidence suggests weakly the opposite, Keynesian conclusion.

Inflation has been a major preoccupation in the years of apparent fiscal crisis, as we have already seen. Figure 5.4 suggests

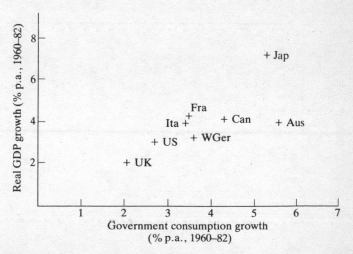

Figure 5.3   Growth performance and government consumption growth in eight major OECD countries, 1960-1982

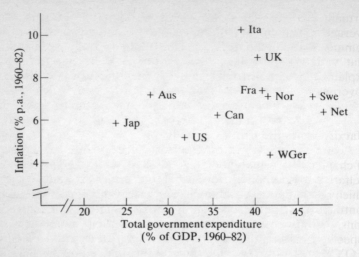

Figure 5.4   Inflation performance and total government expenditure in 11 OECD countries, 1960-1982

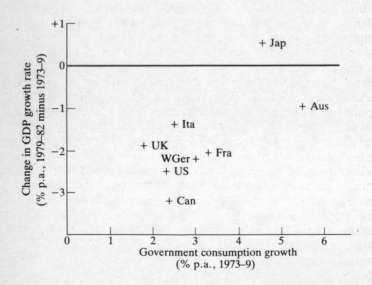

Figure 5.5   Growth performance changes and government growth in eight major OECD countries, 1973-1982

virtually no correlation between overall state spending and average rates of inflation. Rather, it supports our earlier comments about the political nature of inflation, by suggesting that variations (e.g. Italy vs. West Germany) may be better explained by political cultures and the effectiveness of central governments.

Marxist theoretical explanations

In chapter 2 we reviewed marxist accounts of the evolution of the welfare state in capitalist societies. In essence this account is one which sees the welfare state as an adaptation to earlier crises and contradictions, but one which in time sets up its own contradictions. In this chapter we comment further on some economic aspects of the marxist approach.

O'Connor's (1973) *The Fiscal Crisis of the State* was an influential work, as much as anything because of its timing. The essence of its argument can be expressed very briefly. The monopoly sector of the capitalist economy is both the motor force of its growth and the dominant political force in the state. Increasingly, this sector depends for its continued growth on expanded 'social capital'. This includes both 'social investment' in, for example, transport infrastructure and technical education which increase productivity and accumulation, and 'social consumption' (e.g. social insurance) which lowers the 'reproduction' cost of labour and thereby also raises profits. At the same time the growth of the monopoly sector generates increased 'social expenses', including defence (to secure ever-larger overseas markets) and welfare payments for the growing 'surplus' population. Thus, growth is accompanied by a disproportionate growth in state outlays. At the same time as it appropriates the surplus, monopoly capital can and does successfully avoid bearing the tax burden, which therefore falls mainly on monopoly sector workers and the relatively weak and impoverished competitive sector. This system tends to crisis as the powerful, unionized monopoly sector workers resist taxation at the same time as competitive and state sector workers also become disenchanted with the system. Particular features of this model include the very polarized, dualistic model of the economy; high productivity growth in the monopoly sector; the increasingly 'social' (interdependent) character of production, necessitating greater socialization of costs (e.g. education); the 'special character' of the state sector, which combines high wages with low productivity growth (as in the Baumol model); and the tendency for 'special interests' to secure particular, often wasteful, investments (politics as an 'irrational' process). The model is heavily coloured by the American experience of the 1960s and early 1970s, from which O'Connor draws his illustrations.

In his more recent work, Gough (1979) is concerned more specifically with the welfare state and writes from a British perspective. Gough offers a somewhat modified, less deterministic version of O'Connor's model. Less emphasis is placed on the dual economy concept (the monopolistic vs. competitive sectors). There is a more careful analysis of 'reproductive' social expenditure and of who pays for public expenditure as a whole, including the unreproductive social expenses. The position of the working population as a 'fiscally exploited' group is stressed. The possibility of variation in the power position of the working class is discussed, particularly in relation to full employment, and the consequences of this for welfare state expansion representing a 'real gain' for the working class, as opposed to an indirect boost to profits, are drawn out. The fiscal crisis arises when economic growth under full employment becomes unviable in the light of changed international conditions, and as the power of the working class to retain the benefits while passing on the costs of the welfare state lead to rising inflation. However, Gough envisages a 'strategic' response to this by the ruling class, involving a 'restructuring' of the welfare state and a greater centralization of power.

It is not intended here to rehearse a detailed critique of the marxist 'fiscal crisis' model. There are a number of difficulties with it, discussed among others by Heald (1983). The models tend to be discussed in rather general terms and not spelt out in rigorous, mathematical terms with relative quantitative magnitudes specified. It is therefore rather difficult to judge whether the conclusions do indeed follow logically from the premises, or which premises are crucial to the argument. One area which seems to us crucial and not fully explained is the question of how wages, especially (for O'Connor) monopoly sector wages, are determined, since on this hinges (as Gough seems to recognize) the incidence of the fiscal burden, and indeed the incidence of the benefits of potentially 'reproductive' expenditure.

The logical status of the models is not entirely clear. O'Connor appears to be offering a deterministic model in which profound political crisis is inevitable in the not-too-distant future. Gough, on the other hand, appears to be suggesting that crisis may be a phase, which a 'strategic response' by the ruling class can overcome. He seems to suggest that there are choices at this strategic level, for example between corporatism and market discipline types of approach. What is quite clear, though, is that these are not simply economic models, or rather that the economic components alone do not complete the picture which the authors are attempting to draw. There is (certainly in Gough) a set of questions about the political process, within which working-class interests may have certain influence and within which the interests of different sectors of capital may conflict. Most important, however, is the whole sphere of legitimation, since crucial to these models' predictions are questions about how far the system can maintain sufficient legitimacy in the face of growing difficulties (e.g. high unemployment, taxation, etc.) and at what cost.

As pointed out in chapter 2 the control of such a system is likely to rest upon a mixture of measures designed to legitimize and measures designed to repress dissent. Whilst, as we showed, social policies may involve both care and control, the maintenance of order in such a situation may also rest upon more obviously repressive measures. Hence the financial 'burden' upon an economy in crisis will include the cost of policing as well as the cost of social policy. It may be the case that, as new methods of policing emerge, there is at this time a shift away from the softer 'control' measures associated with social policy to harder and more direct forms of control (see McLennan et al., 1984; Saunders and Dearlove, 1984).

An important feature of the marxist political economy approach noted in chapter 2, and to which we now turn, is its similarity in important respects with the new right/market liberal/public choice school's critique. For example, one could cite the shared concern with the uncontrollable growth of state expenditure, the 'waste' inherent in some state activities, the capturing of the state by special interests, or the effect of welfare benefits and taxes on the will to work (Heald, 1983, pp. 267-8). There are also clear parallels between the marxist models and that of Bacon and Eltis (1976). The radical critique of the welfare state developed from the 1970s has perhaps contributed, through intellectual channels, to its declining legitimacy and hence to a passive acceptance of cutbacks in social expenditure.

Alternative explanations

While we have given considerable attention to marxist theory in this chapter, because it has been very influential in social policy thinking in recent years, we would also stress that the fiscal events described here can be accounted for by other kinds of theory. One could, for example, appeal to a 'corporatist' view of the state which explained changes in public spending in terms of the assertion of the primacy of 'the national economy' in policy making. Equally, one could turn to the 'public choice' school which, from a philosophical standpoint of market liberalism, utilizes the methodology of economics to explain political and bureaucratic behaviour. Since arguably this body of theory has been more influential in western policy making in the past decade, it seems appropriate to consider its arguments in this context. Although lack of space prevents us doing this, one could also appeal to ideas about technological and social change, found particularly in the 'futures' literature, to explain some of what may be happening.

Public choice theory has given a new lease of life to right wing critiques of the welfare state, as exemplified in Britain by the output of organizations such as the Institute of Economic Affairs. Much of its output is relevant to arguments about the boundaries between the state and the market, discussed in the next chapter. Its contributions to arguments about the origins of the welfare state were briefly explored in chapter 2. Here we want to review more briefly its contribution to explanations of fiscal crisis. Its contribution can be considered under three broad headings: politics, bureaucracy, and monetarism as a set of doctrines concerning macroeconomic policy.

The seminal works on 'the economics of politics' (Downs, 1957; Buchanan and Tullock, 1962; Breton, 1974; reviewed in Mueller, 1976) are concerned with the question: how would the political system operate if political actors acted rationally in their own interests, with politicians as entrepreneurs seeking to attain the personal benefits of power by selling policies to voters, themselves attempting to maximize their own interests in the light of the limited information available to them. One of the key theoretical propositions is the 'median voter' hypothesis, that policies reflect the preferences of voters in the middle of the range of preferences on the issue involved. From this can be derived predictions that democratic governments will tend to redistribute income and wealth, particularly away from the top end of the distribution and in favour of middle-income groups more than the poor (Culyer, 1980). There is some empirical support for this proposition, as we showed in chapter 3. While failing to achieve the sort of distributional aims generally associated with the welfare state, such redistribution involves progressive taxation on higher earners which market liberals would see as economically damaging in their incentive effects.

Secondly, it is argued (Brittan, 1977; Whiteley, 1980) that

democratic systems tend to generate a 'political business cycle'. Prior to elections, governments maximize popular spending programmes and minimize taxes, whilst after elections economic problems (inflation, balance of payments) necessitate a reversal of policies. As it stands this is a theory of recurrent, but self-correcting, mini-crises; linked to other hypotheses, whereby perhaps spending and expectations increase by a ratchet effect, the system might not be sustainable.

Thirdly, it is arguable that democratic politics embodies a pro-expenditure bias. Spending programmes give high benefits to specific groups – public employees, private contractors, beneficiaries – who find it worthwhile to organize as professional lobbies or pressure groups. The political system is more responsive to such lobbies, which can spend a good deal on persuasion and legitimation of their causes, and by a process of 'log rolling' (vote-trading) large, disparate coalitions of vested interests can secure approval of a whole array of spending programmes. These are paid for by the general taxpayer, a widely diffused interest group within which individuals do not find it worthwhile actively to engage in countering the spending lobbies. Public sector employees are seen as a potent set of pressure groups, and are now numerous enough to exercise voting power as well. However, it could be argued that certain industrial sectors (defence industries, nuclear power, agriculture) are even more effective in this arena.

Finally, with the previous point in mind, it is argued that governments have a natural tendency to obscure the 'bad news' of tax increases by relying on forms of taxation which are difficult to perceive, for example PAYE income tax. Monetarists would argue that inflation (without indexation) is a form of back-door taxation which results from the fiscal irresponsibility of deficit financing.

The 'economics of bureaucracy' literature (Niskanen, 1971; Jackson, 1982) has grown up in parallel, highlighting certain features of public bureaucracy which, it is argued, flow from the same general assumptions of rational, self-interested behaviour. Public bureaus (e.g. ministries) are monopolistic suppliers of policies to politicians/legislatures, and often of the information required to evaluate such policies as well. As such, they are in a position to offer politicians packages which serve to satisfy the politicians whilst creaming off the 'surplus' benefits created by the policy for the advantage of the bureau itself. Niskanen argued that senior bureaucrats have an incentive to maximize their budgets, a view commonly asserted or assumed as a matter of almost common sense in discussion of budgetary behaviour

(Wildavsky, 1964), although this assumption can be questioned as not necessarily plausible in all circumstances (Jackson, 1982). If this were true, and if the bureaucracy had the requisite bargaining power, public programmes would be systematically 'too big'. Again, to stress the monopoly of the supplier neglects the monopsony on the other side of the bargain, which suggests a less determinate outcome. It is also argued that public bureaucracies tend to exhibit productive inefficiency, as discussed in chapter 10, since this meets the interests of bureaucrats without any countervailing pressures from market competition (as with any genuine monopoly). One could also link this cynical view of public bureaucracy to the general, and respectable, view of public budgeting as 'incrementalism' (Lindblom, 1979), with a marked reluctance to question or eliminate established programmes.

Putting all these elements together we do indeed have a recipe for fiscal crisis. Excessive and inefficient redistribution, a political business cycle with a ratchet, the pro-expenditure bias of pressure group politics, monopolistic, inefficient, budget-maximizing bureaus, and incrementalism all combine to exert an unsteady upward trend to public expenditure. Of these elements, the pro-expenditure bias seems the crucial hypothesis. Meanwhile, governments tend to obscure the costs by covert taxation, most notably by deficit financing leading to inflation. Crisis is precipitated by the political backlash to accelerating inflation, tax revolt, the Laffer curve, economic decline created by 'crowding out' (Bacon and Eltis, 1976) and the disincentive effects of taxation. What is less clear is why crisis occurs at a particular juncture, and not earlier, and what happens after the crisis. The theory is much more one of chronic or recurrent mini-crises rather than grand crisis.

It does seem very difficult to account for the relative success of western economies in experiencing something like 25 years of simultaneous economic growth and public expenditure expansion without major crisis. During this period the kind of views embodied in the public choice approach had little influence on policy. It seems almost as though the theory has come to prominence as a consequence of economic crisis. Perhaps one could make the same comment about marxist theory. It also seems a weakness of public choice theory that it is rather static, and ahistorical in approach.

Conclusions

In this chapter we have examined both theoretically and empirically the proposition that welfare states tend to experience, and have actually experienced, a fiscal crisis necessitating a political response detrimental to the continued development of social services and policies. We started by identifying the specific elements or manifestations of fiscal crisis, and examined critically the evidence on these in the British case. While there has been some evidence, and much concern, about these elements since the mid-1970s, we remain sceptical as to how real a crisis these represent. We would reject, as we did in chapter 1, the notion of an economic imperative overriding political debate about priorities, but we would accept that a longer-term economic decline does pose problems for social policy and there are signs of such a trend in Britain especially. Our examination of international evidence highlighted the latter point. It also revealed a common experience in advanced western countries of faltering economic growth, suggesting both a high degree of economic interdependence but also a tendency perhaps for government policies to reinforce economic cycles. Examination of differences in performance between major economies provides little support to the arguments of the right that public expenditure is the root cause of economic problems.

We gave further attention in this chapter to marxist accounts of fiscal crisis, in part because the idea of crisis is so central to marxist theory and in part because this perspective has become so influential in social policy theory. Outlining the principal economic arguments in the work of O'Connor and Gough, we suggested that there are difficulties to be resolved at a theoretical level, illustrated by the example of wage determination.

In the final section of the chapter we outlined an alternative theoretical approach provided by the 'public choice' school. This explains tendencies to fiscal crisis in terms of electoral behaviour, the pro-expenditure bias of pluralist politics, and the behaviour of monopolistic public bureaus, but is not particularly helpful in explaining the timing of any particular crisis. This prompts the thought that, to a degree, one may see the ascendancy of particular theories as consequences of economic events as much as explanatory accounts. Other factors, we feel, need to be introduced to either of these theoretical accounts to provide an adequate overall explanation of the course of events. These include international developments, the role of key natural resources such as oil, particular political choices reflecting in part the electoral fortunes of particular parties, and organizational-level factors.

6

The State and the Market

A Framework for Analysis

Introduction

Analyses of the welfare state have often treated the state and the market as substantially separate spheres of influence. Social policy could be seen as firmly in the realm of the state, and not therefore a relevant subject for the application of market concepts or solutions. We rejected this simple division as unrealistic and unhelpful in our opening chapter. Even in a country such as Britain, with relatively comprehensive state welfare services, the interactions with the market and what Titmuss called 'the social division of welfare' (involving private and subsidized welfare provision) have always been a feature of the scene. International comparisons reveal much greater potential diversity in the boundaries between state and market spheres in relation to particular social services (e.g. health care) (Wilensky, 1975; Heidenheimer et al., 1983; Higgins, 1981).

In the early 1980s the location of the boundaries between the state and market spheres has become a very live policy issue in Britain, and significant changes have occurred. Superficially, this could be attributed largely to the election in 1979, and re-election in 1983, of a Conservative government with more clear-cut ideological commitment to the market than any of its post-war predecessors. However, this shift, or greater state of flux, can also be linked to such factors as the greater fiscal pressure discussed in the previous chapter; to 'restructuring' in other sections of the economy; to technological and social change; and to changing public attitudes, not least attitudes towards the efficacy of large public organizations. With these factors often in common, other western countries are also apparently moving into a period of greater flux and reappraisal in relation to the roles of the state and the market in social policy (OECD, 1981).

There is no shortage of existing tools for analysing the relationship between the state and the market. In chapter 1 we introduced the welfare economic perspective with its typology of sources of 'market failure' and implied complementary roles for the state. There and in chapter 8 we discuss various policy typologies concerned with different ways in which the state intervenes. Useful though these tools are, it is argued here that we need a fuller and more comprehensive framework to analyse the diversity of cases and arguments that increasingly arise in areas where the boundary between the state and the market is in a condition of flux. This chapter aims to sketch out such a framework and apply it to a number of contemporary examples.

Three elements seem essential to such a framework. Firstly, we must clarify the different types of role assigned to the state and the market, particularly the considerable variety of intermediate relationships which are increasingly being explored. Without this clarification, loose statements about 'privatization', 'choice' and 'competition' may be quite misleading. Secondly, we must consider explanations for the direction and form of changes in state/market relationships, the social, economic and political forces and processes generating (or resisting) changes. Thirdly, we must identify the issues which are likely to be critical in normative evaluation of and debate about different forms of relationship. We spell out a range of possibilities under each of these headings before proceeding to examine two cases.

Types of relationship

Social policy is primarily about the provision of services to meet needs. While the state can and often does act as the main organization providing the services, this is not necessarily the only way of implementing a policy that such services should be available. At the other extreme the state could stand aside and rely on a wholly market form of provision – private business producing the service and selling it to clients. In between are a whole variety of mixed or partial modes of state involvement, and it is these which we are particularly interested in here. Not all of these options are mutually exclusive.

(1) *State provision with user charges*. Charges may be used to ration the service, to generate revenue or improve provision standards, and there may be graduated or simpler 'passport' type

remission of charges for categories of low-income or high-need clients. This differs from a wholly market solution in so far as prices are lower, remission of charges is available in some cases, the standard and style of service may be different, and there is greater certainty that the service is actually available comprehensively. (For a fuller discussion of charging see Davies and Reddin, 1978; Judge and Matthews, 1980; Judge, 1981a; Seldon, 1977).

(2)   *State as competitor.* Here the state operates in the market in a rather similar way to private suppliers but seeks to act as a sort of 'market leader', competing on quality and price, and setting an exemplary standard which private firms are forced to follow. This model is rather unusual in practice.

(3)   *State as residual provider, or provider of 'last resort'.* This is much more commonly the state role in welfare; a service of basic minimum standard is available to those unable to secure something better in the market, and is typically rationed by tests of means and of needs and often by its poor image or stigmatized character (Sleeman, 1979, is typical in seeing the welfare state in this role).

(4)   *Contracting, i.e. state provision with bought-in inputs.* The fact that a state agency is responsible for provision of a service does not necessarily mean that all the resources used as input in the production of the service are produced in-house by the state organization. The idea of 'contracting out' elements of services in this way has been pursued energetically by the British government since 1979; in other countries it has often been the case that many of these elements have always been supplied privately under contract. (See Coopers and Lybrand, 1981, for a study of charging and contracting in the local government context.)

(5)   *State purchase of packaged services.* The extreme form of the above approach is where the state simply becomes an intermediary, a sort of collective consumers' representative, and buys complete service packages from suppliers. Judge (1981b) refers to this mode as 'purchase of service contracting' and points out that it is much more common in the USA than in Britain. What is the difference between this and the next category, state as subsidizer? One difference may be that the subsidy is 100 per cent. More fundamentally, in this category the state is still present as an intermediary, setting some at least of the service standards and possibly deciding which clients are allocated to which services.

(6) *State as subsidizer*. Here the state withdraws from its intermediary role and simply retains a financial involvement by agreeing to subsidize (generally at much less than 100 per cent, to avoid abuse and cost escalation) broad categories of expenditure regarded as worthwhile contributors to 'welfare'. Subsidy can be overt in the form of public outlays or less obvious in the form of tax relief (Heald, 1983, pp. 20-2).

(7) *State as regulator*. Again, the state no longer stands between client and supplier, but this time the relationship is legalistic rather than financial. Standards or limits are set on the form of services which may or may not be provided, and the state must police these in some way. Often private suppliers must be registered or licensed. Sometimes this process is linked to subsidy eligibility, as for example with British housing associations.

(8) *State as facilitator or co-ordinator*. While regulation is restrictive, this role is a more positive, enabling one; often involving the exchange of information, provision of advice on good practice, and so on. It may be particularly important in assisting voluntary, community-based, non-commercial suppliers, or small businesses, all of which lack the organizational capacity to cope with a complex regulatory and fiscal environment or to absorb technical information from diverse sources. This role may also involve preventing wasteful duplication of effort and directing suppliers to gaps in provision.

(9) *State as bearer and spreader of risk*. Much of social policy is concerned with overcoming uncertain contingencies of life, and may be likened to insurance; the state is in a better position than any private supplier to spread such risks more broadly. In a sense this is what being 'provider of last resort' implies – insurance for those seen as uninsurable, or bad risks, or those who have failed to insure themselves (see Culyer, 1980, pp. 39-43). However, the state can also be seen as standing in the background as a potential back-up for non-state organizations which may run into difficulty, such as savings institutions or housing associations.

While this kind of typology is clearly useful and probably necessary, there are two senses in which it may be potentially misleading. Firstly, it does not discriminate between different forms of non-state institution or provision, tending to lump them all together as 'the market'. In reality the picture is one of considerable diversity. A broad division would be between commercial (for-profit) organizations and voluntary/non-profit organizations. The whole arena of 'occupational welfare' represents another dimension, where employers take on much of the intermediary role described above in parallel with the state, as well as supplying some services directly. The commercial/non-profit distinction is a difficult one to make. How does one categorize professionals in private practice, who may have a strong service ethic and motivation, or nominally non-profit 'friendly societies' (like the British building societies) whose mode of operation seems barely distinguishable from an insurance company or bank (Boddy, 1980)?

Secondly, by focusing on state roles we tend implicitly to treat the market as 'the norm', deviations from which must be justified in some way. It may be that our cultural conditioning leads us unconsciously into such a stance, and associated beliefs in the efficiency- and freedom-promoting properties of markets (Smith, 1984; Heald, 1983). Another way of approaching the subject would be to say: what potential roles might there be for the market in particular cases? A short list of relevant headings might then include:

(1) competing suppliers: to aid efficiency and keep costs down;
(2) competing suppliers: to generate diversity in services and increase consumer choice;
(3) generate more evidence about preferences;
(4) foster innovation and experiment in forms of service;
(5) involve alternative organizational models to the standard bureaucratic hierarchy characteristics of the state;
(6) devolved self-regulation, as in the professions;
(7) involve 'marketing' skills to generate greater take-up;
(8) involve entrepreneurial and broking skills in bringing together fragmented resources in a complex environment;
(9) bring forth greater 'voluntary' resources (in the broadest sense) to relieve fiscal pressure on the state (i.e. the necessity to raise 'involuntary' taxation).

Judge (1981b, p. 124) offers a rather similar set of categories in his discussion of contracting in the context of personal social services with particular reference to the voluntary sector. We are particularly interested in current changes in the boundaries between the state and the market. Heald (1983, p. 299) suggests that current privatization initiatives fall into four categories: charging, contracting, de-regulation, and complete shifting of activities out of the state sphere. Our typology suggests that the possibilities are broader than this.

Explaining state–market relationships

The second essential element in our framework is to be in a

position to explain how and why particular state–market relationships change or persist, with reference to particular social, economic and political forces and processes. It seems helpful to identify at the outset some general explanatory factors, since detailed examination of case studies does not always bring out strongly enough the importance of common factors. Explanation of general tendencies in social policy was the subject of chapter 2, whilst chapter 8 looks at the explanation of more specific policy shifts.

(1)   *Ideology*. The choice between collectivist/state and market systems is perhaps the dimension of policy choice which is always the most 'ideological'. By this we meant that it is subject to strongly held preferences linked to systematic bodies of ideas which represent undifferentiated mixtures of theory and values. Governments appear to take decisions to 'nationalize' or 'privatize' primarily on ideological grounds, and the boundaries of state and market become more mobile in a period when political parties assume a higher ideological profile. To argue that a change is ideological is to argue that a particular ideology is dominant or at least powerful in certain conditions.

(2)   *Interests*.
(a)   *Private producers*. Politics and power are closely bound up with interests: to be powerful is to further your interests (Lukes, 1974). Pluralist and marxist theories of power (see also the discussion of this theme in chapter 8) are both about interests, but differ in their emphasis on short-term, specific and conscious interests as against longer-term, systematic 'real' interests. Clearly one potentially 'interested' and influential set of parties is the private agencies which do or might engage in providing social services. How interested they are in social services may vary depending on such factors as the opportunities for profit elsewhere. From a pluralist perspective, how influential they are would depend on the particular coalition of interests in power at the time.
(b)   *Public producers*. It is increasingly recognized that those engaged in public authorities producing social services represent a significant pressure group (or set of groups) in the political arena. It may be useful to distinguish between the bureaucracy itself, and different types of bureaucracy (e.g. central and local government), professional organizations and trade unions. The growth of both professionalization and public service union membership were remarkable features of the 1970s in Britain and elsewhere. Opinions differ over how far it is appropriate to characterize the goals of these groups

as the material self-interest of their members as opposed to an expert concern with the welfare of their clients. This theme is explored further in chapter 9.

(3)   *The electoral process*. On the face of it, election results do matter for policy; how much they matter may be arguable. They seem to matter a good deal for the state–market issue because of its ideological significance. Whether election results can be explained in terms of popular preferences on this issue is quite another matter; more plausible explanations, perhaps, include perceptions of the state of the economy, the competence of governments, the style of leaders, and certain events overseas. Having said this, the wider electorate is not uninfluenced by ideological debate, and many voters have direct interests involved as in sections 2 and 3, above. Political parties may try to use specific boundary shifts to secure electoral advantage, the sale of council houses in Britain being a particularly clear example.

(4)   *Fiscal stress*. If there really is a fiscal crisis, a conclusion about which we cannot be confident according to the previous chapter, then this might imply certain kinds of boundary shifts. In fact, only the more radical forms of privatization (or heavy use of charging), significantly ease the fiscal pressure on government, by shifting it on to individuals or families. Fiscal problems are still likely to be used as an argument for such shifts, as for example in a recent celebrated 'leak' of British central government planning (*Economist*, 1982; see also Heald, 1983, ch. 13).

(5)   *Market failure*. The kinds of arguments developed in welfare economics for state intervention (reviewed in chapter 1) are, of course, normative arguments, albeit with a logical/technical component. However, this does not mean they have no explanatory role. If the market fails to produce an efficient outcome, due for example to monopoly, economies of scale, externalities or whatever, then there is the potential for certain groups to gain if a 'successful' intervention can be secured. In theory, these groups would gain more than enough to compensate the losers and still be better off. This compensation could take the form of coalition-building deals ('log-rolling'). Therefore, there is a certain pressure in the system to intervene in the market where there would otherwise be serious failures from an efficiency point of view. Certainly these pressures may not overcome inequalities in political power as between gainers and losers in some cases, but they should not be dismissed. A limitation of this explanatory factor is its static character; it will

not explain changes unless the technical character of a service changes; it may be more useful in explaining non-changes, or why particular forms of state–market relationships are adopted rather than others. No discussion of the 'market failure' perspective would be complete, in any case, without some reference to the parallel phenomenon of 'state failure' (Niskanen, 1971; IEA, 1978; Jackson, 1982). Doubts about the efficacy of the state, in other words, limit the force of market failure arguments, and such doubts are spreading in intellectual circles (Le Grand and Robinson, 1984; Webster, 1981).

(6) *Technical and social innovation.* The way people live, and consequently the needs they manifest for social services, are to some extent influenced by technology, while the possible ways of providing services to meet needs are also dependent on this factor. Gershuny (1982, 1983) identifies 'social innovation' as a fundamental influence on the development of the economy and employment. Private motor transport would be an example. Probably the most significant long-term trend of this kind is that towards 'the self-service economy', and arguably this has implications for the boundary between the state and the market.

Critical issues for evaluation

If we are concerned with evaluating proposals for change in the state-market boundary, or engaging in debate about such policies, then it is important to recognize that while a considerable number of diverse kinds of argument are involved, there are similarities in the general form of these arguments from case to case. They deal with the broad areas of market effectiveness, equity, the organizational perspective, sociocultural issues, and alternatives.

(1) *Effectiveness of market processes.* The strength of the market is supposed to lie in its greater efficiency and sensitivity to consumer requirements. Such properties cannot be assumed to be present in practice in particular cases; neither should they be cynically dismissed out of hand. As chapter 1 indicated, it is possible to specify the assumptions required to arrive at the theoretical proposition that a market is efficient. Most important among these are the presence of competition between, ideally, a large number of suppliers, the attainment of an 'equilibrium' between demand and supply, and the availability to consumers of adequate information on which to base choices. As we saw in chapter 4, there are important examples in the social services where consumers are not regarded as competent to make

decisions and the state or professionals act as intermediaries.

(2)　*Equity*. Ideas about equity are fundamental to social policy, as we saw in chapter 3. Equity embraces the equal treatment of equals and the appropriately unequal (most would say progressively redistributive) treatment of unequals (Weale, 1978), and the question of social 'rights'. Conventionally we tend to assume that market solutions are less equitable than state provision, since the former are heavily influenced by 'ability to pay'. More recently this assumption has been challenged (Le Grand, 1982); there may be systematic inequities generated by the conventional operation of state services. A closer examination of specific forms of provision and rationing is required before we can pronounce on this issue. We would include also under this heading equity issues relating to employment in social services, for example pay, security, conditions of employment and the implementation of 'equal opportunities' policies.

(3)　*Sociocultural issues*. In chapter 1 we saw that one of the most potent ideas in the social administration tradition was the idea that social services involved a different quality of transaction between consumer and producer from the commercial situation, and that this in itself was important in promoting desirable values, of altruism, community awareness, sharing, and so on. To some extent this concerns the nature of organizations providing services, but goes somewhat wider. It raises aspects of the well-rehearsed selectivity/universality debate (Davies and Reddin, 1978; Sleeman, 1979). This is evident, for example, with a service such as public housing which may be shifted across the boundary between a broadly based high-quality service and a residual form of provision for the poor (Forrest and Murie, 1983).

(4)　*Alternatives*. As our first set of categories ('types of relationship') illustrated, there are more than two alternatives in the division of responsibility between the state and the market. Yet very often in debate the existence of other alternatives is not considered. If the problem is seen to be one of unresponsiveness to consumer requirements, for example, solutions other than privatization may be available and more effective: examples include the provision of more information to clients and granting to them of more formal power to choose; competing public agencies; and appeals procedures. Technology is often a force for change, yet there are usually alternative technical possibilities open for a society if it has the collective will and ability to choose them.

Case studies

In the first part of this chapter we have outlined a framework for the analysis of changes in state–market relationships in the provision of social services. The framework is general in its applicability and has been presented in general terms. We now utilize this framework to analyse two specific cases of change in the boundary between the roles of state and market. These cases are of interest as contemporary areas of policy debate in Britain; but they parallel changes taking place in other western countries, and sometimes draw on alternative models of service provision assumed to exist elsewhere. Of our two cases, the first is a conventional mainstream social services one: social care of the elderly. The other is of interest as an example of a policy outside the conventional definition of social policy where, we argue, similar issues arise: public transport.

Social security funding of private residential care for the elderly

In the early 1980s the British social security regulations and practices have been amended to enable an elderly person in a privately run home to claim relatively high charges directly from the national social security system. The practical effect has been a rapid expansion in private residential care for the elderly and some decline in both the numbers in public (local authority) homes and the waiting lists for admission (Johnson, 1983; Murray, 1984). Potentially, such a measure opens the possibility of a whole sector of welfare, currently the biggest item in local authority social service budgets, being 'privatized'. Whether the change goes this far in practice depends on how generous the social security system is, how it relates to regulatory measures, and how adequate a standard of care the private sector is able to provide.

In terms of our typology this phenomenon can be seen as either one of state purchase of a package, or as one of very high state subsidy (at up to 100 per cent for some people) combined with regulation and some residual state provision. As such it is easily explicable in terms of a strong ideological commitment to private (and voluntary) enterprise. It seems quite consistent with past arguments from the Institute of Economic Affairs (Seldon, 1977) that there is no logical necessity for the state to actually provide such services, given its objectives, merely to provide adequate income-maintenance. However, there is a very big difference between a normal old age pension and the cost of labour-intensive residential care. This policy obviously furthers the interests of private providers and indeed has provided an opportunity for many small businesses to start (Johnson, 1983 and 1983b; Murray, 1984). This policy change coincided with tight financial restraints on local authority services, growing numbers of very elderly and also a long and bitter dispute over pay in the public residential care sector. A possible interpretation of the policy is an attempt to counter 'creeping professionalization' in the public sector. It is patently obvious that this policy makes no contribution to solving any fiscal crisis; rather the reverse. Unless social security outlays are more tightly rationed, total public expenditure is likely to expand, because of the extent of unmet demand, and in addition the residual public providers may experience the reverse of 'economies of scale' (Knapp, 1984). The policy, as it at one stage appeared, of giving an open-ended 100 per cent subsidy, seems non-viable financially. At the time of writing the government has drawn back a little from its initially almost open-ended commitment.

As the financial commitment is tightened up the critical evaluative issue will be whether and how far an adequate quality of care can be ensured. Both the client and the social security agency are in a weak position to assess and control this (Johnson, 1983b; Challis, 1983). The public authorities will have to successfully engineer a change of role, from provider to inspectorate, a test of their organizational flexibility. From an equity point of view there may be a danger of the service being allocated less consistently to those in most need. The local authority homes may suffer (e.g. from stigma) as a 'residual' form of care. Pay and working conditions for a group who have always been relatively badly off could deteriorate with the dominance of a very fragmented non-unionized private sector.

This case study is particularly interesting as a possible harbinger of a future 'social security state', in which the primary social role of the state is confined to financial transfers to individuals and a degree of regulation of services themselves.

Public transport

Our second example concerns a service outside the traditional boundaries of social policy, but one in which the state has intervened extensively and which is arguably important for giving people access to a range of opportunities (work, shopping, leisure) which are important for their overall welfare. It is also a case study which raises most of the issues set out in our framework for this chapter. We concentrate on bus services here, as these are the main mode involved in local public transport.

Historically, bus services in Britain developed under private enterprise but subsequently became subject to extensive regulation, partial nationalization and municipalization (Mulley and Glaister, 1983). Although users are normally charged, the industry has always been characterized by heavy 'cross-subsidization' between profitable and unprofitable services, and has more recently received increasing subsidy from national or local government. With rising affluence and car ownership the industry has been in decline, and issues arise about the continued maintenance of services of any kind in more rural areas. At the time of writing, the government in Britain is seeking to pursue radical policies of de-regulation as well as a reduction in public expenditure on subsidies (Department of Transport, 1984).

Most elements of our typology of state roles are represented here. The level of charges (i.e. fares) is a key policy issue. State (national and local) operators compete with private operators and other modes of transport. Buses are increasingly seen as a 'residual' form of provision for those without access to private transport. Central and local government enter contracts for services from private operators, including specific-purpose services (e.g. school transport), as well as public 'stage carriage' services where operators may tender on the basis of service levels and/or required subsidies. Since the 1930s, bus services have been closely regulated by bodies known as 'traffic commissioners', but this approach is now being rejected (Mulley and Glaister, 1983). Local authorities have a duty to plan and co-ordinate services in their areas, including co-ordination with other modes of transport and land-use planning. Pro-market advocates suggest that greater use of private enterprise and market forces will increase efficiency, lower costs, widen choice, foster innovation, involve more entrepreneurial and marketing rather than bureaucratic skills, and so on.

Similarly, in explaining changes in public transport policy most of the categories in our framework are relevant. The concept of public transport itself, if opposed to private transport, is ideologically charged. So is the choice between an integrated, regulated and subsidized system and a free market system, or the choice between a monopoly public operator and a system of tendering and contracting involving private operators. The producers themselves, public and private, represent significant lobbies. Public transport has proved to be a significant electoral issue at local government level, particularly in the major cities. The battle between the Greater London Council and the London Borough of Bromley over a cheap fares/high subsidy policy, fought in the courts in 1981, illustrated both this point and the relevance of public transport to the issue of fiscal stress. Public transport subsidy in the urban areas was one of the major growth areas of local authority expenditure in the late 1970s and early 1980s. As we explain below, public transport raises a number of 'market failure' issues. It is also the most important example, in this chapter, of the significance of 'technical and social innovation'. Private car ownership represents an alternative technical mode of provision which, from a consumer's point of view, provides an altogether superior service in most circumstances to public transport. It also supports a 'suburban' life style which, as it becomes more dominant, militates against the capability of public transport to compete. At the same time, as wages rise and use falls, the economics of bus operation become less favourable.

Market failure problems arise in this case because of a combination of increasing returns to scale, local monopoly, and externalities. On a given route the cost per passenger falls sharply as the number of passengers increases. A number of consequences flow from this. Firstly, conventional economic theory suggests that, for maximum efficiency (benefits-costs), prices should be low to encourage people to use the service; specifically, fares should relate to marginal costs, which are below average costs. This implies that subsidies are efficient (Glaister, 1984). Secondly, increasing returns to scale tend to lead to a 'natural' monopoly situation – one dominant supplier on a particular route can undercut new competitors. Yet, as we all know, monopoly breeds inefficiency, both in terms of higher fares/poorer service and in the sense that poor management and inefficient working practices are protected. Yet the introduction of competition appears to be inefficient by creating costly duplication. Also, experience with the pre-regulation era and the recent experiments with de-regulation suggest that rather 'degenerate' forms of competition may develop where routes are sufficiently densely populated to offer any profits to operators. For example, different operators set services to depart at the same times rather than spacing them out, or tend to run slightly ahead of timetable to cream off passengers waiting for the next service. Safety and reliability standards may suffer as well. Where routes are thinly populated, services are unprofitable and de-regulation may not encourage anyone to offer them without subsidy.

Competition generally eliminates cross-subsidy. Thus, paradoxically, it may increase tax-financed public expenditure if it is decided that the same network of unprofitable routes must still be maintained (Andrews and Stonham, 1984). Subsidies are also argued to be justified on 'externality' grounds; namely that more attractive/cheap bus services cause people to switch from car to bus and thereby reduce congestion. Empirical support for this proposition is weak, except in very dense areas such as London (Glaister, 1984); without further measures like parking controls and other limits on car access to congested areas, and bus priority schemes, the impact on congestion is likely to be small.

Equity issues are also raised by public transport policies. These are probably more significant in relation to the policy of reducing subsidy than they are with respect to de-regulation and competition. The main effects of subsidy reduction will be reduction in service quality (especially frequencies) and higher fares. Bus users are drawn mainly from lower-income households (Department of the Environment, 1976) and are also dispropor-tionately women, children, young people and elderly. This impact can be seen as regressive in terms of both income levels and degrees of mobility (i.e. the least mobile become less mobile). If de-regulation eliminates cross-subsidy and this is not replaced by public subsidy, services will disappear altogether from more rural areas. This is an example of 'territorial (in)equity'.

The bus industry is in an increasingly difficult position as a result of technical, social and economic changes. Are there any alternatives to ever-increasing subsidies or the scenario just painted, which might be more effective and/or equitable? Without going into any detail, the sort of possibilities to be explored include the encouragement of intermediate forms of transport between the public and the private (e.g. taxis, car-sharing), the facilitation of cheap private transport (e.g. bicycle routes, etc.), the control of car use in congested areas, the encouragement of voluntary community initiatives (e.g. volunteer-driven minibuses), the integration of stage carriage with other services (e.g. school journeys, mail deliveries, etc.). In other words, technical and social innovation may call for an innovative approach to policy.

Conclusion

The principal aim of this chapter has been to show, through an analytical framework applied to a couple of important examples, that the choices between state and market forms of provision of social services are complex. The rhetoric of debates about privatization is rarely illuminating on the real chocies involved and their implications, although it is clearly important in highlighting key elements in the political process generating changes in the state–market relationship.

We first identified a number of different ways in which the state may operate in relation to the market in the social policy field. In one of the cases considered, public transport, raising user charges and thereby, hopefully, reducing public subsidy is a significant element. In both cases we can interpret current changes as a shift towards a more clearly 'residual' role for public services. The idea of the state as an active competitor setting exemplary standards has received little attention, although public transport could be cited as an example. This illustrates a general tendency we highlighted, in our discussion of the typology, to treat market provision as a norm which is relatively unquestioned whilst the state's role is subjected to ever-more-searching scrutiny.

Contracting for service inputs or outputs is a major new area of interest in Britain, illustrated by both cases. On present evidence these devices may be interpreted as much as levers to secure more efficiency within public organizations, by weakening the bargaining power of public employees. While the state may retain or even increase its regulatory role in some of these cases, active 'de-regulation' is also a policy in some other cases, notably public transport. Similarly, there may be a growing need for the state to develop its facilitation/co-ordination role where greater use of small-scale private, voluntary or informal modes of provision are employed, as in both of the cases discussed here, yet at the same time pressures for de-regulation push in the opposite direction.

In explaining shifts in policy in this chapter we adopted an eclectic approach. It is tempting to see ideology as a dominant force here, because the central ideological issue in western societies is between collectivism and market individualism. Certainly, some of these cases seem to exhibit privatization being pursued in Britain at the time of writing, at almost any cost, regardless of its economic rationality or otherwise. Some would explain this partly in terms of interests, with capital seeking new areas for profit in a climate where other areas of market activity have become less attractive owing to recession and international competition. Privatization both reinforces and is facilitated by a weakening of the power of organized labour in a period of high unemployment; but some cases not discussed in detail here, for example the stimulation of home ownership, also illustrate the significance of more specific ideologies cutting across the main dimension identified above, as well as the importance of 'electoral market-place' explanations. Although not developed here, the ideology of localism is another cross-current which has been significant both in the evolution and in the frustration of privatization policies.

Fiscal stress might not be expected to be a major factor leading to more market-oriented modes of social policy. There is some of this logic present in cases of reducing public subsidy, such as public transport, but it is not necessarily the dominant motive. Both of these case studies involve modes of relationship which either do not much affect public expenditure (contracting) or which may even increase it, as with care of the elderly, in so far as social security commitments remain open-ended, or public transport if minimal rural and suburban services have to be maintained without cross-subsidy.

Market failure arguments are still, in our view, relevant to the evaluation of different service modes. However, they appear to be less influential in explaining actual policy changes in the present ideological and fiscal climate (e.g. public transport). To some extent they are balanced in intellectual argument by concerns about the failings of state bureaucracies. Technical and social innovation are more significant factors in some cases, particularly transport.

The most important issues in evaluation probably centre around equity. Changes involving high charges and lower subsidies (e.g. transport) tend to worsen the situation of relatively deprived groups. We would also wish to stress that equity issues in the labour market are raised by contracting policies, with potentially adverse effects on the primary distribution of rewards. It is significant that the main targets for contracting ventures are aspects of social services provided by lower-paid, lower-status manual workers, many of them women, rather than the relatively privileged professional groups.

It is difficult to offer such clear comments on the social and cultural impact of the kind of changes discussed in this chapter. To argue that service providers in a 'mixed economy of welfare' will in future be less imbued with an ethic of service, community concern and altruism is to assume that these features are dominant in the motivation, outlook and style of service providers in traditional public agencies. There is growing recognition of the credibility problem this poses for the welfare state. A distinct kind of argument which may have more substance, at least in cases like public transport, is that current changes reinforce a trend to 'privatization' of life styles and a decline in communal, shared activities and experiences. It is concerns about issues of this kind which lead some, in the pursuit of welfare goals, to look much more hopefully towards alternatives to traditional state provision *and* the market. These form the subject of the next chapter.

7

Social Care, the Family and the Community

Introduction

While the focus of this book is upon public social policy it is necessary to consider the way in which public policy, and particularly the public provision of social care, relates to and interacts with private activities. This involves not merely issues about the relationship between the state and the market, as explored in chapter 6, but also a consideration of the many ways in which individuals tackle, or are helped to tackle, their own social problems with little or no involvement of the machinery of the state. They may buy such assistance, but probably more important than any help secured in that way is help from family, neighbours and others in the community, including voluntary organizations.

In modern industrial society this assistance, which we shall give the general name of social care (to embrace the whole range of private and public help in personal services, kind and cash) often involves a complex mixture of care from non-state sources with care from the state. The elements in this mixture need to be examined in terms of their relationships to each other, as phenomena which are likely to interact and affect the character of each other. However if we take a historical view we can see the more formal and organized forms of social care as relatively recent additions to the help available to individuals, super-imposed on top of, and thereby transforming, older patterns of more informal care principally provided by family and neigh-bours. Those forms of care provided by the state are amongst the most formally organized and most recent additions to the overall package. Yet the state, or governing institutions at the sub-state level, have had an interest in the social care package, which goes back rather further than a study of its main formal activities may suggest. This ancient concern was particularly motivated by the extent to which the breakdown of informal patterns of care had implications for public order. Social unrest, or the movement of unsupported beggars and vagrants around the country, were seen as occurring when patterns of informal care had broken down. This reminds us of the close relationship between issues about care and issues about control, which we discussed in chapter 2. While our emphasis in this chapter is upon care we must not lose sight of the care/control relationship. Just as the state is a provider of control as well as care, so too are the family and the community.

In order to explore the ways in which the various forms of care are inter-related the next section of this chapter outlines some of the features formal caring institutions have developed in Britain.

Features of social care in Britain

Looking at the early development of social care in Britain, by the end of the nineteenth century family and informal community care had been supplemented by a variety of public, private and charitable institutions. An ethos of self-help, implying individual family provision to meet emergencies, influenced the policies of both public and voluntary agencies. We should, however, emphasize two other closely related things of dominating importance as far as social policy was concerned. One was the emphasis upon the family as the key grouping in society. It is a little difficult to say what this implied as far as the distinction between the nuclear and the extended family was concerned. It is recognized that internal migration has severed some of the links between extended families. The rules about interdependence used under the Poor Law placed an emphasis upon the household, not the extended family. Yet many households were still in some sense extended families. The work of Rowntree cited in chapter 3 provides a good indication of late nineteenth-century perspectives on the family, of a comparatively extended kind since it included adult unmarried children, as a resource-sharing unit. The other crucially important related element, in the emphasis placed in Victorian thinking on family life and family obligations, is the idea of the dominance of the male bread-winner. Thinking about social security or housing needs was dominated by this concept. Child care and education policies similarly reflected this perspective. The female-headed household secured minimal assistance from any source, particularly if there was any grounds for suspicion that the woman was responsible for her and her family's predicament. Unmarried mothers, in particular, were treated very harshly. As arguments began to emerge about state responsibilities in respect of the unemployed it was the male unemployed who were their concern. It is true that there had been early state intervention concerned with the working conditions of women and children, but these found support from philanthropists who wanted to protect these 'social dependents' and from male workers who wanted protection from their competition.

What happened in the twentieth century to alter the picture of the mixed provision of welfare, with family and voluntary care dominant, which we have presented for nineteenth-century Britain? There is a popularly propagated picture of the impact of the coming of the welfare state which suggests that public social policy, developed between about 1906 and 1970, entirely supplanted the older forms of care. Such a picture is sometimes painted in the arguments of the New Right, who argue now for turning back the clock (see Boyson, 1971). Before going on to look at what that turning back might imply we want to show that it is nonsense to suggest that non-public forms of social care have not survived from the nineteenth century. We will do this by looking at the forms of non-public care which have remained of significance in each of the main areas of social policy.

In the social security system a number of significant values have been retained about the interdependence of the family unit and about incentives to make additional or separate private provision against contingencies. Within social insurance, although changes have occurred to cope with the extent to which women go into paid employment, the rules are still built around a view of the male as the breadwinner and as the supporter of dependents. Beveridge saw social insurance as a particularly desirable approach to social security because in the absence of a means test individuals are free to supplement state provision with private provision. The problem about this, however, is that it also offers an argument for the maintenance of benefit levels close to subsistence level, an argument that governments have gladly accepted. In the one area where this principle has been eroded, pensions, what has resulted instead is a public/private compromise under which many employees are contracted out of the state graduated pension scheme into private ones, and given support from the taxation system to do so.

As far as the social assistance element in the British social security system is concerned, that is supplementary benefits and related means-tested benefits, the unit upon which calculations of needs and means is based has remained the nuclear family. With the ending of the Poor Law the household means test was abandoned, but adult (non-dependent) members of their parents' household are normally expected to make contributions towards rent. Wives are treated as 'dependents' in these schemes, except in rare situations where it is conceded that 'role reversal' has occurred. The system treats unmarried partners as if they were married, and this creates difficulty with more marginal relationships and as a consequence generates harassment of women claimants where they are suspected of having involvements with men. Social assistance does not, except to a very slight degree in allowing small amounts of earnings and some benefit from payments from charitable sources, provide scope for the private supplementation of benefits. On the contrary, in recent years unofficial 'private enterprise' to enhance supplementary benefit incomes has been countered by campaigns to discover, and prosecute, such rule-breaking. In this respect the tendency over the past 20 years for social insurance to decline and social assistance to increase in importance in the British social security system has diminished the scope for the private enhancement of welfare. This remark particularly applies to relief for the unemployed, but very much less so to income maintenance for pensioners.

The national health service seems to provide a comprehensive public service for the sick. However, private medicine is not prevented in Britain. Hence a small private sector has survived, and is, at the time of writing, tending to grow. It is not the case, however, except for a minute fraction of the population, that the private sector provides a completely separate system of health care. Rather the private sector is dependent upon, some would say 'parasitic upon', the public sector. Doctors are able to combine public and private work. Correspondingly patients often combine public and private care. For example, they consult health service doctors and then use the private sector to jump queues for non-urgent operations, or to supplement low-quality national health service care. Similarly mixtures of public and private care occur in the dentistry and optical services; national health service patients are able to pay for better forms of complex dental treatment and for preferred spectacle frames.

The most important way in which the state health service is combined with private care involves a quite different sort of private care. It is a form of care which is seldom discussed but of enormous importance. Most of the care of the sick is done outside the health service by carers, most of whom are close relatives of the sick, who work for nothing. We refer, of course, to the fact that only a minute proportion of the total care of the sick is provided in hospital; most of it is provided in the home. This may seem a trivial point to make, but it is surely a central part of the evidence that the state does not provide cradle-to-grave care. It still depends fundamentally upon the family, above all, and to a lesser extent friends, neighbours and voluntary organizations to provide the routine day-to-day care of individuals who are dependent – as infants, when sick, when disabled and in the last stages of life. That dependence has considerable importance for the relationship between the state and the family, and especially for women who are disproportionately called upon to play the caring roles (see Land, 1978; Finch and Groves, 1980; Walker, 1982).

The remarks in the preceding paragraph apply equally, or perhaps even more powerfully, to the personal social services. It was suggested in chapter 3 that these services have remained to some extent under the influence of the Poor Law view that help should only be extended to the very deprived who have no-one else to whom they can turn. Studies of elderly people who go into local authority care have shown how relatively few of them have nearby relatives to whom they can turn for help (see Walker, 1982). Other domiciliary services also tend to be rationed according to the availability of help from families or neighbours. An old person with relatives nearby, especially a daughter, is less likely to secure a home help or the delivery of meals. Community care is not a new policy for the personal social services; it has been an ever-present reality throughout their short history, as it was the taken-for-granted system of care for most people in the days of the Poor Law.

A feature of both health and social services care is that the boundaries between informal care and public care are peculiarly inflexible. Individuals who are shifted between the sectors move between systems of almost total family care to systems of almost total state care. There are some attempts to develop intervening measures, in particular domiciliary support for private carers, but, as was suggested in the previous paragraph, the rationing of these services is often decisive in sharpening the dividing line. Systems of subsidy to carers are poorly developed. As a consequence it is possible to have side-by-side individuals with enormous burdens of responsibility for care, and cases of total neglect of needy individuals by relatives and their communities. There are few mechanisms for determining acceptable burdens or protecting the rights of carers.

The Charity Organization Society played a key role in the history of social work (Woodroffe, 1962). Whilst most modern social workers would no longer wish to see themselves as experts in distinguishing between the deserving and the undeserving poor, it remains the case that a principal concern of public social work is with preventing family failure and dealing with the consequences of that failure. Hence, again, whilst 'community social work' is seen as the new concern of the profession (Barclay Report, 1982), at least since the formation of the local authority social services departments in 1970, if not before, a central concern of social work has been with the adequacy of family and community support networks. Perhaps the contemporary shift in emphasis is rather more towards the recognition of the community element and away from what is now seen as an undue emphasis upon the nuclear family. Certainly, however, social workers have never been able to concern themselves with more than a minute proportion of all the social and emotional problems in the community as a whole. They generally only encounter, and are generally only able to deal with, situations where private support systems are going very wrong.

The two remaining areas of social policy which we want to discuss, housing and education, provide an interesting contrast. Housing was, up to the First World War, with the exception of limited slum clearance activities, an area of almost purely private provision. Since that time the state, in the form of the local authority landlord, has largely replaced the private landlord. Yet at the same time housing has continued to be a significant area of private, market-related, activity, because of the extent to which houses are purchased. The owner-occupied sector has grown dramatically. It is still growing; a growth reinforced by government pressures to force local authorities to sell council houses to their tenants. Since nearly everyone with the resources to make a choice in the market-place chooses to be an owner-occupier rather than a tenant, we can describe this as still an area of public policy dominated by the private sector.

The provision of education, by contrast, became state-dominated in Britain in the late nineteenth century and has remained so. There is a private sector providing around 6 per cent of all school places, mostly in the secondary sector. Publicly provided schools are free, and so is most higher education. The input into education provided by families consists, therefore, in financial support of children through the education process and in the general emotional support and encouragement necessary if the child is to make the best possible use of the educational system. This 'private' element in the education system, like the care required for the health and social services system, must not be under-rated. After all the strong correlation between educational success and family and class background has been shown to be considerably influenced by the support and encouragement middle-class parents give to their children (Halsey et al., 1980; Jenks, 1979; Bouden, 1973).

Having briefly reviewed the public/private interface and balance in Britain's social policy system, in the last part of this section we will comment briefly on the way in which the current Conservative government is, or would like to, alter that balance.

As suggested above there has been a great deal of talk about the role of community care in the health and personal social services. We suggested that there is nothing new about this. Inasmuch as the New Right's stance on public services in general is one of reducing expenditure, community care is the necessary alternative. However, there have been attempts to approach this subject in a rather more sophisticated way. There has built up, over the past 20-30 years, a strong battery of arguments against institutional care, whether for children, the elderly or the mentally or physically handicapped. From the point of view of health service and social services professionals, commitment to community care involves the more effective planning and organization of domiciliary caring services to support the family and voluntary care already available. The negative aspect of community care is the devolution of more responsibility to already overburdened private networks, the positive aspect the development of effective public services to aid and support these networks. Where the balance lies between the two depends upon the resources available in the public sector, and the effective deployment of those resources. If it can involve the redeployment of resources hitherto extravagantly used in institutional care then positive community care may be achieved at lower costs; but research evidence on the shift from institutional to community care suggests that this redeployment is not an easy process (Walker, 1982).

In education the main shift that has actually occurred under the Conservatives has entailed the squeezing of educational budgets rather than any significant privatization. The main consequence of this has been increased pressure on parents to pay for education-related activities, though in the worst cases schools have been so starved of resources that parents have been forced individually to buy textbooks and collectively to raise school funds for books and equipment. A related development has been the shift away from a subsidized school meal service, putting the provision of meals for children, other than the most deprived, on a quasi-commercial basis open to further privatization (see Wilding, 1983, ch. 9).

These examples from education show how interwoven are those forms of privatization which involve a shift from state provision to market provision, and those which simply limit the availability of services from the state, thereby throwing greater burdens on the family and the community. Similar observations might clearly be made about declining state provision in the fields of social security and housing.

By concentrating in this chapter on issues about the relationship between the state, on the one hand, and the family and community, on the other, our aim is to show that changes in the role of the former involve much more than increases or decreases in the role of markets. We will expound this point more fully in the rest of this chapter.

Issues about the public/private interface: a wider perspective

We have also suggested, somewhat tentatively, some of the ways British social policies are related to assumptions about the family and the community. We now want to look at some of the wider questions about the analysis of social policy raised by that discussion.

The revolution in social anthropology which occurred in the 1920s taught the importance of not assuming that the cultural features of one society will necessarily be repeated in another. It was shown that human social organization could embrace a variety of widely different ways of constructing family and community relationships. This challenged the carrying of simple ethnocentric assumptions from one society to another. It also taught that social arrangements within a society should not necessarily be taken for granted; new ways of organizing family relationships may emerge and be just as viable as the ones they replace.

There are lessons here at various levels for the study of social policy. One, that has not been learnt by all students of comparative social policy, is that one should not assume that particular social institutions can readily be translated from one society to another. A related false assumption has been that the process of industrialization necessarily bring in its wake the development of forms of social policy similar to those already established in societies that have already been through the industrialization process. Of course, a great deal of copying goes on, but that does not make it either inevitable or appropriate. Decisions in the development of social policy must be seen as choices. These are made, of course, in a context of economic, cultural and ideological constraints, but nevertheless they are choices, indeed to some extent choices about which of those constraints to accept and which to challenge. As Higgins has argued:

> it will not be an entirely free choice but one at least which is sufficiently flexible to prevent all industrial societies tumbling headlong into the melting pot of convergence. . . . The fact that choice exists also means that while some nations will wish to accord a high priority to public expenditure on social welfare other nations may not. (Higgins, 1981, p. 160)

These observations, however, need to be applied not merely to comparative analysis but also to analysis of the choices made within a society. Social policies do not merely emerge in the form they do because of a particular family system or economic system; they must be seen as the result of choices in favour of those systems. These choices then reinforce those systems, and the ideologies that sustain them. Hence, British social policy, particularly social security policy, does not just have patriarchal characteristics because of the strength of the patriarchal family model in its formative years, it also supports that view of family relationships.

Let us look more deeply at the concepts of 'family' and 'community', amplifying the above observations (a) that societies with different family and community structures will evolve different ways of relating public social policy to private social life, and (b) that even within a society neither family or community forms nor the relationship of social policy to them need remain constant over time.

The family

In our discussion of the characteristics of British social policy we showed how various different concepts of the family crop up at different times and in relation to different social policies.

In social security policy the boundaries used to identify family responsibilities have shrunk since Tudor times, but they clearly could shrink further to define out of concern sexual partners to whom the claimant is not married, or to remove entirely the notional responsibilities of adult children. There is a related issue here of the definition of adulthood. There has been a tendency for the dividing point between childhood and adulthood to be moved backwards, from 21 towards 16 or younger. At the same time ambiguities remain. In Britain sexual adulthood is generally seen as commencing at 16, but other laws (relating to child care by local authorities, and, of course, to voting) see adulthood as beginning at 18. There are still also some relics of the previous laws providing for 21 as the age of majority, and for the purposes of support for higher education dependency can continue some years beyond 21. At the time of writing the burden upon the social security system of unemployed new entrants to the labour market has led to some attempts by governments to shift the age of 'adulthood' for social security claimants in their own right upwards from 16.

Logically the process of eliminating the concept of dependency for women and children in social policy could be taken to the point at which only the individual applicant for benefit is taken 'into account'.

In personal social services policy the quality of nuclear family care for children is a central concern. Yet when concerned with care for the elderly extended family considerations are brought into play if there are younger relatives in the household, or even nearby, who do or might participate in the caring process. Such extended family members regularly participate, as was shown above, in health care. Issues about the family role in these, and other, situations are widely debated. In such a debate issues about what *can* be the role of the family in a modern industrial society, and arguments about what that role *should* be, are often freely mixed together. We want here to try to separate them out a little by raising some issues from evidence on the nature of family life and then going on to some of the fiercely argued ideological perspectives.

A debate about the role of the family at any point in time needs to take as its starting point some facts about family life at that time. These are, of course, not immutable; but they surely provide an important starting point. Here are some facts about the modern British family.

> The so-called 'typical' family of a married couple with father in employment and mother at home, with two dependent children, represents only 1 in 20 of all house-holds at any point in time, but a substantial proportion of families will pass through this stage at some point in their lives. (Family Policy Studies Centre, 1984, p. 1)

Thus one 'household' in five is a single person living alone and one in four is a childless married couple. On the basis of present trends, out of every three marriages two are likely to end in death and one in divorce. Most divorced people re-marry, however. Nine out of ten married women will have children at some stage, but only one woman in four will have three or more children. About half of all mothers of dependent children have paid employment, but only about 15 per cent work full-time. The elderly proportion of the British population has grown rapidly up to the 1980s, but is likely to remain comparatively steady up to the end of the century. One person in seven is over 65. However the very elderly proportion is likely to go on rising a little. Most elderly people remain in their own nuclear family – 34 per cent alone and 43 per cent with a spouse (Rimmer, 1981, p. 58).

We see, then, in modern British society, a pattern of life in which single-person households are a quite common feature both early in the adult life cycle and in old age, and in which households without dependent children are a frequent occurrence. Yet this is also a pattern in which parenthood is still an expectation of most adults at some time; what is significant about it is that it dominates a comparatively small part of the total adult life. Two other features of family life are associated with this – one is the likelihood of paid employment for women and the other is the considerable possibility of divorce. Finally, it is a pattern in which extended families in the same household are rare, and most people remain in nuclear families even in their later years.

Hence there is a pattern of family life in which social policies might be expected to operate with assumptions about the continuing dominance of the conventional nuclear family of parents and children, but where households which are differently constituted are sufficiently frequent to make the rigid use of those assumptions inappropriate. It is a pattern in which it is not surprising that policy assumptions based upon extended family notions have diminished in importance. It might be argued that they should have diminished more totally than they have.

In comparing the way in which social policies are related to the family structure in different countries at least three issues need to be examined carefully: variations in nuclear family size associated with different birth rates, variations in the extent of female labour market participation, and variations in the importance of the extended family. Proposals to take policy ideas – on social security or on other forms of social care, for example – from one society to another need to take variations like these into account.

But we should not simply see specific policy proposals as appropriate or inappropriate in relation to a family structure in existence at a particular point in time. As we stressed earlier in this chapter, the relationship between policy and social structure is a dynamic one in which specific policies may sustain or undermine particular social arrangements. Hence what makes many of the arguments about social policy and the family very heated is that the former are recognized as preventing, or perhaps contributing to, changes in the latter.

Let us look briefly at two examples, involving social policy in one case as a potential agent of change, in the other as a reinforcer of the *status quo*. In societies where the extended family remains of key importance not only for the care of members but also for their income maintenance the development of social security policies and of public caring agencies is seen as a threat to traditional family life. In some of the rapidly developing Chinese societies (Taiwan and Hong Kong, for example) urbanization and industrialization is altering the economic role of the extended family. Is the development of social policies to aid the nuclear family a necessary accompaniment of this economic change, or are they likely to accelerate the decline of the traditional extended family? Some Chinese observers of this situation see dangers in the development of individual, or nuclear family-based policies, which may undermine traditional patterns of care and mutual obligation.

Our second example concerns the British welfare state which is seen, particularly by feminists, as supporting the maintenance of the male-dominated nuclear family, making it difficult to establish new behaviour forms in which individuals, particularly females, can develop their own life styles. As Bennett puts it:

> The Welfare State treats the family as a unit, but a unit comprising different parts with different functions. Women are seen as financially dependent, but have no rights of access to men's income – either from wages or benefits. Women are supposed to care, in private and with little help, for those who are physically dependent. In fact, the nature of the Welfare State's provision for the family depends to a large extent on its views about the role of women. When the Welfare State mentions 'the family', women are never far from its mind. (Bennett, in Segal (ed.), 1984, p. 191; see also Wilson, 1977)

Hence we may conclude this discussion of the issues about the family by recognizing that arguments about the family and social policy are not only concerned with policy choices in their own right but also with the impact of those policy choices upon wider patterns of social life. We will find similar issues in the next section when we look at the concept of community.

The community

The concept of community has been the subject of much controversy amongst sociologists. It has been applied to an assortment of qualitatively different phenomena. Hillery (1955) identified 94 different definitions of community. Whilst the figure of 94 clearly exaggerates the range of meanings applied to the concept, there are important differences between definitions in the extent to which they place emphasis upon (a) geographical proximity, and (b) concerns about the quality of social inter-action. Dennis (1958) has shown how the concept has been variously defined as meaning 'locality', meaning 'social inter-course', and as meaning 'social control'. This third sense implies a community defined by a common culture where the community group has common opinions and autonomous systems of control over its members. Related to this third issue of social control are questions about the extent to which people within a so-called community have any effective control over the economic and political institutions which determine their well-being. Proposi-tions about the role of the community in our lives, and especially about community care, frequently invoke a simplified ideal. This is what Halsey (1969) has referred to as: 'The persistent evidence of a romantic protest against the complexity of modern urban society – the idea of a decentralized world in which neighbours could and should completely satisfy each others' needs and legitimate demands for health, wealth and happiness'.

We can explore some of these points about the concept of com-munity by examining the likely social characteristics of an area where the needs of the deprived and disadvantaged are likely to be particularly great, an inner-urban area in economic decline (see, for example, the Inner Area Study of Lambeth: Shankland et al., 1977). Such an area is likely to have an elderly population who were born there, or who moved there early in their adult life. They will probably live in old owner-occupied houses or will have been rehoused by the local authority in particular parts of larger housing projects (the foot of tower blocks, for example). They will have previously secured their livelihoods from industry that has now moved out of the area. The younger of their former colleagues will probably have moved out with it. Their children will have moved elsewhere for work or suburban housing: a long way away if they were 'upwardly mobile' or if the whole region is in economic decline, or otherwise out to the fringes of the urban area. This dispersal will have often been enhanced by local authority rehousing policies, shifting younger working-class people to large peripheral estates. Whilst in some places this dispersal process will have just left commercial properties or even undeveloped sites, if the area enjoyed any degree of economic prosperity during the 1950s and 1960s then new people will have come into the area. A significant element in this new population will have been immigrants from the Commonwealth. These will have established new social institutions relating to their needs and cultures. These immigrants, however, are unlikely to form just one cultural group in the area, but a number depending upon their place of origin (Rex and Moore, 1967; Rex and Tomlinson, 1979). But they too, like the older 'native' element in the area, are likely to have experienced fragmentation and dispersal as housing renewal moved some of them from the houses they originally occupied into local authority properties and as changing employment opportunities forced movement. Finally, the area is likely to have a group of very recent arrivals whose attachment to it is particularly slight – for example, transient workers, students, and young white-collar workers starting their 'housing careers' in cheap old houses.

The old locality identifications applied to the area (the name of a village, for example, originally embraced into the growing town) will often not correspond with even the lowest unit in the system of government, the electoral ward of the borough or city. It is almost certain that there will be no single autonomous unit of local government relating to that area alone. In addition whatever local government unit there is will be likely to be heavily dependent upon (a) resources from central government to tackle the problems of the area and (b) collaboration from other local administrative units (health districts, for example) which possibly do not share coterminous boundaries with it even at the lowest level. Furthermore, the administrators and professionals concerned with, or working within, the area are very unlikely to be residents of the area themselves. Finally the economic fortunes of the area will certainly not be determined by decisions made within it. Crucial decisions affecting its prosperity will be made by economic elites without local roots; inded they may well be the managers of multinational companies (Dennis, 1958; Bennington in Lees and Smith, 1975).

We have described here, then, an area of a kind common in advanced industrial cities, to which a variety of policy initiatives carrying the label 'community' have been applied. Thus, if it is in England and Wales, it may experience, or have experienced, any or all of the following. Local health and social services authorities will be operating within it a variety of domiciliary care policies which they are likely to describe as 'community care'. The local authority social services and education departments may employ community workers who try, according to their terms of reference and ideologies, to stimulate group activities, self-help or even perhaps political and pressure group action amongst residents. In the 1970s the area may have been the base for one of the nationally funded Community Development Projects, involving action and research to try to tackle the social problems of the area. The area will be one amongst several represented by an appointed Community Health Council for the Health District in which it lies; this body is supposed to advance consumer interests in the health service. If there is a significant black population in the area there will probably be a Community Relations Council for the local authority area within which it falls; this has a mandate to work to improve race relations and represent the interests of ethnic minorities.

Each of these sorts of initiative have been the subject of extensive analysis from both academic and political perspectives (on community care see Walker, 1982; Hadley and Hatch, 1981; on community work see Thomas, 1983; Jones and Mayo, 1974; on Community Development Projects see Higgins et al., 1983; CDP, 1977; on Community Health Councils see Klein and Lewis, 1976; Levitt, 1980; on Community Relations Councils see Hill and Issacharoff, 1971). In each case it has been shown that the social structure of an area of this kind makes the straightforward application of community concepts very difficult. Certainly such areas are very heterogeneous, and at best can be described as containing several communities who are interlocked and who may have key affiliations well outside specific geographical boundaries (see Rex and Moore, 1967; Rex and Tomlinson, 1979). But many would want to go further, to describe areas of this kind to be too disorganized, with a population too fragmented and alienated for community concepts to be applicable at all.

It may be objected that we have deliberately used the worst case to expose the problems about the use of the concept of community in social policy. This is a fair point, though it must be stressed that the kind of area we have described is typically one in which experiments in community action, community work and community care have occurred. To some extent these involve attempts to give this kind of area a community life which it is believed to lack and other areas to possess (Cheetham and Hill, 1973). Initiatives have been developed or proposed which counterbalance political devolution with the provision of resources to redress territorial inequality. (This is a theme to which we will return in chapter 11.) To widen our discussion let us look at some of the other ways in which issues about the concept of community emerge in the analysis of social policy.

A considerable amount of attention has been given to the creation of 'communities' in new settlements. Public housing policies which merely decant large numbers of people to new suburbs have been criticized for the way in which they break traditional family and community links (Young and Wilmott, 1957). Accordingly extensive efforts have been made to engender new communities in such places (Cherry, 1973; Eversley, 1973). The evidence suggests that this aspect of social engineering is problematical, and that in many respects communities can only emerge over time as new social networks are established. Ironically conflict between the residents of these new areas and the policy makers – over schools, amenities, repairs programmes, refuse disposal, etc. – seem to play an important part in the building of community links and community organizations, perhaps a bigger part than the social engineering activities of the policy makers (see discussion in Frankenburg, 1971).

An important argument in discussions of community building has been between those who advocate heterogeneity and those who espouse homogeneity. The ideal of creating a socially heterogeneous community has had a considerable influence upon the planners of new towns and suburbs. Generally their plans have been undermined by the extent to which housing choices occur in a market structured not only by price and rent differentials between houses of different quality, but also by differentials determined by the social statutes of different residential districts. Heterogeneity, where it has been achieved, often operates in practice over a comparatively narrow social band, and even then, after the social engineers have completed their work, residential movements may tend to push areas back towards homogeneity. However, if our concept of community is seen as entailing strong social cohesion then residential heterogeneity may be seen as a disadvantage for the development of a community structure.

Some of the efforts of utopian planners to achieve socially heterogeneous communities for egalitarian reasons can be seen as foundering because the wider society remained unequal. But another ideology motivated some planning of this kind – the search for the re-establishment of heterogeneous village communities containing people of all 'social ranks'. This ideal involves a very different approach to this ambiguous concept of community, a search for an interdependence based upon deference and the acceptance of social differentials. This is one of the senses in which the 'quest for community' involves a search for a stable form of 'social control'.

Very often the concept of community is used much more loosely than it is in the concerns about quite small geographical areas discussed above. Large local government units are often referred to as if they were communities, and arguments about the development of community care or community participation are seen as applying in general terms to extensive populations. These are very often socially heterogeneous. An important group of consequences follow. Where forms of participation and political involvement are concerned the community voice which is strengthened is largely that voice that is powerful already: the voice of the section of the community which is generally not disadvantaged (see Simmie, 1974). Where large formal forms of voluntary care are involved, what similarly tends to happen is that, as opposed to the strengthening of patterns of neighbourliness, the help comes from those best able to engage in voluntary activities – the relatively prosperous (see, for example, Holme and Maizels, 1978). Formal community care, therefore, is largely provided by the well-to-do for those less fortunate than themselves. We do not wish to imply that there is anything wrong in this – we are trying to avoid making such judgements here. All we wish to suggest is that when community care means this sort of formal voluntary care it implies something very different from the extension of care by families and neighbours. It may, in practice, have many features very like the kinds of care provided by professionals. Indeed it raises difficult problems for professionals about the boundaries between their services and those of volunteers (see Holme and Maizels, 1978). It clearly may, too, carry with it stigmatizing and social control connotations. That was certainly, as we suggested earlier in the chapter, how such voluntary work was seen in Victorian Britain. Some of the problems of combining formal and informal care have been well explored in the work of Abrams (see Abrams, 1984).

Just as there are problems about the heterogeneous concept of community, so too are there problems about the homogeneous one. Perhaps the most powerful example of the homogeneous community is the ghetto (see Krausz, 1971, p. 93). Such a community is internally strong because it is externally weak; its strength is a defensive reaction to hostility and discrimination. The community within a ghetto turns inward, developing its own institutions, safeguarding its own culture, and operating its own system of social control. When individuals within the ghetto deal with the outside world they derive what strength they have from the solidarity of the support they secure from their own community.

The ghetto is an extreme form of a phenomenon common

within most modern societies, a community (not necessarily neatly defined geographically) united by bonds of ethnicity, culture, national identity or religion (or of course some combination of these) in a wider society which tends to discriminate against it. The bonds of community operate positively to provide support and a sense of identity, but they also operate negatively to make penetration into the outside world difficult. Individuals who want to succeed outside gain strength from their roots but are likely to need to sever the links with them to assimilate. This paradox gives a problematic dualism to social policy interventions from the state. As we have seen, for example, social security policy entails specific stances on family life. Education policy tends to impose the majority culture, and medical and social care similarly embodies specific cultural assumptions. Hence such policies reinforce a dominant culture. Yet if they did not do so at all they would reinforce the separation of the minority. Imagine a separate system of social security, an education system with the minority language as the main medium of instruction, a health service cut off from the major institutions of the dominant society. Such a system could be separate but equal; it would be much more likely to be separate but unequal. There is such a system in South Africa, though of course there the dominant group are a numerical minority.

We are, of course, talking about tendencies here and emphasizing extremes. Of course, there are half-way positions for the British case – for example, in education: good instruction in English, but also teaching of the minority group language, teaching of history which is not dominated by the majority perspective and so on. What, however, we want to emphasize is that a responsiveness to the concerns of minority communities may only too easily imply an abandoning of a community to its own resources. Moreover if minority status implies, as it usually does in nation-states, a deprived status then those resources will be inherently inadequate.

Finally let us return to the issues of culture and social control within homogeneous communities. Some of the things that make a minority community different, and some of the aspects of social control within that community, may be phenomena which at one and the same time give it strength and make the majority society most hostile to it. Two minority community phenomena, for example, which are most disturbing to 'liberal' opinion in the British Isles concern the subordination of women in Muslim communities and the operation of violent physical forms of discipline, both within some migrant households and even more problematically within the cohesive working-class communities (both Catholic and Protestant) of Northern Ireland. These may be described as forms of 'community care', forms which keep many 'social problems' away from the concerns of the public social services. Does the growth of community care entail more delegation of responsibility for dealing with moral questions of this kind to family and community groups?

Conclusions: the mixed economy of welfare

In the first half of this chapter we stressed the way in which public social policy must be seen as supplementing and inter-acting with a great deal of private social care. It is quite false to expect to find in an advanced industrial society either a system in which public care has entirely supplanted private care or a system where public policies do not impinge at all upon private care. We may describe the pattern throughout such societies as a mixed economy of welfare, with, as was shown in chapter 6, the private commercial sector also playing a significant role. Nevertheless there are great variations between societies, and within any one society over time, in the ways in which the boundaries between public and private care are drawn. Those boundaries are, moreover, permeable and ambiguous.

A great deal of debate about the 'proper' role of public social policy in society concerns the boundary between public and private care. It is a debate which tends to be conducted with great passion since it concerns questions about the role of the family and about the relationship between the individual and the community. Public policy interventions are both influenced by, and influence, perspectives on family and community. Arguments that public policy developments are forms of social engineering designed to modify family or community structures seems to us to embody half-truths, since it is equally possible to show how ideologies about family or community have influenced or constrained policies. The interactions are complex, and this chapter has been able to do no more than suggest some of the ways in which they need to be analysed.

8

Interpreting Policy Making and Implementation

Introduction

Chapter 2 examined general theories which have been developed to try to explain why advanced industrial societies tend to have a set of state institutions and policies of a kind which have led to their being described as 'welfare states'. At the end of that chapter it was suggested, however, that the various macro-sociological theories available do not satisfactorily answer more detailed questions about the sources of social policy developments. This chapter will shift to examine the more micro-kinds of explanation which have been advanced to help with the understanding of how specific policies evolve. It will therefore tackle some of the issues raised in chapter 2 in a different way; but it will also examine the ways in which micro-explanations relate to the larger macro-theories.

A chapter of this kind must necessarily start by considering what is meant by policy. This leads on to two closely related issues. The first of these is the exploration of what might be understood to be the *policy-making* process, and of the relationship between that process and the *policy-implementation* process. The second is the case for distinguishing *different types of policy*, which might be expected to experience very different policy-making and implementation histories. After that it proceeds to look at some ways of analysing the policy process, looking at approaches rooted in pluralist political science and exploring the limitations of these. It then looks at comparative studies of policy making and ends by considering a model which has been used in two valuable policy process analyses.

Defining policy

We have already discussed the concept of policy at the beginning of chapter 1. All we want to do here is underline a few points particularly relevant to the study of the policy-making and implementation process. In our earlier discussion we gave particular attention to Jenkins's approach to the definition of policy; but there are many alternative definitions to which we might have turned (for example in Friend et al., 1974, p. 40; Heclo, 1972, p. 85; Anderson, 1975, p. 3).

Should we conclude from the lack of consensus about a definition that it does not really matter how policy is defined, adopting perhaps the characteristic pragmatism of a former British civil servant who asserted 'Policy is rather like the elephant – you recognize it when you see it but cannot easily define it' (Cunningham, 1963, p. 229). Readers may conclude that our position is rather like this as we are not going to add our definition to the collection; but our stance is certainly not to treat policy as somehow self-evident – rather, we are concerned that the various attempts to define policy tend to try to tie down something which is essentially contested and contentious. We recognize that we may, in the ensuing discussion, get a little trapped by the language we use. Literature about policy, its making and its implementation, tends to treat it as a self-evident concept. We prefer instead to recognize, as Barrett and Fudge have argued, that 'policy cannot be regarded as a constant' (Barrett and Fudge, 1981, p. 251), that policy analysis involves studying the continuing interplay through 'political action' (in the widest sense) between different policy goals. In this sense policy may be regarded as '*property*, something owned by one group, with which they identify and feel a sense of possession' (p. 271), or as 'the expression of *political intention*' (p. 275, our emphasis). The advantages of this approach are particularly evident when we examine below the policy making-implementation relationship. It also deals effectively with the issue of 'symbolic policies' identified by Edelman (1971) and others where politicians seek merely to give the impression that they are aware of problems and engaged in action.

Our view, therefore, is that to attempt to provide an authoritative definition of policy runs the risk of treating as concrete something which is not, and perhaps of taking it for granted that political behaviour is specifically goal-directed. This is not to say that we may not identify situations in which policy making and implementation is concerned with the translation of goals into action, but that we should beware of the extent to which usage of the concept of policy involves the assumption that this is generally and self-evidently what is taking place wherever political and administration action is occurring.

Our stance in discussing policy making and implementation together is closely related to our view of the concept of policy. The notion that there are two distinct phases in the policy process, with policy being first made and then implemented, is one which has been challenged by a number of recent discussions of the implementation process, in some of which one of us has been a contributor (Elmore, 1980; Hjern and Porter, 1981; Barrett and Hill, 1984). It is recognized that the distinction is based upon an important value assumption in democratic government, that there should be a group of politicians who are answerable to the electorate who make policy, and that those policies should be implemented by others whose duty it is to carry out the will of their political masters. In questioning whether that distinction is always made in practice, we are neither trying to assert that it is rarely or never made nor to argue that it should not be made. Once again, however, policy analysis should not be predetermined by such assumptions, particularly when they carry a heavy loading of traditionally accepted values. There is a great deal of empirical evidence to suggest (a) that 'policies' leave that part of the political system which is conventionally seen as concerned with policy making still highly uncertain or ambiguous, or indeed even sometimes containing contradictions; and (b) that actors in the part of the system seen as concerned with implementation frequently operate in ways which create or transform or subvert what might have been regarded as the 'policies' handed down to them.

We therefore prefer to treat the policy process as involving a flow of activities in which concrete system outputs on the ground are determined by activities and interactions throughout the whole policy process. What is perhaps important about the policy-implementation distinction, in addition to its role in relation to democratic values, is that it draws attention to the structural discontinuities likely to exist within the policy process. Hence the policy-*making* process may be seen as referring to development up to the point where legislation is enacted, and *implementation* to the process from then on. Changes in actors are often involved, from politicians and their advisers to administrators. Often different levels of government are concerned, legislation being provided by national government and implementation by sub-national or local government.

In fact to outline these structural discontinuities draws

attention to the ways in which they may mislead. Legislation is often enacted in skeletal form, its translation into action depending upon subordinate regulations, guidance notes and interpretations. Many studies have shown how these later phenomena really shape what is perceived as policy (see Hill, 1984; Barrett, 1979). Many key actors operate on both sides of our distinction, civil servants both formulate and implement the legislation. Politicians do not necessarily cease to try to intervene in the policy process once the law-making process has ended. Finally, we find the policy-making processes occurring at all levels of government, sub-national governmental bodies seeing themselves as policy-making within the broad statutory structure provided by central government. Moreover they do not simply passively take the legislation handed down to them, they operate within the initial policy-making process to try to get the legislation they want or to get rid of the legislation they already have but do not like.

So we clearly must use even the notion that the policy making-implementation distinction relates to structural discontinuities with some care. We may perhaps adopt the image of the implementation process provided by Dunsire, which suggests that it involves the successive 'concretization' of action to embrace within this the policy-making process too. Hence the break between policy making and implementation may be at the point where, to continue the concrete analogy, a critical hardening occurs. But we need to beware another couple of misleading assumptions – that hardening does occur or that there are logically separable stages in that process. Above all we would prefer the question about the relationship between the hardening process and the system in which it occurs to be the subject of empirical investigation and not something taken for granted as a result of the concepts we use. If the distinction between politics and administration is important for the realization of democratic government then there is likely to be a *right* place for policy making to end so that implementation does not further transform policy. It is then important to identify whether in some substantive policy areas this kind of 'break' is achieved, how it is achieved and whether it could be similarly achieved in other areas.

Types of policy

It may seem rather inconsistent to move on to issues about policy typologies after a discussion which has rejected any attempt to give a hard definition to policy. What, however, we are concerned with here is policy content, the substantive issues with which public policy interventions are concerned. Our discussion of these will, it is hoped, further explain the stance we have taken in the previous section.

In chapter 1 we looked at the way welfare economists, in particular the Musgraves (Musgrave and Mugrave, 1975) have attempted to analyse different forms of public policy interventions in terms of a typology. That was developed to try to help with answers to some of the normative questions about justifications for state interventions. You may recall, in particular, their distinction between 'allocation', 'distribution' and 'stabilization'. In the field of political science an alternative, but not entirely different, approach to policy classification has been developed by Lowi (1972), and elaborated subsequently by others, to try to characterize different forms of public policy.

The Lowi typology originally had three categories, but he subsequently added a fourth. The categories are:

(1) *Distributive policy*. This is where the government is involved with the distribution of new resources. This is seen as applying to government subsidies, for example, but perhaps the clearest example of this category is nineteenth-century land policies in the United States where the government was engaged in distributing rights to the use of new land.
(2) *Redistributive policy*. In this case government intervention aims at shifting resources from some individuals to others. Clearly tax and social security policies come into this category, together with the provision of subsidized services and policies which give rights to previously deprived or unequal groups.
(3) *Regulatory policy*. This involves government action to prevent and control individual activities. This category includes policing and law enforcement, but also most government interference with the free working of the market economy for other than explicitly redistributive ends.
(4) *Constituent policy*. This is Lowi's additional fourth category, recognizing that much government activity involves setting up agencies and generally formulating and re-formulating the machinery of government.

A rather similar typology to Lowi's is provided by Austin in an article which particularly applies this kind of approach to the analysis of social policy. His typology, like Lowi's original one, leaves out 'constituent policy'.

Austin's threefold categorization is expressed in terms of

'services' rather than 'policy types'. He says 'all human service programmes can be classified as falling within one, or a specific combination' of '*universal, redistributive* and *behaviour change/ social control* services' (Austin, 1983, p. 344, our emphasis). Let us examine his three categories a little more:

(1) *Universal services.* These are 'individually consumed services that are collectively provided for universal utilisation. The public good created by universal services consists of a benefit to the community, or the general society, that comes from universal, or nearly universal, utilization . . .' (Austin, 1983, p. 345). The main example given is education.

(2) *Redistributive services.* Austin sees these services as particular characteristics of urbanized and industrialized societies where communal and familial moral obligations no longer suffice to protect vulnerable individuals. His main examples are obviously income transfer payments.

(3) *Behaviour change/social control services.* Austin says these are 'often described as treatment programmes or "people-changing" programmes' (Austin, 1983, p. 350). He goes on 'The public good benefit consists of changes in the pattern of behaviour among categories of individuals whose behaviours are considered to have significant consequences for the community as a whole' (ibid.).

These typologies have been developed to assist with the analysis of the dynamics of the policy process. The contention is that different types of policy raise different kinds of social and political issues and can therefore expect to experience different dynamics in the policy-making and implementation process. In particular the interest constellations involved in decision making in respect of each of these three types is expected to be different. Naturally particular attention has been given here to the respective gainers and losers from both redistributive and regulatory policies, distributive and universal policies tend to be seen as less controversial. The users of these typologies have not been unaware that they involve 'ideal types'. Hence actual policies may be analysed as mixed types. It has also been recognized that there may be differences of degree within the types. Policies may be more or less redistributive or regulatory. Clearly the more they challenge the existing interest structures the more the conflict they will experience.

Readers will notice that in the discussion in the previous paragraph attention has been focused upon only two of the types. We have some doubt about the importance of the distributive type. It seems to us that except in the very unusual 'open frontier' situation most distributive policies are in fact to some degree redistributive. Indeed even nineteenth-century American land policy often involved redistribution – away from the Indians! Austin, of course, does not use the distributive label, but instead calls his similar category 'universal'; but his main example, education, is redistributive in general with resources going from other taxpayers towards those receiving education, and may involve many other more explicitly redistributive aspects as particular types of education are favoured against others.

The fourth category in Lowi's typology, by contrast, seems very important, but in a rather different way. The way in which any specific government activity delivery system is structured may be of quite fundamental importance for what it delivers. Moreover, does Lowi include the financing of government activity within his constituent policy category? We often see situations in which social policy is under threat much more because of the changes in the structure of the delivery system or in the pattern of financing than because of what we might call substantive policy change (see, for example, Webb and Wistow, 1982). This is a theme to which we will return later.

In addition to these reservations about how two of Lowi's four types are handled, we must also add that there is an important respect in which the other two are inter-related. Reference was made in chapters 1 and 2 to the ways in which many contemporary social policy analysts have seen redistributive initiatives as inherently regulatory. An influential study of income maintenance policies in the United States was, significantly, entitled *Regulating the Poor*. In their introduction its authors explained:

> We shall argue that expansive relief policies are designed to mute civil disorder, and restrictive ones to reinforce work norms. In other words, relief policies are cyclical – liberal or restrictive depending on the problems of regulation in the larger society with which government must contend. (Piven and Cloward, 1972, p. xiii)

Clearly the fact that policies which are redistributive may also appear to be, or be regarded as, regulatory is damaging to any notion of relatively distinct policy types. What is more it brings us back to our earlier argument that policies are complex and ambiguous. Not only do they often appear different to different observers, they also contain different features with distinctly different aspects. Income maintenance policies may both redistribute and regulate. Whilst which facet is of greater importance may be a matter of ideologically biased judgement, it is also likely to depend upon how they are conceived in detail and how they are operated on the ground.

The typologies advanced by Lowi and Austin are designed to help us analyse the way policies and interests relate, to facilitate, in Austin's words, a 'political economy' approach to policy analysis. Yet they tend to prove more difficult to use in practice. Our criticisms have focused upon the ways in which the types tend to merge in actual examples. We might equally have questioned whether there were not other, equally helpful, ways of developing policy typologies. These typologies do not handle ideological and moral components in policy particularly satisfactorily. Policies about the preservation of the family and the protection of religion, for example, will tend to fit uneasily into the categories. They contain regulatory and distributive aspects, but are not easily handled in these terms. For example, the control of abortion is in a sense a regulatory policy but it is very different in kind from the main items in that category. Austin's transformation of the regulatory category into 'behaviour change/ social control services' does seem to include it, but his emphasis is misleadingly more upon change, even if only change of individuals' behaviour rather than the maintenance of the *status quo*. The typologies, in general, apply more satisfactorily to active government interventions than to the equally important efforts to prevent change and maintain a pre-existing order.

However such typologies are important in raising the general proposition that policy content will affect, and be affected by, interest patterns in our political system. Some kinds of policy initiatives will therefore be more likely than others, and where the rarer kinds emerge they are likely to experience a rougher passage through the policy process. If the typologies have helped to sharpen attention to this then perhaps the attention they have been given has been worthwhile.

Let us see now whether an approach to the production of a policy typology similarly rooted in a political economy approach, but in a more marxist one, is likely to prove more fruitful. This is expressed in terms of the functions of the state, rather than types of policy and has already been explored in chapters 1, 2 and 5. Here we will look at the rather different way it has been used by some contemporary political scientists. It tends to identify functions with types of policy, but does not imply any exact equation between the two. Hence it tackles the mixed types issue in rather a different way. The approach largely derives from O'Connor's (1973) categories of public spending – as 'social expenses', 'social investment' and 'social consumption'. Offe's (1984) distinction between productive and allocative activities of the state is also relevant. Particular expositions of this approach are provided in the work of Cawson (1982) and of Saunders (in Boddy and Fudge, 1984). They see the state as performing three functions – in respect of the maintenance of *production* processes, the *consumption* processes, and *legitimation* (in which category they include coercion – the other aspect of the 'maintenance of social order', Cawson, 1982, p. 72).

This categorization is designed to help to handle the analysis of the complexity and diversity of the activities of the state. As was shown in chapter 2, O'Connor's original formulation was developed to analyse how contemporary governmental activity could still be explained within a marxist framework which sees the state as subservient to the interests of capital, and to suggest how such activity produces contradictions for the capitalist system. In its more recent formulations it has been seen as a 'dual state' theory, showing how the close connections between the interests of capital and the role of the state have been to some extent loosened. Hence for Cawson 'the insertion of consumption processes within the democratic state opens them up to a range of non-capitalist interests which shape both the level and pattern of welfare provision' (Cawson, 1982, p. 78). A particular aspect of this has been the way in which the interests of welfare producers – professionals and bureaucrats – play an important role in policy development (see Cawson, 1982; also Dunleavy, 1981).

Another issue which this typology has been used to explore is the division of functions between central and local government. In this model central government has been seen as principally concerned with production issues, which themselves have some primacy over consumption issues and set the limits for state expenditure, while consumption issues are often delegated to the local level. Then a pattern of political conflict is likely to occur at the local level which may have different characteristics to the production-based class conflict at national level (see Boddy and Fudge, 1984). Our interests as consumers are often patterned differently from the way our interests as producers are structured.

The analysis does not deal so fully with the legitimation issues. These are associated with many consumption policies (as O'Connor's analysis suggests). It is also, for many of the analyses which use this sort of model (see, in particular, Offe, 1984), the case that the growing conflict between consumption demands and the constraints arising from the limits to the surplus provided by the production process produces a 'legitimation crisis'. In this crisis consumption itself is less able to function as a legitimizing force, and there is accordingly a need for a shift towards more coercive ways of maintaining social order.

What are the potential problems about this approach towards a policy typology? First, its source lies in a theory about the relationship between a capitalist economy and the state, about the role of the latter as principally determined by the former, and about the *functions* it therefore has to perform. Whereas a theory like Lowi's sees the relationship between state and economy as one in which the state is an autonomous actor which encounters interests as it seeks to develop policies, this kind of theory explains all, or most (since many modern exponents of this theory recognize a degree of state autonomy), state action in terms of the dominance of that interest structure. It is a functionist kind of theory, with a view of the relationship between state and society in which the role of the latter is largely determined by the system maintenance needs of the former.

Where the Lowi typology requires that we label specific policies as redistributive, etc., and thus attribute purposes to policies and those who promote them, this theory attributes functions which may be quite independent of the purposes of the actors involved. They are deduced from a general theory of state and society.

This leads us to the second problem area. Like the Lowi approach, this kind of theory also acknowledges the existence of mixed types. In this case it is, of course, policies serving more than one function. If we look at some of those policies we find the three functions very mixed together. For example, education is an investment in a productive resource, a valued consumption 'good' and of key importance for legitimation of the existing social order. Whilst this mixed type problem is inevitable it becomes more serious when the theory is used to explain the division of responsibilities between levels of government, or the pattern of interest interaction which is associated with policy making and implementation. The kinds of observations which have been developed about central-local relations or about consumer and producer interest structures are of a very general kind (see the exposition by Saunders and criticism by Dunleavy in Boddy and Fudge, 1984). Above all, as all its exponents make clear, the dominance of production processes continually threatens the relative autonomy of consumption processes. This is a fundamental feature of this kind of theory, since its roots lie in attempts to provide dynamic explanations of conflict and development processes in modern capitalist society (O'Connor, 1973; Offe, 1984).

We must conclude our review of policy typologies by concluding that it is not possible to provide solid and water-tight typologies of policy content. What we have instead are approaches which draw our attention to some of the interactions between questions about power and interests on the one hand and the issues with which specific policies may be concerned on the other. Both of the theoretical approaches examined here do this, and thus help to sharpen our awareness of the relationship between the study of policy and the study of power. We will take this further in the next section by looking at ways of analysing the policy process systematically.

Analysing the policy process

Probably the most widely used approach to analysing the policy process involves the development of some sort of systems model. This implies inputs and some sort of policy development system with outputs and outcomes. Most of the formulations adopted are based upon Easton's (1965) model of the political system. What this involves is set out diagrammatically by Jenkins (1978) (see figure 8.1).

This sort of diagram can, of course, be elaborated enormously. Embellishments might include:

(1) the further subdivision of the central system showing the decision process as involving several stages, during which interactions continue with the environment;
(2) the recognition that, similarly, there are many more 'feedback' loops than merely that shown here between the beginning and the end of the process;
(3) the identification, as suggested earlier in this chapter, of an implementation process, and not merely a simple policy output element, which interacts strongly with the earlier parts of the policy process.

Many writers have recognized the need to elaborate the 'demands', 'supports' and 'resources' elements in this kind of model. One of the most important analyses of these elements for the study of social policy is provided in a book by Hall et al. (1975). Using a model rather like Easton's they analyse several case studies to try to advance 'propositions about what determines the priority that an issue attains' (Hall et al., 1975, p. 475). They conclude that the progress of policy issues through the system depends principally upon three criteria: legitimacy, feasibility and support. Let us look a little more at what they say about each of these.

(1) *Legitimacy.* Hall and her colleagues say the question that

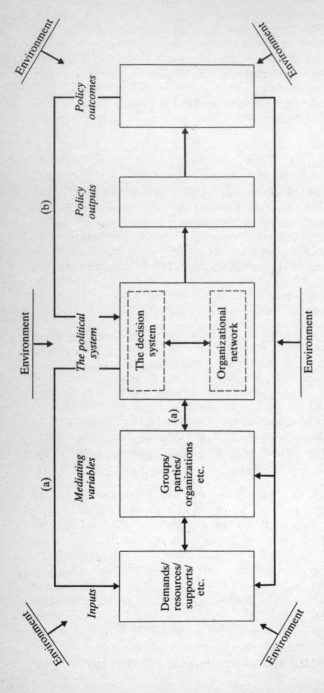

Figure 8.1 Easton's (1965) model of the political system

Environmental variables:
Socioeconomic
Physical
Political
N.B. Environmental variables vary with time.

must be asked on this is 'is this an issue with which government considers it should be concerned'. The answer to such a question will depend upon features internal to the system – governmental ideologies – and external factors – the state of opinion amongst the public and important interest groups. They suggest it is 'useful to think in terms of prevailing *levels* of legitimacy' (p. 476).

(2) *Feasibility.* Three elements are identified in the notion of feasibility. Hall et al. say 'First, feasibility is, in its broadest sense, determined by the prevailing structure and distribution of theoretical and technical knowledge' (p. 479). Their second point is that the concept of feasibility 'is not entirely independent of who does the judging'. Their last point is that feasibility 'is rarely immediately apparent' (pp. 479-80). Judgements have to be made which have as their particular concerns questions about resources, collaboration and administrative capacity.

(3) *Support.* Hall et al. argue on this as follows: 'Because policy change alters, or is thought to alter, some features of an existing distribution of power, influence, status or values, inevitably it will create some satisfaction and some discontent. The notion of the political feasibility of an issue is closely connected with its implications for this balance. Two considerations determine how it is estimated by authorities. The first is *whose* discontents and *whose* satisfactions are involved, and the second is the general state of the reservoir of support' (p. 483).

In their conclusions Hall et al. go on to argue that there will be factors affecting the 'image' of an issue which influence its progress within the system. Here they raise some questions about policy 'content' of a much more specific kind than those outlined in our earlier discussion of typologies. They consider questions about the associations between the issue under study and other issues, the scope of the issue, the relationship between the issue and trends or developments in society which affect its importance and the quality of the information available on the issue.

In this section they also address the question of the source of the demand. It is interesting that they seem to give this subject a rather less prominent place in their analysis than do many other pluralist analyses of the policy process. Their focus is upon a government dealing with issues, which may arise on the agenda for a variety of reasons including having been put there by the government itself. Other writers have seen issues as much more clearly exogenously generated, as coming as demands from specific groups. There may well be an interesting difference of emphasis here between American and British versions of pluralist theory, with the former seeing government most clearly as mediation between demands, while the latter is more inclined to ascribe a role to governmental programmes and ideologies. However, the two approaches may come together at another level, as those programmes may themselves be the products of demands.

It is clearly important for any analysis of the importance of groups outside government as sources of demands and supports to deal with a whole range of questions about the strength of these various pressures. We have described the work of Hall et al., together with the main intellectual sources on which it draws, as pluralist. Unlike marxist theory this perspective sees the policy process as to some extent an open and competitive one. Responses are being made to pressures, calculations are made about support, and the end result is a series of choices. The alternative marxist perspective is to see governmental action as much more specifically responses to the specific requirements of the capitalist state.

These differences, however, are to some extent matters of degree. There is a variety of ways in which pluralist and marxist perspectives may be partly combined. It is only in their really strong formulations that they are quite incompatible. The strongest positions on either side involve on the marxist side a functionist determinism with state autonomy of minimal importance and on the pluralist side a theoretical and methodological stance which asserts that demands upon the political system must be studied as separable empirical phenomena. Those who try to fuse these two perspectives have to grapple with difficult theoretical and logical problems, but there is a significant body of middle-ground work. In the last part of this section we will outline some of the ways in which propositions from both pluralist and marxist studies of the policy process may be brought together.

The recognition that there are substantial inequalities of power within societies is by no means absent from pluralist theory. In that sort of theory the ultimate control of elites by non-elites is what makes the system open (see Dahl, 1961). It is, therefore, perfectly compatible with the general perspective of pluralist theory to move towards an alternative formulation in which inequalities are cumulative, some groups are so weak that their effective political participation is minimal, and elites are acknowledged as very difficult to control. One finds that sort of perspective in, for example, C. Wright Mills' analyses of power in

America (Mills, 1956). But one may take that a step further to tie an analysis of the relationship between elites and non-elites into a class theory of society, which then sees the pursuance of class interests as a central characteristic of the political process and elites as closely tied into a dominant class.

A related step of some importance in the transformation of pluralist theories has entailed the recognition that power is exercised in a variety of ways, some of which are much less open to straightforward empirical study. Bachrach and Baratz (1970) show that non-decisions, organizing and keeping issues off the agenda, may be as important as decisions in the political system. Their insights were taken further by Lukes who described three faces of power: that which can be identified in relation to decisions, that which is manifested in non-decisions, and that which involves the shaping of people's attitudes and preferences so that no visible conflict occurs at all (Lukes, 1974). A critical concept here is the marxist one of 'false consciousness'. There is an important divide between those theorists who see preferences and choices as essentially manipulated and those who do not accept that such phenomena are significant for political behaviour.

Just as modifications of the pluralist position have made possible its restatement in ways which bring it close to the marxist view of power, so too has marxist theory been developed in ways which conceive of a more open kind of power structure than that embodied in Marx's view of the state as the executive committee of the ruling class. Even some of Marx's own work conceded that the class structure might not be so simple as that postulated in the notion of a dichotomous bourgeoisie-proletariat conflict. However, he argued that those features making for greater complexity in his time would gradually be eliminated, or become irrelevant, as the class struggle intensified. Some modern marxist students of society have been ready to acknowledge that the structural complexity has continued, or even that the structure has become more complex. That implies, particularly when the structural complexities are within the ranks of the bourgeoisie, some degree of pluralism within the system. The particular manifestation of it seen by some theorists (Poulantzas, 1973) within the bourgeoisie has been described as the existence of 'fractions' within capital.

Perhaps an even more important development in some marxist or neo-marxist work has involved a recognition of the state as a partly autonomous actor within the policy process. Marx's 'executive committee' remark belongs to a period when the institutions of government were still minimal. Modern marxists have been forced to re-analyse the power structure in the face of the enormous growth of the machinery of government. They have generally been unwilling to concede to the critics of marxism (Weber, for example, 1947) that state bureaucracy is a significant power in its own right, or that public servants form a 'new class' (Djilas, 1957). Some have conceded that the state has some degree of autonomy, particularly when confronted by conflicting demands from different fragments of capital. Some of the more functionalist marxist theories have portrayed this autonomy as used in the long-run interests of capitalism, when short-run demands conflict with that interest (see Poulantzas, 1973).

Arguments about the importance of the state may be seen as challenging both traditional marxist theory and traditional pluralist theory. Whilst theorists influenced by Max Weber have provided that challenge in their analyses of bureaucracy (Mills, 1956; Lipset, 1960; Kingsley, 1944), Nordlinger (1981) has emphasized the extent to which policy choices may be analysed as 'state preferences'. He does not attempt a detailed analysis of what this means, in terms of the internal structure of the state institutions, but instead seeks to show how there is room for the exercise of 'state preferences' in a variety of situations in which societal preferences are expressed without unanimity or effective force.

An alternative treatment of the contemporary influence of the state involves seeing it, or some of its functionaries, as tackling decision problems through a complex bargaining process involving the most powerful of the pressure groups. A version of this viewpoint, which has grown out of those pluralist theories which stress the roles of a limited number of powerful groups, speaks of 'post-parliamentary democracy' (Richardson and Jordan, 1979). From this perspective policy is settled by a number of 'policy communities', in which pressure groups and government interact. The compositions of these communities vary according to the issue. A version of this perspective close to the marxist viewpoint would stress that the policy community which settles the central issues about the management of the economy is dominated by capitalist interests. Corporatist theory (see Middlemass, 1979; Winkler, 1976) accepts the importance of this rather closed policy community, agreeing with the marxists that it is perhaps beside the point to describe it as 'democracy', but is likely to argue that trade unions are also key participants.

Each of these versions of the 'post-parliamentary democracy' thesis raises questions about the extent of the existence of policy communities other than that concerned with the management of the economy. We referred earlier to the work of Cawson and

Saunders in developing the O'Connor typology to emphasize the politics of consumption. Policy communities concerned with consumption may be more open to participation by weak, consumer-based pressure groups and idealistic cause groups (Richardson and Jordan, 1979). They may also be dominated by the bureaucrats and professionals which provide the service in question (Cawson, 1982).

We have described here, then, a variety of ways in which pluralist and marxist analyses of the policy process have developed and may converge. The extent of that convergence is, of course, hotly contested. It is a matter of debate to what extent they are competing paradigms offering mutually contradictory explanations (see Alford in Lindberg et al., 1975). Clearly many marxists concede little to the pluralist position and vice-versa. For some writers substantial amounts of the theory on either side is incompatible with that on the other. A significant number of marxists espouse a perspective which is deterministic, seeing economic imperatives as crucial determinants of social and political life, whilst most pluralists are methodological individualists rejecting general theory and regarding the arguments about the system of power as essentially resolvable by empirical investigation. In this discussion, like many contemporary analysts, we have been trying to ride both the marxist and the pluralist horse. Some philosophers of social sciences would argue that we are bound to fall!

Comparative studies of the policy process

One way of studying the policy process which tries to offer an objective approach to identifying influences upon policy is to focus upon *outputs* and, if possible, *outcomes*, and to try to identify the *inputs* which determine them. The comparison of different governments or local authorities seems to offer a way to do this statistically, examining specific output variables from a number of places and using correlational techniques to try to see which input variables are associated with them. However, we saw in chapter 2 that this approach has not been particularly successful for cross-national analysis. It has only been possible to identify very general indices of level of socioeconomic development, and has led to crude convergence theories which see an association between the overall growth of welfare state expenditure and industrialization (Wilensky, 1975).

Nevertheless this sort of comparative method has also been used to compare the outputs of different local authorities within individual states. In such cases it is very much easier to secure a range of broadly comparable variables to use in the analysis, and to work with a sufficient number of relatively similar authorities to facilitate a deeper correlational analysis. In both Europe and the United States a number of studies of this kind have been undertaken (see Aiken and Mott, 1970; Bonjean et al., 1971; Alt, 1971; Newton and Sharpe, 1977; Dye, 1976; Foster et al., 1980). An interesting feature of the debate about the policy process engendered by this work has been the discussion of the respective importance of general social environmental factors on the one hand, and political party and system inputs on the other, in explaining public expenditure outputs. Whilst there has been a tendency for many of the studies, particularly in the United States, to emphasize the former, some European studies (see Aiken and Depré, 1980) and particularly some British studies (see Boaden, 1971; Alt, 1971; Jackman and Sellars, 1978; Sharpe and Newton, 1984) have suggested circumstances in which party political control is important.

However, whilst some of these studies, like that of Boaden (1971), suggest reassuring conclusions on the relevance of the democratic process in determining policy outputs, there remain difficulties about using these studies to help to explain the policy process. First, whilst we have spoken of them as concerned to explain output, that is normally interpreted in terms of the most readily quantifiable measure of output, that is expenditure. It may be argued that expenditure is not a true output measure, but just a measure of the cost of achieving an output. Certainly moreover, as will be stressed in chapter 10, 'output' measures must not be confused with outcomes. Second, these studies do not to any significant degree deal with the 'black box' lying between inputs and outputs (see figure 8.1). Moreover even where correlations are established these, of course, only account for part of the relationship; and in any case a correlation does not *explain* how a relationship has occurred. Correlation evidence can at best show that the evidence is, or is not, consistent with specified hypotheses about systematic relationships. Because so little can be measured, the reader of analyses of this kind is likely to be left with an uneasy feeling that other, unmeasured variables, really explain the perceived relationship. A powerful body of techniques is often deployed to provide a conclusion, that necessarily has to be expressed cautiously and hedged around with reservations. The main defence of the technique is that, as we shall see, it is very much more objective than any of the available alternatives. It is a pity that little has been done to link analyses of this kind with other, more qualitative, exploratory methods.

As suggested above, the case for the abandonment of quantitative techniques has been more readily made in the context of cross-national studies than of intra-national studies. What then is the alternative? One answer to that question may be to abandon comparative studies, to regard it as hopeless to make satisfactory comparisons. Another answer is to regard such research as 'intelligent tourism', a possible conclusion suggested by Knoepfel and Larrue (1984); but a number of writers have sought to make a case for such research. Joan Higgins (1981) explores this issue using the major theoretical debates to suggest a number of categories of analysis – comparing the role of the state in social policy, the influence of religion, different ideologies on welfare and the work ethic and different perspectives on the role of the private sector. She suggests, therefore, that her approach 'is not "grand theory" but it aims to establish general guidelines for analysing policy in specific cases' (p. 171).

Ashford (1982, 1984), another exponent of comparative research, argues for an approach he calls 'structural analysis' which begins where other analyses leave off.

Another pioneer of qualitative comparative work is Hugh Heclo (1974). His approach, in his comparative study of social security policies in Britain and Sweden, is very like Ashford's. By shifting to and fro between passages examining relatively similar events in policy development in the two countries he provides an insight which lays a strong emphasis upon understanding the policy process through understanding the way the political system operates. In his conclusions he seeks to disentangle the relative importance of socioeconomic development, elections, parties, interest groups, and administrators in the two countries. His results again, of course, lead towards no simple conclusions.

It seems to us that the value to the reader of studies such as Ashford's and Heclo's lies in the extent to which they provide insights on the way the process works, and particularly in the extent to which they make one think again about often taken for granted assumptions about one's own system.

Comparative work involving separate national researchers needs rather more of a framework for a compare-and-contrast exercise. An important attempt to develop such a framework has been made by Peter Knoepfel and Helmut Weidner (1982). It was designed for a comparative study of air pollution control policies. As such it is probably difficult to apply outside that specific policy context. However it embodies certain more general ideas, and as such was adopted by Roger Whitmore to use for the analysis of the structure of the system developed in Britain for the operation of policy aimed at the prevention or reduction of child abuse by parents (Whitmore, 1984). Although Whitmore's was not a comparative study his adaptation of the framework to another policy analysis task suggests ways in which it may be made more widely usable.

Another reason for giving attention to Knoepfel and Weidner's framework is that it deals with another issue that has been a concern of this chapter – the need for an approach to policy analysis which can handle together those processes generally conceived of as policy making and those regarded as implementation.

The central idea in both the papers we want to discuss is a core element surrounded by a series of shells (Knoepfel and Weidner, 1982) or onion layers (Whitmore, 1984). The development and implementation of policy can only be explained by attention to each element in these series of concentric circles. The inner elements are perhaps of more fundamental importance, but the limitations of two-dimensional drawing prevent an entirely effective representation of the multi-dimensionality of the interactions entailed in the process as a whole.

The core element is the most problematic part of these models. Knoepfel and Weidner treat concrete air quality standards as their core, Whitmore treats the general issue of child abuse as his. What an analysis of this kind seems to need is a central issue or standard on which there is a high measure of agreement. One can then analyse the ways in which different interests impinge upon it, and thus may undermine or distort it as concrete actions are determined. In the air pollution case we would suggest that the core element should be not a concrete air quality standard but the general agreement on the desirability of keeping our air sufficiently pure to avoid poisoning ourselves. There is consensus at that level, but as soon as you move away from that general proposition that consensus disappears. Thus Whitmore's example of the undesirability of child abuse represents a simple common point of agreement.

The first problem about this is that it is possible to conceive of policy issues where it is much harder to find a common point of agreement, for example on an issue such as abortion. Can we proceed in this way to identify generalized consensus points for most issues? Certainly one of our earliest propositions in this book was that there seem to be a variety of social issues which are all tackled in some way in advanced industrial societies – the provision of education, the alleviation of poverty, the treatment of illness, etc. Yet, as we showed in chapter 4, the concept of 'need' for such services is not generally subject to consensus.

Is it necessary for the purposes of analysis to try to establish a core issue on which there is consensus? Perhaps not, but what is important is to try to analyse the fundamental dimensions of a policy issue. This may be done by recognizing the alternative perspectives evident at the core, and the interests identified with those. Or it may be done, as Whitmore has in his article, by looking at the divisions of perspective at the next level. Whitmore analyses these as competing 'policy paradigms'. In the case of child abuse he sees two – one which attributes this problem to deprivation, the other which see 'bad parenting' as the key issue. He argues that the first of these interpretations states the problem in a way which requires substantial redistribution for its solution, whilst the second requires specific remedial action by groups of professionals to prevent or deal with individual cases of family failure. He suggests, therefore, that the first solution challenges substantial economic interests, while the second provides scope for developing professional groups to make a case for the special skills in tackling the 'child abuse syndrome'. In this way he explains how the second explanation has become the dominant paradigm. In a comparative analysis we would want to explore the extent to which paradigms differed from country to country, and to try to explain why.

The subsequent rings in the model then deal more fully with the phenomena which need to be taken into account in interpreting the translation of core, or near to core, concerns into action. The labels for these rings in the Knoepfel and Weidner model and in the Whitmore model are set out side by side in Table 8.1. What the outer rings remind us is that if a policy output is to have any real impact then the kinds of issues which they represent must be tackled. They focus attention upon the issues concerning organization and financing, and the nature of administrative actions on the ground. To an overwhelming extent the actual output of social policy depends upon (a) the provision of resources, (b) the overall form of organization, including the roles assigned to different levels of government, and (c) the activities of key actors at the policy delivery end of the system. In connection with each of these issues the interest conflicts observable near the core may recur.

In relation to air pollution Knoepfel and Weidner are able to show how apparently very dissimilar control systems in different countries arrive at very similar outcomes. They operate in similar social and economic conditions, and the system differences mean that specific interest groups need to operate to protect themselves at different parts of the system in different countries. For effective use of the model it is most important to ask the kinds of questions Knoepfel and Weidner (1982) do about a checklist of

Table 8.1   Core/shell models of the policy process

	Knoepfel and Weidner model	Whitmore model
Core	Ambient air quality standards	The issue of child abuse
Shells		The competing policy paradigms, one of which is dominant
	Measuring methods, monitoring and network evaluation	The monitoring framework
	Emission, product, process standards	Inter-organizational resource dependencies
	Organizations, financing	Administrative structure and processes
	Administrative instruments processes	Fieldwork/client interface

possible interest groups. They do this in terms of three separate systems: the sociocultural (legitimatory) system, the economic system, and the politico-administrative system (pp. 90-1).

A problem which the model does not appear to cover very satisfactorily is what may be termed the question of interaction with other issues, particularly adjacent policy issues. Much important work on the study of implementation has stressed the need to see any new initiative as entering a very crowded policy space (Elmore, 1980) and to see ground-level actors as making choices both about the ways they may put different resources together (Hjern and Porter, 1981) and about the things they will select to do from amongst the excessive demands upon them (Lipsky, 1980). Perhaps the model may be elaborated to deal with this. Whitmore has made a start in this direction by introducing issues about inter-organizational relationships and about the worker-client interface into the model.

We do not believe that there is any easy *key* to the comparative analysis of the policy process any more than there is any easy way to defining policy. We have chosen to conclude this chapter with a discussion of one particular model for research, particularly comparative research. It is a model which has uses inasmuch as it sensitizes analysts to the issues to be considered. We do not offer it as the best approach to analysis; merely as one we regard as useful. It is in no sense predictive; it merely provides a framework for analysis. We have stressed the value of the model because Knoepfel and Weidner, and Whitmore in his adaptation of it, succeed in bringing together the micro-issues about specific policies with the macro-issues about their wider contexts.

9

Bureaucrats and Professionals in Social Policy Delivery

Introduction

An extensive amount of policy analysis literature, particularly in more recent times, has recognized that the behaviour of people who are responsible for the delivery of services, particularly of the more personal kinds of services, plays an important part in the determination of the character of those services. This is a theme which was raised at several points in chapter 8. We want to follow it through more fully here. It is, however, quite difficult to provide a straightforward account of the contribution to the analysis of social policy made by this literature as there is a number of complex and sometimes conflicting threads within it. First, an important distinction must be made between those accounts of 'front-line' or 'street-level' or 'coal-face' official behaviour which see this as essentially a control issue for those responsible for policy, and those which do not make the assumption that simple analysis of the phenomenon as a control problem is an adequate approach to the issue. Analysts in the second group, moreover, themselves vary between those who focus, as we did in chapter 8, on the essential complexity of the so-called policy input, those who see high front-line discretion as an inevitable feature of complicated policy delivery systems, and those who are concerned with the structural sources of power of some front-line workers, including above all those who are often described as 'professionals'. Whilst an integrated account of the sources of 'front-line' policy output determination needs to weave together these various threads the fact is that they focus attention on very different parts of the overall phenomenon and need to be explored separately.

Hence in this chapter we will look first at the approaches to

this issue which focus upon it principally as a control phenomenon. A section on discretion will then take this definition of
the problem forward in a way which both accepts that view and
also exposes some of its limitations. Then, examinations of
Lipsky's 'street-level bureaucracy' thesis, analyses of 'gatekeeping' roles and exploration of professionalism in social policy
administration will further develop various aspects of the
weaknesses of the control perspective.

The control perspective

As the study of policy implementation became a fashionable sub-
topic within policy analysis a number of works were published
which saw 'implementation deficit' as a problem for top-level
policy makers and proceeded to set out a series of prescriptions
on how this problem might be minimized (see Sabatier and
Mazmanian, 1979; Williams, 1971; Gunn, 1978). These prescriptions typically include statements about securing clarity in policy
goals, keeping the structure responsible for the implementation
process as simple as possible and maintaining effective control
over implementing actors. It is, of course, the second and third of
these which we want to look at here, but we will find that our
analysis will return from time to time to the first, since it is in fact
the inherent unlikelihood of simple policy goals which is a central
source of difficulties.

Concerns about over-elaborate structures, particularly ones
containing a large number of hierarchical layers, have been a
major preoccupation of administration textbooks for the public
and private sectors alike for a long while. Herbert Simon, as one
of his examples of the conflicting 'proverbs' of administration,
examined the way in which arguments that the numbers of levels
in administrative hierarchies should be limited come into conflict
with arguments that individual 'spans of control' should be kept
small (Simon, 1945, pp. 27-8).

We have here, then, issues about control within hierarchies
which have been the traditional concerns of 'management
science' ever since it became recognized that control of complex
organizations can be problematical. We do not propose to go into
issues of this kind in this book; but at the same time it is not our
intention in brushing over them to suggest that these issues are
unimportant – merely that to analyse social policy implementation problems in this way is to examine only part of the story.

In the implementation literature another aspect of this problem
has emerged: the presence of inter-organizational clearance

problems in implementation chains. Hence, Pressman and Wildavsky (1973) illustrated the very complex inter-organizational linkages for the operation of a specific employment creation policy, and demonstrated mathematically that proportionately very small amounts of disagreement at each individual clearance point could lead to very large 'implementation deficits' where a number of such points are involved in translating policy into action.

Analyses of administration by Hood (1976) and by Dunsire (1978a, b) have explored issues of this kind theoretically, using the notion of 'perfect administration' rather as economists use the notion of 'perfect competition'. They recognize therefore that a great deal of inefficiency gets into complex systems. Dunsire analyses administrative operations as a series of programmes and asserts that 'Such programmes, and programmes within programmes, form the bureaucracy's repertory of responses to presenting problems; and the degree of appropriateness of final output to presented problem is limited (at maximum) to the combinatorial possibilities of the repertory' (Dunsire, 1978b, p. 13). This kind of analysis is clearly appropriate both for the complex inter-organizational implementation chain, and for intra-organizational situations of a high degree of complexity in which individual divisions enjoy some elements of autonomy.

Prescriptions to deal with this kind of problem typically come in the form of advice to ensure simplicity in the relationship between task and agency. This is an issue that has been a particular preoccupation of American studies. It relates above all to the tendency of Federal initiatives to create new agencies which then have to manage complicated relationships with older agencies in order to carry out tasks. Again we do not wish to quarrel with the general common-sense concern to try to keep administrative mandates simple, but it must be recognized that behind such issues lie political conflicts and dilemmas which were the original creators of the complexity.

Another way to take the issues about complexity is to see them as symptoms of 'big government'. In this case two alternative kinds of prescription follow. One is the suggestion that government is trying to do too much; it is taking on new tasks which inevitably conflict with earlier tasks, or it is trying to secure social and economic effects which involve complex activities because they extend beyond areas which it can easily control. When taken in this direction the analysis of implementation deficits becomes a part of the case against active government (see King, 1975; Brittan, 1975). The alternative prescription is the 'small is beautiful' one, which sees decentralization as the key to simplifying the implementation process (Hadley and Hatch, 1981).

Since we see the complexity of implementation as something closely related to the complexity of the policy process, and thus ultimately to the complexity of politics, we find the logic of these kinds of conclusions more satisfactory than the logic involved in the derivation of prescriptions for better management from the study of the implementation process. We believe we can deal more effectively with the issues about so-called implementation deficit by looking carefully at some of the particular manifestations of front-line staff behaviour than by looking for generalizable control issues.

The issue of discretion

Much that has been written about discretion takes as its starting point the notion of it as a problem, a problem for control. Bankowski and Nelken have thus suggested that 'Practical and theoretical concern over discretion is best seen not as an invitation to study a particular area of decision-making, but as an index of anxiety over the possibilities of unregulated decision-making. Concern over discretion constitutes a social problem?' (in Adler and Asquith, 1981, p. 247). Hence in the study of social policy the use of the concept of discretion has been very strongly linked with a normative issue, a concern about rights. Interest in the phenomenon of discretion can be seen as emerging from the examination of the welfare state as the provider of social rights. The issue emerged in Britain as it became recognized that the complex administration machinery for the delivery of social policy might not deliver benefits as rights, in the sense that Titmuss (1968) and Marshall (1975) had analysed them. Thus Townsend (1975) made the problem of discretion one of the central planks in his arguments for universalism in social security, a theme which was then taken up and argued effectively in various publications from the Child Poverty Action Group. Where policies could not be formulated in ways which made rights quite clear-cut, some writers, moreover, have been prepared to argue that at least strong rule structures should be used to limit the freedom of action of front-line staff. The issue has been summed up by Donnison with particular reference to the British supplementary benefits system as follows: 'Do you want administrative flexibility, policies shaped . . . to the infinite variety of human needs? Or do you want legal precision, policies shaped by Parliament and the lawyers in tribunals and courts, and "proportional justice" treating broad categories of people in predictable and reasonably consistent ways? Do you want discretion or rights?' (Donnison, 1982, p. 93). Yet to make sense of this argument we need to be a great deal clearer about what we mean by discretion, and how it manifests itself in relation to the policy output at stake. Our starting point should be not that very emotive and ideologically charged argument that has developed in Britain over the administration of means tests, but instead attempts which have been made by organizational sociologists to identify the discretionary elements in work tasks.

Such sociologists' have shown how all work, however closely controlled and supervised, involves some degree of discretion. Wherever work is delegated, the person who delegates loses some amount of control. To approach the concept in this way is, of course, to examine it from the perspective of superordinate authority. Viewed the other way round the equivalent phenomenon is rules which apparently guarantee benefits or services but nevertheless have to be interpreted by intermediaries. It may be important to distinguish here the phenomenon of 'judgement', involving applying rules to actual situations, from much broader examples of discretion where the rule constraints are limited (this is done in the writings of Bull, 1980; and Donnison, 1982, pp. 93-4). In our view, however, this is only a difference of degree. Certainly few officials operate in contexts in which discretion is entirely unstructured.

Running through much organization theory, and in particular through the work of those writers who were seeking to help those they saw as 'in control' of organizations to determine the right way to approach the delegation of tasks, is therefore a concern about the balance between rules and discretion, even when different words are used. Hence Simon, in his *Administrative Behaviour* (1945), emphasized the importance of the various 'premises' upon which decisions are based. Rule-making and control within organizations is concerned with the specification of premises for subordinates.

If the analysis of discretion is approached in terms of propositions about limits to control, questions then need to be examined about the sources of those limits. This is an issue that has been explored by Jowell (1973) in examining the legal control of discretion. We may identify several questions which need to be asked about the limits to control over front-line work tasks, for example:

(1) Does it involve making choices between competing tasks? As students of police activities have stressed, there are always

more potential crime prevention tasks than police, so choices have to be made about where to patrol, who to stop, when to limit action against minor offences, etc. Similarly, social workers have to decide which of the many families for whom they have responsibility are most likely to require their support.

(2) Do decisions involve judgements for which is it inherently difficult to provide unambiguous and universally applicable guidelines? Many tasks concern the evaluation of the standards (good child care, for example) or the determination of the extent of need (for rehousing, for example), where it is impossible to provide clear objective yardsticks in advance (see the discussion of these issues in Jowell, 1973).

(3) Does the subordinate need to possess a degree of expertise in order to perform the task which makes him or her the best judge of the action required? One of the classics of organizational sociology, Michael Crozier's *The Bureaucratic Phenomenon* (1964), showed how maintenance engineers were in a very powerful position in a factory because only they could deal with breakdowns. We need to take account both of the many forms of expertise found in public sevice work, and also the very fact that anyone with delegated responsibilities acquires some expertise inasmuch as he or she tends to have more direct experience than a superior. Inevitably, teachers who become heads or social workers who become managers tend, in due course, to find that lack of use lessens some skills. What is even more important is that it is the front-line workers, not their supervisors, who have the clearest sense of the needs of specific pupils and clients.

These are all questions about tasks which make them logically difficult to predetermine. Then in addition there are various limitations to control related, as already suggested, to explicit difficulties of supervision. In social policy a lot of front-line work is done in places inevitably far from the scrutiny of supervisors, in people's homes, for example.

Next there is a further, more complex, range of reasons why discretion may be allowed. Fox, coming to the examination of this issue from a concern with industrial relations, has related rule imposition to low-trust relationships. He picks up the 'top-down' concern with detailed prescription and shows how this creates or reinforces low trust relations: 'The role occupant perceives superordinates as behaving as if they believe he cannot be trusted, of his own volition, to deliver a work performance which fully accords with the goals they wish to see pursued or the values they wish to see observed' (Fox, 1974, p. 26). A vicious circle may be expected to ensue. The subordinate, who perceives he or she is not trusted, feels little commitment to the effective performance of his task. This affects the way he or she carries out the remaining discretionary parts of his work. The superior's response is to try to tighten control, and further reduce the discretionary elements. The irreducible minimum of discretion left leaves the subordinate with some weapons against his superior; he performs his prescribed task in a rigid, unimaginative and slow way. Low motivation in a rule-bound context produces restriction of output, working to rule, industrial sabotage and strikes. In public administration there is often another person, a member of the public, rather than a machine, to feel the effects of low official morale. The very rules which have been promulgated to guarantee a consistent service to the public may be used against them.

In this way problems of rule enforcement become the basis of the case for allowing discretion. Some rather similar phenomena may emerge by different routes. Some may be defined as discretion, others as rule breaking. The former emerges from a recognition of limits to control, a concession of autonomy because of the recognition of the power and status of implementers. This is the 'high-trust' situation described by Fox, and applies to much professional discretion within public administration. The latter is seized by low-level staff regarded as 'subordinates' rather than 'implementers' whom, in practice, superiors fail to control. One is legitimated, the other regarded – by the dominant elements in the hierarchy – as illegitimate. To the member of the public 'on the receiving end' they may be indistinguishable.

Where discretion is regarded as legitimate, our analysis needs to take into account the power of the groups of officials who secure this autonomy, this claim to discretion. The degree of freedom which they acquire may be very much greater than that made necessary by the logical limits to control outlined above. The issue of the need for trust may be extended to arguments about the rights of officials to autonomy. It may also be supported by arguments that such officials have a clearer conception of the best interests of the public than do those who seek to control them. In two particular contexts, which often in practice come together, the debate about such autonomy takes a particularly value-charged form; one of these concerns the rights of officials to a measure of freedom from control by their political masters; the other concerns the prerogatives of officials defined, or defining themselves, as professionals.

So far our discussion of discretion has, even if it has raised doubts about the validity of simplistic control strategies, remained (except perhaps for the passing reference to professionalism) within the broad parameters of managerial concern about the *best way* to influence policy implementation. But the sources of discretion may be somewhere within the underlying debate about policy choice. In an analysis of his role as a 'front-line' official in a relief agency one of the authors analysed many of the sources of his discretion as rooted in a 'failure' of policy makers to resolve critical value problems (Hill, 1969). The dilemma of balancing 'hard' and 'soft' requirements in a relief system, which could have been resolved by political choice, was left to the implementing official. Similar examples can be found in many areas of social policy, for instance the difficult balance between 'care' and 'control' required of social workers. One can also find unresolved value issues in rationing responsibilities. In medicine, for example, we often find the allocation of scarce treatments such as kidney machines, explicitly left in the hands of practitioners.

The word 'failure' was put in quotation marks above, since the context in which it was used involved a value position, which was certainly taken in the original article mentioned there, that policy makers *should* have resolved the problem. Our concern here is rather to stress that they often do not do so, as our analysis in chapter 8 suggested, and that the fact that they do not do so must be analysed in terms of the considerable value conflict likely to be associated with many areas of social policy (see Prosser in Adler and Asquith, 1981). This brings us back full-circle to the initial statement in this section about the way so much analysis of discretion sees it as a value problem. Our stance is partly to agree and partly to disagree with that view. Discretion is in our view an inevitable feature of policy implementation. Our reasons for arguing this are partly derived from a logical analysis of organizational decision making and partly from the observation of limits to decision-making closure as a political phenomenon. The two are, of course, related. In fields where actions are difficult to structure and predetermine decisions are taken (or, of course, not taken) about where to try to limit discretion and where not to. The value problems are associated with those choices.

The street-level bureaucracy viewpoint

A very different perspective to that in this chapter so far, of seeing implementation issues in control terms, is that offered by Michael Lipsky and his colleagues (Lipsky, 1980; Prottas, 1979; Weatherley, 1979). They see front-line staff in social policy implementation agencies as isolated people trying to provide services in the face of conflicting hierarchical requirements, great pressure from the public and inadequate resources. Lipsky describes front-line workers in the public sector as 'street-level bureaucrats'. He argues in his book *Street-level Bureaucracy* that the process of street-level policy making does not involve, as might be hoped, the advancement of the ideals many bring to personal service work, but rather development of practices which enable officials to cope with the pressures they face. He says:

> people often enter public employment . . . with at least some commitment to service. Yet the very nature of this work prevents them from coming close to the ideal conception of their jobs. Large classes or huge caseloads and inadequate resources combine with the uncertainties of method and unpredictability of clients to defeat their aspirations as service workers. (Lipsky, 1980, p. xii)

Working under pressure, front-line officials find themselves sacrificing their wider ideals to the need to get through their day-to-day work. The need to deal with large quantities of work – getting benefits out on time, ensuring that everyone in a queue gets at least some attention – undermines its quality. Simplified practices have to be developed to cope with otherwise over-complex tasks.

Lipsky speaks of a paradox about front-line work. Officials appear to the public outside as having considerable discretion, indeed even sometimes considerable power; but they do not see themselves like that. They feel they are merely 'cogs in a system', constrained by their 'bureaucratic' roles. How is this paradox to be explained? It is, of course, partly a consequence of the very weak and vulnerable position of many members of the public who seek help from these officials. In this sense relatively powerless officials are nevertheless very powerful people as far as their clients are concerned. Moreover, those clients rarely have a clear view about where that power really lies. It is often extremely difficult, for clients and sometimes for the officials themselves, to distinguish agency policy from individual official discretion.

However, there is more to Lipsky's paradox than this. Front-line officials make choices about the use of scarce resources. From this perspective their power is limited by scarcity; nevertheless they still have responsibility for crucial choices about resource use. For example, social services staff may feel that they have very inadequate budgets for aids to the disabled, for the provision of telephones and so on. In this sense they are very constrained; but they often have very considerable discretion to decide to whom those scarce benefits should go. Similar observations might be made about another form of rationing – the rationing of individual workers' time.

Lipsky sees the street-level bureaucrat's *freedom* to make policy as largely used to provide *him or herself* with a more manageable task and environment. He talks of 'defenses against discretion', emphasizing the extent to which street-level bureaucrats develop rigid practices which may be described by the observer as involving rule conformity even though the rules are imposed upon themselves. He stresses patterns of practice as 'survival mechanisms', a perspective also used in a British study of social workers by Carol Satyamurti, *Occupational Survival* (1981), where she speaks of the use of 'strategies of survival' by social workers under pressure which led people with the 'best of intentions' nearly always to do 'less for clients than they might have', and often behave in 'ways that were positively damaging' (Satyamurti, 1981, p. 82). Difficult work environments lead to the adoption of techniques which enable clients to be 'managed', and therefore probably to disregard of the workers' original ideals.

A problem about matching limited resources to apparently much greater needs is recognized by all sensitive members of social services agencies. Accordingly, therefore, considerable efforts are made to identify priorities and to develop rational ways to allocate resources, as suggested in chapter 4. The problem is that, according to Lipsky, 'theoretically there is no limit to the demand for free public goods' (Lipsky, 1980, p. 81). Therefore it is important to accept that welfare agencies will always feel under pressure. Lipsky says that the resource problem for street-level bureaucrats is often irresolvable 'either because the number of people treated . . . is only a fraction of the number that could be treated, or because their theoretical obligations call for higher quality treatment than it is possible to provide to individual clients' (p. 37). Adjustments to case-loads further the quality of the work but leave the worry about quantity and vice-versa. It is always possible to make out cases for new resources.

A substantial section of Lipsky's book deals with the way in which street-level bureaucrats categorize their clients and respond in stereotyped ways to their needs. This draws on a large body of American research, particularly on police discretion, which has shown how distinctions are made between different kinds of citizens, which enable officials to develop certain responses in uncertain situations (see, for example, Brown, 1981). In the social policy areas we may note how the distinction between the 'deserving' and the 'undeserving' poor regularly resurfaces in decision making. There is evidence of the use of simplistic grading systems to govern the allocation of houses, and of judgemental responses to some types of social security claimants. Even the more professional services are not free of this kind of stereotyping, influencing decisions about 'treatability' or 'teachability'.

Lipsky's view is that such stereotyping is a necessary feature of 'street-level' work. He argues that such is the need for street-level bureaucrats to differentiate clients 'that it seems as useful to assume bias (however modest) and ask why it sometimes does not occur, as to assume equality of treatment and ask why it is regularly abridged'. We need to categorize people whenever our tasks require us to choose between them.

Lipsky's position involves, as was stressed above, seeing ideals of service as undermined by work pressures. There are two more radical directions in which his argument might have been taken. One of these is to argue that these ideals of service are necessarily very fragile. Bureaucratic employment offers secure work in which individuals manipulate and control individuals whose social positions are inherently weaker. Professional or semi-professional ideals are merely a smokescreen behind which more self-interested concerns can be protected. Hence it may be argued that the true interests of street-level bureaucrats and their clients are more at variance that he suggests. The former sustain or enhance their power at the expense of those 'below' them and thereby make their contribution to the overall maintenance of the *status quo*.

The other radical criticism of Lipsky's perspective is that it gives insufficient attention to the extent to which the desire of basic-grade public servants to provide an effective service may be more fundamentally undermined further up the system. This was explored at the end of the previous section on discretion, where we argued that decision issues may have been explicitly left unresolved.

Lipsky regards most of those whose work he examines – teachers, social workers, etc. – as semi-professionals. In one chapter he analyses the extent to which greater professionalism provides a way forward from the 'street-level bureaucracy' dilemma. The fact that their discretion is hard to control suggests that 'street-level bureaucrats should be professionals whose relatively altruistic behaviour, high standards and self-monitoring substitute for what the society cannot dictate' (Lipsky, 1980, p. 201). However, he comes to conclusions on this rather like those of other recent radical observers of professionalism in social policy. We will look at this professionalism theme more fully in the section after next. First we want to look at another way of looking at the issues in this chapter, a way which takes the perspective of the recipient of benefits and services as its starting point.

Gatekeeping

A number of writers have focused attention upon the way in which individuals seeking benefits and services are likely to have to make their cases in the first place to an official who plays a 'gatekeeper' role. The original formulation of this concept of 'gatekeeping' is in a brief discussion by Lewin (1947). The idea has been taken forward by Deutscher (Deutscher and Thompson, 1968) in the United States and by Foster (1983) in Britain. In describing Deutscher's work Hall, who has made one of the few empirical studies of gatekeeping, says 'His basic argument is simple. Man is increasingly required to come into contact with large-scale bureaucratic organisations. When entering any such organisation a person must encounter some form of gatekeeper "who will determine just how far he will get and how long it will take him" ' (Hall, 1974, pp. 31-2).

Organizations where the gatekeeper role is likely to be particularly significant will have two important characteristics:

(1) There will be an excess of demands over resources, or at least a lack of fit between the ways in which demands come in and resources are provided.
(2) There will be no market mechanism which effects the accommodation between demands and resources.

Hence, gatekeeping, although not necessarily entirely absent in other situations, is a salient characteristic of bureaucratic rationing mechanisms.

Peggy Foster (1983), in her account of welfare rationing processes, uses the gatekeeper concept to embrace a wide range of rationing activities. She includes within it not merely receptionist roles played by officials whose duties are confined to something not far advanced from the actual physical responsi-bility of opening and closing the 'gate' – that is those who simply make appointments for others – but also individuals who themselves have the ultimate responsibility for rationing benefits and services (including themselves as the providers of the services). While it is recognized that the distinction embodied in the preceding sentence may be a difficult one to make in practice – there are many hybrid examples where people have decision responsibilities for some services but are referral agents for others (general practitioners in respect of more specialist medical services, for example) – Foster does rather confuse the picture by grouping these activities together. Even though there may be grey areas, there is an important distinction to be made, with important policy and organizational control implications, between (a) rationing which occurs implicitly, without overt official recognition and therefore often without adequate scope for redress, through the gatekeeping activities of staff who appear to have a routine job; and (b) that which occurs when readily recognizable decision takers say 'no'.

Certainly Hall's study (1974) was concerned with the first of these phenomena, the way in which receptionists in social services departments had an impact upon the rationing of social work services. His study had a significant influence upon intake procedures in British social services departments, encouraging the development of practices which involved social workers more directly in intake processes. Drawing the distinction between these two types of rationing in the way we have done highlights the issue about the extent to which rationing occurs as a relatively irrational process, where activities undertaken to protect receptionists themselves, or more particularly the front-line staff immediately 'behind' them, from pressure plays a fundamental role in the allocation system.

However, the question must remain: is the rationing behaviour of the legitimate decision takers who are protected in this way markedly more rational? Much of the data quoted in Foster's book, particularly with reference to medical decisions, suggests that it is not so; but much more research needs to be done on the various screening and sorting processes which occur. At the same time important issues which must also be explored concern the relative strengths and weaknesses of bureaucratic or professional, as compared with market-type, rationing processes. Some of these were explored in chapter 6.

The question raised by our distinction between types of gatekeeper brings us back again to the issue raised but not discussed at the end of the previous section: does professionalism make a difference? This is what we must turn to now.

Professions

Public servants who are generally recognized as professionals play a key role in the delivery of many social policies. This is particularly true of health services and of education, with the extent of professionalization being lower in the personal social services and much lower in areas where the key concerns are the delivery of material benefits such as housing and social security. Where professions are recognized as involved, they are often able to secure much more than simply a degree of autonomy in the determination of service delivery. They are generally involved in management structures, it being accepted that professionals should be managed by fellow-professionals, and this involvement implies therefore elements of participation in parts of the policy process well before the implementation stage. This has been a particular characteristic of health services where doctors have been sufficiently powerful to secure some involvement in the determination of the basic character of publicly supplied services (see Ham, 1982; Alford, 1972).

What then are professions, and why do they secure such influence in the policy process? Various attempts have been made to identify the characteristics of professions, and to explain their power in terms of those characteristics. This has been described as the 'trait' approach (see Greenwood, 1957). It implies that professions are special kinds of occupations with distinctive characteristics, and is often taken a stage further to be linked with a functionalist explanation of the role of the professions in society. Professions are seen as embodying moral characteristics of service necessary for the common good of society. Their power is justified in terms of their contributions to service, which need to be protected against baser forces in society (see the discussion in Johnson, 1972, pp. 12-14).

However perhaps the most important element in the 'trait' definition of professions is expertise. Most discussions of professional power acknowledge that expertise – particularly expertise in matters concerning illness, life and death, as is the case with medicine – makes it more difficult to resist claims of autonomy and a right to participate in decision making.

But does the possession of necessary expertise in itself explain the power of the professions in social policy? While this element in professional power should not be dismissed we agree with some of the more recent radical critiques of professional power that it does not offer a sufficient explanation on its own. The claims to an inaccessible expertise by many of the groups described as professions are distinctly thin. This is particularly the case as far as teachers and social workers are concerned. Some theorists deal with this problem by speaking of them as 'semi-professions' (Etzioni, 1969), and arguing that the limited nature of their expertise is reflected in their comparatively weak power positions. Recently even the claims to expertise by doctors have come under attack (Illich, 1975; Kennedy, 1983). Clearly there are many aspects of medical practice which are either based upon comparatively weak scientific foundations or are fairly comprehensible to non-medical people. Doctors have been attacked for the mystification of simple phenomena, and for the unnecessary medicalization or at least over-medicalization of issues (childbirth and the care of the mentally handicapped, for example). What, therefore, has been brought under scrutiny is the significance of the legal and organizational framework which reserves particular issues and particular forms of health care practice to a specific group of people who have undergone an elaborate training and socialization process controlled by representatives of the profession.

Hence, recent approaches to the explanation of the phenomenon of professional power have emphasized not so much expertise as the social and political processes which have granted, and still protect, the monopoly over the exercise and development of that expertise. Wilding puts the issue like this: 'Professions gain power and influence as experts who are technically and politically useful to governments. Their use, and the granting of power to them, is legitimated by the technocratic rationality which is part of the ideology of advanced industrial society' (Wilding, 1982, p. 17). That approach puts the explanation of professional power very much in terms of the relationship to the state. Other theorists have emphasized rather more the way in which professional power is supported by class power (Johnson, 1972; Parry and Parry, 1976) and by links with other professional and commercial interests (Dunleavy, 1981). In his work Dunleavy has drawn particular attention to the way in which professionals who are in both public and private practice (architects, lawyers, accountants, etc.) bring to public sector work links with private sector interests and commitments to private sector values. Taken together these analyses of professional power, however, offer an overall approach to its explanation which emphasize its relationship to other sources of power rather than the intrinsic qualities of the professions.

Not surprisingly perspectives of this kind on professional power give short shrift to those claims for professionalism which emphasize altruism and service ethics. They draw attention to the extent to which protection of the privileges of the profession also figure prominently in formal codes of conduct, and see concerns about malpractice as motivated by a desire to ensure that the professional monopoly remains unchallenged. If a profession wants to retain its power it must demonstrate that it is able to discipline its own deviants. Of course this kind of control may be in the public interest; the profession may be protecting the unsuspecting public from incompetent practitioners; but it is increasingly questioned (a) whether such control is particularly thorough, and (b) whether it should be a private form of control and not one shared with the lay public (Klein, 1973).

This brings us back to the issue raised earlier about the extent to which professionalism provides a framework for control over the exercise of discretion. We see now that the first problem about this is that the argument is to some extent circular. Professionalism is used as an argument for more discretion, but is also offered as an approach to its control. From the perspective of a concern about professional power, discretion is part of the problem. Second, it is far from certain that professional monopolies are not greater evils than the forms of discretion and 'street-level' behaviour they profess to bring under control. It is this view which leads Lipsky (1980, ch. 13) to argue that enhanced professionalism is only a satisfactory solution to what he sees as the problems of street-level bureaucracy if professions can be rendered more publicly accountable. Wilding's conclusion (1982) is similar: the need for more effective partnerships between professions and society. Yet, since he equally sees that professional power is rooted in wider inequalities of power, he ends his analysis by endorsing Bernard Shaw's conclusion that 'the social solution of the medical problem depends on that large, slowly advancing pettishly resisted integration of society, generally called Socialism' (Shaw, 1947, p. 67). To this Wilding adds his own gloss: 'The argument is a simple one – only through political change of this kind with new values and ideologies and with a new approach to economic, social and political relationships will the professions emerge clearly as public servants working with their clients for mutually agreed ends and purposes' (Wilding, 1982, p. 148).

Conclusions

This chapter started with a discussion of social service delivery issues which looked at solutions to weaknesses and problems within the system in top-down control terms. It proceeded to look at this as particularly an issue about discretion, accordingly more complex than simple control strategies allow. It then shifted to analyses which emphasize the complexities of the roles of front-line staff. By ending with an examination of professionalism it was able to scrutinize critically that view of organizational control which suggests that if bureaucratic modes of dominance have limitations then the professional model may offer a better way to organize policy delivery. We found ourselves in agreement with Lipsky and with Wilding in finding the attraction of this solution limited by unease about the power of the professions and about the sources of that power.

If we find both bureaucracy and professionalism as offering weak modes of control over service delivery in social policy, we must relate these observations to the issues about market modes of control. At one stage in the chapter we explicitly referred to this in seeing the issue of 'gatekeepers' as one which is of much less importance when market techniques are used to ration benefits and services. Similarly we find some writers, for example Eliot Friedson (1970), arguing that market solutions can be adopted to deal with professional power, offering members of the public as consumers choice between competing professionals.

The problems about market solutions for issues of this kind have already been explored in chapters 4 and 6. Our purpose in this chapter has been to show that it is inevitable that either bureaucratic or professional modes of service delivery partly disperse power to those responsible for the provision of the service. We also showed that some of the decision-making freedom possessed by front-line staff arises because decisions are not taken elsewhere in the system. It is not self-evident that either of these ways in which power is distributed is necessarily undesirable. They seem to clash with an ideal of democratic decision making in which power is concentrated in the hands of elected policy-making bodies and service delivery is merely administration, the translation of policy goals into action. However if, as this chapter and the last chapter have shown, reality does not often correspond with this ideal, we still need to ask whether (a) the extent to which systems depart from that ideal is serious, and (b) the presence of participation in the formulation of services by those responsible for their delivery is necessarily undesirable (they would often, for example, claim to know much more about real needs on the ground than the politicians and managers who nominally control the services). Finally there may be ways in which the elements of democracy missing from the 'top-down' model can be injected through forms of participation close to the delivery level. This is a theme to which we will return in chapter 11.

10

The Pursuit of Efficiency

Introduction

This book is being prepared at a time when the pursuit of efficiency in the provision of social services, particularly in the public sector, is high on the agendas of government in Britain and elsewhere. The following quotation from a recently reformed organization with an explicit mission to 'Improve Economy, Efficiency and Effectiveness in Local Government' is symptomatic of the concerns and processes involved.

> The management challenge facing Local Government has not become any easier in the past year. Indeed, in many respects, the situation has become more difficult. The need for many of the services provided by local authorities is increasing inexorably, fuelled by demographic, economic and social trends which they can do little to influence. Conversely, other trends are reducing the numbers of children coming into care, the number of pupils in secondary education and the number of planning applications. At the same time, resources to meet new needs are limited. Central support is being reduced in real terms; and local ratepayers not unnaturally oppose steep increases in their rates, and are encouraged to do so by the government as well as the media. Councils thus face conflicting demands for more and better services, but all at lower or no greater cost to ratepayers. Unless these situations are managed effectively, the outlook is bleak: frustrated councils, disillusioned residents and demoralised employees. (Audit Commission, 1984, p. (i), para 3)

The picture painted is one of increasing demands confronting diminishing resources, the central element in the scenario of 'fiscal crisis' examined in chapter 5. Yet at the same time the quotation hints at opportunities created by change, as some traditional demands decline, if only the organizations involved – in this instance local government – show the capacity to adapt and redeploy resources. This quotation also hints at important psychological and political dimensions to the problem, relating to morale, motivation and sense of purpose. In other words, analysis of the problem should pay attention to organizational and political process as well as to techniques of measurement, planning, evaluation and monitoring.

It would be wrong to pretend that a concern with efficiency is wholly new in social policy. It has always been present in the minds of administrators concerned with achieving the most they can from available resources; and efficiency has always been the central goal or ethic of management training and research, as well as the discipline of economics. Nevertheless, it seems reasonable to argue that political and intellectual climates do change over time in such a way that in certain periods, such as the time of writing, efficiency goals come more to the forefront and achieve higher legitimacy relative to other enduring goals such as equity, freedom and participation.

The efficiency goal has certain attractions which give it special political force. In particular it suggests or assumes that an organization or a society can achieve net gains in its achievement of desired objectives – welfare, to use a common term – even after allowing for the cost of resources employed, and resources are in general always scarce. If this is seen to be so, there is clearly a greater chance of wide agreement, even consensus, about the changes involved than is the case with policies on distribution, which clearly involve losers as well as gainers. In other words, efficiency ought to be a 'positive-sum game' rather than a 'zero-sum game'. In practice, specific efficiency policies do not always operate like this. They may create losers, overtly or covertly. For example, policies to save public expenditure in an environment of high unemployment may make certain former public employees a good deal worse off.

This is one reason why efficiency is more contentious in the social policy arena than elsewhere, since social policy practitioners and commentators are quite sensitive to distributional issues. The culture of the social services is probably more hostile to efficiency notions and initiatives for other reasons as well. They often carry with them connotations of market, commercial and managerial values which appear to conflict with an ethos of service, altruism and caring, as discussed in chapter 1. However, some economists and others have argued that such reactions betray a confusion and perhaps some blindness to the influence of service producers' own private interests, and that what is needed is clearer thinking, in particular about the distinction between ends and means (Culyer, 1980; Williams and Anderson, 1975; Knapp, 1984).

The remainder of this chapter is divided into three sections. The first explores the definition of some key concepts and distinctions relevant to 'economy, efficiency and effectiveness'. The second deals with the role of measurement in the identification and classification of opportunities for improving efficiency. The third examines a range of essentially process explanations for the emergence or persistence of shortfalls in efficiency. The chapter concludes with some observations on the political economy of efficiency in the social services.

A framework of concepts and definitions

Different writers use a number of similar-sounding terms like 'efficiency' and 'effectiveness' in ways which, although similar and overlapping, are not always identical. It is necessary to introduce a number of further terms at this point, terms like 'input' and 'output', in order to clarify definitions, and these definitions form a mutually interdependent and, hopefully, consistent set. Thus, it may be helpful to provide an overall framework to show how these concepts fit together, and it is probably easiest to do this diagrammatically. Figure 10.1 represents such a framework, which we term 'a model of the production of welfare'. This formulation is similar although not identical to one employed by Knapp (1984). It also bears a superficial resemblance to Easton and Jenkins's 'systems' model of the policy process (chapter 8) but the reader should be aware that the content and context here are somewhat different – the production of social services and their impact on welfare, rather than the process by which policies are generated, which may be thought of as a somewhat higher-order system. The essence of the model in figure 10.1 is that a production process transforms inputs into outputs, which in conjunction with other factors impact on the welfare of individuals and society. Policy and the social, economic and physical environment each impinge on several different stages of the model. Factors like technology and the quality of management also impinge on the production stage. Broken lines indicate influences which may operate in some cases, while solid lines represent relationships which normally apply.

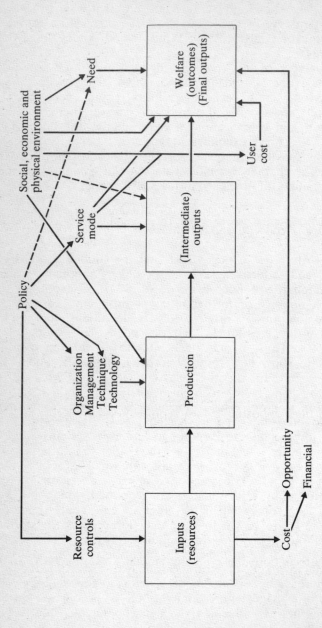

Figure 10.1 A model of the production of welfare

Some definitions

(1) *Inputs* are the resources employed in the production of services, for example staff, buildings, land, equipment, fuel.

(2) *Outputs* are taken here as the definable, immediate services produced and delivered by the agencies under study; examples include a place in an old people's home, a publicly rented house, a home nursing visit, a general practitioner consultation, a year's primary schooling for one child; some writers (e.g. Knapp, 1984) call these 'intermediate outputs'.

(3) *Production* is the process by which inputs are transformed into outputs.

(4) *Welfare* is the state of well-being of the individuals defined as the primary clients of the service, together with the well-being of other individuals or groups (e.g. carers, relatives, neighbours, communities) indirectly affected by the provision of the service and/or the well-being of the primary clients; well-being may be as subjectively assessed by the individuals concerned, or as assessed by relevant professionals, or as measured in terms of reduced shortfalls on defined scales of requirements, coping, etc. related to the objectives of the service. This definition implies a relationship with 'need'; welfare is the extent to which need is met. Other terms used for this concept include 'outcomes' or 'final outputs'.

(5) *Cost* is the measure of what must be given up in order to secure the resource inputs; commonly, these are measured by financial outlays; however, it is generally accepted that the concept of 'opportunity cost' is superior in principle; if what is given up is assumed to be some alternative social service then opportunity cost represents a notional parallel production process and the value of this is assessed in terms of the objective of that service, i.e. welfare; if it is what the money would buy in the economy at large, then financial outlay may be an appropriate value.

(6) *Service mode* refers to the different ways of providing services to meet the needs of a particular client group, for example, the choice between geriatric hospitals, public and private old persons' homes, and intensive domiciliary care in the case of very dependent elderly people. Clearly, service mode affects both the type and amount of outputs and the welfare of clients and others.

(7) *User costs* are resources, time, energy, etc. given up by clients and others affected (e.g. carers) in the process of using the service, e.g. the time and travel costs of hospital

visits, the anxiety associated with lack of information. User costs are often very different under different service modes, may well vary according to the environment (e.g. travel distances to hospitals depend on the density of settlement), and are often ignored in measures of the cost or efficiency of services.

(8) *Need* definition was discussed at length in chapter 4; in this context need should be defined in a manner consistent with the definition of welfare; needs are obviously a function of individual client characteristics and the broader environment.

(9) *Quasi-inputs* is a term sometimes used (as is 'non-resource inputs') to refer to the influence of the environment on welfare outcomes, e.g. the influence of home environment on educational attainment.

We are now in a position to define the main focus of attention in this chapter.

(10) *Efficiency* is the relationship between outputs and inputs, allowing for the influence of factors outside the control of the agencies in question (e.g. technology, environment); greater efficiency is achieved by increasing the output from given inputs or by reducing the inputs required to produce a given output.

(11) *Effectiveness* is the extent to which a service increases welfare, allowing for environmental conditions.

(12) *Cost-effectiveness* is the relationship between the cost of inputs and the increase in welfare achieved by a service, allowing for the influence of factors outside agencies' control; greater cost-effectiveness is achieved by reducing inputs for a given level of welfare increase or by increasing welfare for a given level of inputs.

(13) *Benefits* are a monetary valuation of the increase in welfare associated with a service; conventionally these rely on individual valuations or indirect estimates thereof.

(14) *Cost–benefit analysis* attempts to compare the net difference between benefits and costs as defined above (i.e. all in monetary terms), including indirect effects as well as effects on primary clients and taxpayers.

(15) *Economy* (as in the Audit Commission approach) may mean, narrowly, minimizing the cost of a given set of resources, for example by use of contracting, leasing, bulk purchase, etc.; it may also be interpreted more broadly by some commentators, as minimizing agency expenditure.

Economics and efficiency

Because efficiency is so central to economics it is worth commenting on the way the term is used in this discipline. For a somewhat fuller discussion still geared to a public and social policy context, see Heald (1983, pp. 85-9) or Culyer (1980, pp. 10-24). Economists are most interested in what they call 'allocative efficiency', which corresponds to cost-benefit analysis as defined above – in other words it is a broad concept. It subdivides into 'technical efficiency' – minimizing the resource cost of given outputs through an appropriate choice of production technique – which equates with our earlier definition of 'efficiency' as commonly used in public and social administration; and 'exchange efficiency' – maximizing the welfare benefit of a given resource budget by choosing the right mix of output relative to people's preferences – which corresponds to effectiveness with the proviso that it is subjective individual preferences which are normally counted. The overall allocative efficiency criterion is generally known as the Pareto principle, that an efficient allocation is one where no-one can be made better off without someone else being made worse off; after allowing for gainers compensating losers, this corresponds to the 'net gain for society' alluded to earlier. Heald and Culyer discuss the value judgements underlying this approach, as does Sugden (1981, ch. 1). While economists often assume that, in the production process, the best use will be made of available resources for any chosen technique, some (especially Leibenstein, 1976) have identified an additional dimension of 'X-inefficiency', also referred to as 'managerial inefficiency' or 'organizational slack'. In other words, agencies do not always make the most (in terms of output) of their available resources and chosen techniques. This problem is seen as particularly prevalent in large and non-competitive organizations, including many in the public sector.

The conventional economic approach is limited in its treatment of effectiveness – the right-hand end of figure 10.1 – by its emphasis on individual preferences, in the social policy context. There is no consensus that this value judgement is the right or only sensible approach to social services which are often (a) highly redistributive; (b) directed to people with limited ability to exercise choice (children, the mentally disordered, some elderly people); (c) involving legitimate professional judgements; and (d) involving collective social judgements about priorities. It is much more helpful in analysing issues of productive efficiency. The economic theory of production highlights four distinctive issues:

(1) that there is usually a *choice of techniques* of production, that
different techniques involve different combinations of inputs,
and that the efficient choice will vary if the relative costs or
availability of different inputs change;

(2) that there may be *(dis)economies* of scale in producing some
services, due for example to indivisible or fixed inputs, the
nature of technology, or the process of distributing a service
geographically;

(3) that there may be *managerial inefficiency* if incentives and
accountability mechanisms are inadequate;

(4) that *technology* changes the general level of efficiency over
time, often in an uneven way as between different time
periods and different products, and often in a way which
alters the appropriate choice of technique or scale of
production.

To illustrate some of these possibilities, figure 10.2 utilizes the
standard microeconomic textbook analysis of the relationship
between cost of production and level of output for a public
service before and after a significant technological change. Unit
costs (measured on the vertical axis) fall as output increases up to
a certain level (X1 in the first case, X5 in the second), beyond
which costs increase somewhat. In other words, there are
economies of scale up to a certain level, but these are not
unlimited. Average costs per unit (AC) are distinguished from
marginal costs (MC), the increase in total costs associated with
one unit of output. MV is the 'marginal value' or 'demand' curve
(see chapter 4, and Culyer, 1980, ch. 2 for a fuller discussion). In
a fully competitive market situation, firms would produce X1 at
minimum cost C1, but we are not considering this situation here;
one agency dominates the particular market (say in a particular
locality), enjoying a local monopoly either as a matter of policy
or because of its natural economies of scale advantage. How
much should it produce, and at what cost? The social optimum is
X3 at a cost just above C1 (marginal cost = marginal value is the
standard allocative efficiency condition). But there is a danger
that, like any monopolist, the service agency may prefer to
supply less output at a higher apparent cost; thus X2 may be
supplied at a supposed cost of C4 within the same budget as X3
at C1. But C4 is not the true cost here; the agency is absorbing
surplus revenue of C4-C2 in the form of 'organizational slack'
·(Jackson, 1982, ch. 5 discusses this possibility).

The effect of the technological change (figure 10.2(b)) is to
lower the general cost curve and increase the extent of scale
economies (not all technologies necessarily have this effect). The

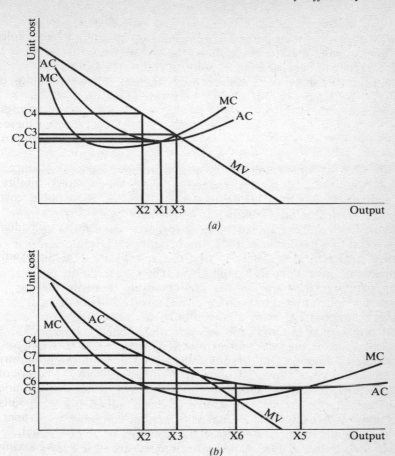

Figure 10.2 Cost of production and level of output: (a) period 1 – before technological change; (b) period 2 – after technological change

optimum output now is X6 at a cost of C6. This could be accommodated with a slightly higher budget than previously – technology does not necessarily lower expenditure.

This second case illustrates the point that it is not necessarily appropriate to seek the lowest cost level of output; in this case, X5 is too high a level of output for the demand it would meet or benefits it would create. However, the same danger remains here as in the previous case; namely of the monopolistic agency supplying less than optimal output, such as X2 at C4. Technological change may be absorbed in organizational slack and may widen discrepancies between actual and potential effectiveness, all within a constant budget and unchanging apparent unit costs. The particular feature which allows this to happen is the ability of the agency to conceal from its political client (the local authority, say) the true shape of its efficient cost function, a key proposition in the 'economics of bureaucracy' literature (Jackson, 1982, ch. 5; Niskanen, 1971).

Opportunity cost

The idea of opportunity cost is a distinctive element in the contribution of economics. Indeed, some 'policy analysis' from other disciplines have highlighted it as the most, even the only, useful contribution (Jenkins, 1978; Wildavsky, 1979). Opportunity cost is the value of benefits forgone when resources are devoted to a particular activity, the benefits of those resources in their next-best uses. There is a particular useful discussion with practical illustrations in Knapp (1984, ch. 4). He points out that opportunity costs are, in the final analysis, benefits forgone, which implies that the common criticism of cost-benefit analysis that (paraphrasing many commentators and students) 'costs are uncontroversial but you can't measure most benefits' is somewhat misplaced; he suggests that in practice costs are often wrongly calculated anyway. Opportunity costs are normally different from accounting costs (financial outlays) – sometimes greater, sometimes less, sometimes zero.

Capital costs are a major source of error, although it must be conceded that the right treatment of capital continues to divide the accountancy profession (see the columns of *Public Finance and Accountancy*, 1983-4). Another crucial area for questioning is the cost of employees; in any situation where there is a probability that the people involved would otherwise be unemployed, it is arguable that the opportunity cost is less than the financial outlays, possibly even zero. We say 'arguable', since this issue does depend on the view taken of the wider nature and causes of unemployment, a focus of great controversy in mainstream economics (Cuthbertson, 1979; Heald, 1983, ch. 3). A third area of great significance and uncertainty concerns the opportunity cost of voluntary and family resources in social care.

Measuring efficiency

A clear implication of the framework set out in the previous section is that we cannot measure efficiency without measuring output. If we are concerned with the efficiency of production we must relate costed inputs to units of output. If we are concerned with effectiveness we also require measures of welfare and an understanding of the contribution which service outputs make to this alongside other factors. There was a considerable upsurge of interest in output measurement in the public sector in the early 1970s, but this was accompanied by a rapid recognition of the difficulties of finding adequate and comprehensive measures (Shonfield and Shaw, 1972; CIPFA, 1974). Perhaps this experience illustrates the danger of premature disillusionment arising from both an attempt to be comprehensive and a failure to distinguish outputs as defined here from welfare outcomes. It is more realistic to adopt a selective approach, concentrating either on production or on the achievement of welfare goals and focusing on important services which are capable of yielding reasonable measures. Our own preferred definition of 'output' referred to *definable* service units, and we listed a number of examples.

There are two general difficulties with output measurement. The first is that social service outputs typically involve a package of different elements, with the composition of the package varying in different cases. In other words, output is often multi-dimensional. For example, publicly rented houses vary in terms of their type, space, amenities, location and state of repair. To compound the problem, some elements may be essentially qualitative and therefore difficult to measure or standardize. For example, the quality of care provided in old people's homes can vary considerably. Some responses to this problem can lead directly to the second general difficulty, that the output measures used might turn out to be essentially input measures. A well-known example is the use of pupil:teacher ratios as a measure of the quality of schooling. If inputs are used to measure output, little useful information about efficiency can be derived from ratios of outputs to inputs. That there are pitfalls and difficulties in the measurement of output is not a reason for abandoning the attempt.

Any attempt to measure the efficiency of a service involves comparisons. Calculating ratios of output to input will not allow judgements to be made of performance without some yardstick against which such ratios can be compared. In general, four distinct kinds of comparison can be identified:

(1) comparisons with the past performance of the same agency;
(2) comparisons with the performance of other similar agencies;
(3) comparisons with the performance of other different agencies;

(4) comparisons with some theoretical model which generates 'ideal' performance standards.

We discuss each of these in turn.

Comparisons over time are both commonplace and superficially attractive. The managers of service agencies are likely to regard it as part of their normal function to monitor inputs and outputs, and the data required are readily to hand, within their control, and familiar enough for problems of interpretation to be appreciated. At the same time, the obvious dangers arising in comparisons with other agencies, dangers essentially of not comparing like with like, seem to be avoided.

However, this approach is not without its own dangers and limitations. Firstly, much depends on the nature of the starting point: how adequate was the level of efficiency in the past? Without external comparisons there is no real check on this. If the same managers or staff were involved it may be uncomfortable to own up to past deficiencies, and an apparent gain in efficiency may be interpreted by others as evidence confirming suspicions that the agency is poorly managed or could get by with less resources. Thus to be useful this approach requires an open and self-critical attitude by managers and staff and an organizational climate in which such openness is not 'punished'.

Secondly, as our discussion of the economic perspective on efficiency showed, technology is important in comparisons over time. Two different kinds of situation create dangers here. On the one hand, technology may be developing in a way which allows significant gains in efficiency to be realized (as in figure 10.2). For example, new information technology based on microcomputers and telecommunications may offer considerable scope for change in services which involve a large element of information handling – the payment of welfare benefits, the provision of welfare rights advice, the allocation of public housing, employment placement services. In this situation one would expect some efficiency gains to be realized, even if management was only half aware of the possibilities. On the other hand, many social services are essentially personal services involving the direct interaction between workers and clients. Such services offer limited scope for productivity gains of the kind which are commonplace in industry. The normal relationship between outputs and inputs here is effectively constant over time. With the advance in productivity elsewhere in the economy, wages and salaries rise over time and the real cost of these labour-intensive services rises as a consequence (Baumol and Oates, 1979, pp. 147-56). If the emphasis in efficiency assessment is placed on measures of cost-effectiveness, 'cost' or 'economy' as defined above, the performance of the service will appear to deteriorate over time. If this in turn puts pressure on management to hold costs constant, the likely result is a dilution of the quality of the service provided. The significance of this 'problem of affluence' for the social services and public expenditure as a whole has already been mentioned in the chapter on fiscal crisis.

These two issues, concerning the starting point for comparisons and the role of technological change, are the principal general issues which affect comparisons over time. In particular cases, other issues may also arise which involve changes in relevant factors outside the immediate control of the service agency. The demand for the service may decline, for example, at a rate faster than the existing structure of provision can adapt to. In many western countries, falling birthrates are reducing numbers of schoolchildren, and it is difficult to reduce inputs of teachers and schools at a commensurate rate without upsetting the quality of service (e.g. curriculum content) or the users' costs (e.g. travel) (Bailey, 1982 and 1984).

Given these difficulties, and particularly the first one, it is natural to seek external comparisons and especially tempting to compare apparently *similar agencies*. Thus the Audit Commission places considerable reliance on comparisons between local authorities in England and Wales in relation to their costs and performance in delivering specific services. It can be argued that local authorities are similar as organizations (Stewart, 1983) and provide particular services within a common national framework of legislation, policy guidance and professionalism. Similarly, a particular service authority may compare the performance of individual service units (schools, homes, social work teams), or comparisons may be made between such units located within different authorities. Such comparisons are not necessarily popular or uncontroversial – local government has shown some resistance to what may be presented as 'league tables' – but they are almost inescapable in any serious attempt at measuring performance.

The difficulties and dangers in this approach may be summed up as follows:

(1) Are you really comparing like with like?
(2) Once some degree of unalikeness has been conceded, can you separately quantify the influence of differences outside and within the control of agencies?
(3) Given the significance of quality dimensions of output in the

social services, can you be confident about your answers to (1) and (2) above?

Let us pursue these questions in the case of between-local authority comparisons. How might local authorities differ? From figure 10.1 we can see that broadly they may differ in their policies, assuming some degree of local discretion, and in their social, economic and physical environments.

Policy differences are within local authorities' control, and they impinge on the production of welfare in a number of different ways as figure 10.1 indicates. Some of these ways have efficiency implications, but others relate more to objectives, priorities and effectiveness. Authorities may differ in how they organize and manage their services, and while these differences may be labelled as 'policy' differences ('our authority has a policy of decentralized management') it seems fair to expose such differences to questioning in terms of efficiency. If the organizational difference is intended to influence welfare outcomes through some change in service objectives or priorities, the case is more complex; instead of a straight cost-effectiveness comparison, one may be trading welfare gains against higher costs or vice-versa. This situation typically arises where 'service mode' differs, perhaps changing quite substantially the role performed by particular agencies. If the policy difference extends to a different definition of objectives and priorities – in short, a different definition of needs – then of course it becomes difficult to even quantify a trade-off in the way suggested above. Comparative measures of effectiveness require a common welfare yardstick. The link from 'policy' to 'needs' in figure 10.1 is shown as a broken line to indicate that this is not always an issue; for some services, national policy or professional consensus may provide a given definition of need. Policy may be expressed primarily in terms of resource constraints, which again represents an index of priority, albeit a crude and implicit one. Particular forms of resource constraint (e.g. manpower reductions or freezes) might be exposed to efficiency questioning from the point of view of inconsistency with the requirements of producing desired outputs efficiently. Finally, policy may impinge positively or negatively on the crucial qualitative aspects of service delivery. A 'decentralization' policy may be motived by a desire to improve the quality of the relationship between staff and clients. A resource control policy may force the quality of service down as staff attempt to cover the same or greater needs/demands more thinly.

The 'environmental' influences on the production of welfare

are more extensive still than policy influences. Production of services is affected by factors like how dispersed a population is: in sparsely populated areas, schools and class sizes are smaller and more resources are devoted to transport. For non-compulsory services, depending on the rationing technique used, there may be variations in output related to variations in effective demand, which in turn reflect environmental conditions. The number of classes and students involved in adult education is an example, demand relating to such factors as density and socioeconomic status. Environmental influences on needs for services are generally well recognized, even to the extent of being institutionalized in systems of grant distribution (Bramley et al., 1983; Bennett, 1982; Foster et al., 1980), although this body of knowledge may still be ignored or discounted in comparative work concerned with efficiency (contrast for example the Audit Inspectorate's (1983) study of the elderly with Bebbington and Davies (1980)). To the extent that outcomes have been studied in this comparative mode (Challis, 1981; Lord, 1983) there has been no difficulty identifying environmental influences; rather, it is the influence of specific services on outcomes which is difficult to quantify or even, in some cases, to identify. The issue of user costs is relatively neglected, although it has received some attention in the context of health care alternatives. In general, environmental influences are widely recognized in principle but imperfectly in practice; the problem is to develop adequate, quantitative models of the influence of environmental factors on the production process or on states of welfare.

To summarize this discussion, efficiency comparisons between 'similar' agencies like local authorities must recognize potential variations stemming from policy differences, and environmental differences. Policy differences are within local agency control and may be open to questioning from an efficiency perspective, but where they involve differences in objectives, priorities or service quality standards it may be difficult to separate issues of managerial efficiency, and even issues of effectiveness, from legitimate differences in policy intentions. Environmental influences are complex and it may be difficult to quantify the extent to which differences in costs between local agencies are due to environmental factors. One of the difficulties here is that environment may influence policy, via the local political process – for example, local authorities in poorer urban areas may, on average, pursue more 'socialist' policies – and indeed a considerable literature has developed around this kind of influence (Sharpe and Newton, 1984; Dye, 1976; Jackman and Sellars, 1978). Uncertainties about the precise influence of environmental factors may be amplified in the apparent measures of relative efficiency which emerge from the comparison. This is because efficiency, particularly of the general managerial (X-efficiency) kind, tends to emerge as a residual element of variation after the analysis has allowed for policy and environment. Residuals accumulate all the errors, biases and omissions of the preceding analysis, including simple errors or inconsistencies of measurement. The latter are a continuing feature of published local authority expenditure information: for example, there is not full consistency in the way particular items are coded to different expenditure headings.

A popular line of approach to inter-authority comparisons is to select a limited number of comparator authorities judged to be 'very similar' to a particular authority: this approach is naturally attractive in studies undertaken by individual authorities, or by auditors or consultants involved with an individual authority. In this context, considerable interest has been shown in cluster analyses of local authorities in Britain using large numbers of census indicators (Webber and Craig, 1976; Imber, 1977; Craig, 1984); such studies either group authorities in 'families' or identify 'nearest neighbours'. The advantage of this approach is that, by concentrating on a limited number of comparators, more effort can be devoted to collecting detailed information from those authorities; in addition, it may be assumed that most environmental influences are being held constant, and attention can focus on differences in management or perhaps differences in policy. The emphasis shifts from statistical modelling towards a case study approach, within which a more detailed account of performance differences may be offered. The disadvantage of relying on clusters in this way is that the analyst may bypass explicit consideration of relevant dimensions of similarity or difference. The clustering models referred to use large numbers of indicators, but many of these may not be relevant to the service in question. At the same time, the measures of similarity are averaged, and apparent overall similarity may conceal significant differences in crucially relevant indicators. Given that no two authorities are identical, it is difficult to dismiss environmental influences without a view about their quantitative effect (e.g. on costs), which this approach does not yield.

Comparing the performance of *different types of agency* in producing a certain general kind of service, notably comparisons between statutory, voluntary and private sector agencies, is clearly a more ambitious undertaking. Underlying similarities of legislation, organization, aims and ethos are being removed from the analysis, so that 'like with like' comparisons seem ever more remote. This is doubtless why relatively few such comparisons have been carried out. But with the current interest in privatization and the voluntary sector as alternatives to direct public services (see chapter 6), it seems inevitable that more attempts will be made at performance comparison.

Of the areas where greater differences may arise, the underlying policy objectives of the organization would seem to be a key area. While it may be reasonable to argue that a concern with some concept of welfare is central to public agencies, it is less obvious that this is the case in private organizations which must make some level of profit to remain in business. In other words, private organizations may well restrict their concerns to what we have termed outputs. Voluntary organizations may be concerned with more particular notions of need than public agencies. In order to manage an economically viable service, private or voluntary agencies may be more selective in the clients they deal with. The measurement of cost on a comparable basis is also much more problematic here. The different sectors use different accounting conventions and are characterized by different sources of 'bias' in cost measures: for example, British local authorities understate the opportunity cost of capital assets relative to private sector practice; private sector accounts are more affected by taxation, overstating some resource costs; voluntary sector accounts arguably understate the opportunity costs of volunteers.

One public service for which extensive inter-sectoral comparisons have been made is refuse collection. This is no coincidence, the reason being the same as that for this service being a prime candidate for privatization: the output of the service is relatively standardized and relatively easy to monitor. Issues about service quality, need, welfare and so forth are not very significant. Savas (1980) provides a useful summary of a number of studies of this service, which have typically compared municipal direct provision with contracting and private market solutions (see chapter 6).

In the social welfare services field a particularly interesting recent study is that of day care for the elderly, by Knapp and Missiakoulis (1982). This proposes and demonstrates a methodology involving the statistical estimation of a 'cost function' using data from individual establishments drawn from three sectors (two public, one voluntary). The cost function relates unit costs to a variety of service mode and organizational characteristics (size of centre, occupancy, design, activities and treatments provided, etc.) and also factors related to need (e.g. client characteristics). The main conclusion emerging is that simple average unit costs can be quite misleading, since sectors vary systematically in the clients they handle and the detailed services they provide. Particularly interesting are the findings on scale economies, one of the issues illustrated by figure 10.2. While public sector day centres apparently show economies of scale, the opposite applies to voluntary centres, perhaps reflecting different approaches to management and the availability of voluntary care resources.

Our fourth general approach to efficiency measurement through comparisons, using *'theoretical' models*, is both important and distinctive, and involves doing more than just comparing average values of actual data on costs, inputs and outputs from real-world organizations. In this approach the production process is broken down into some of its component parts, and measures are constructed using some prior reasoning and professional judgement as well as some more specific empirical data. The quote marks around 'theoretical' imply this qualification, that some prior reasoning is employed and that empirical data are not necessarily ignored; we do not wish to imply that 'theoretical' should be taken as a term of abuse! An alternative term would be 'synthetic'. The main attractions of this approach are twofold. Firstly, it helps to get away from the relativistic emphasis on the comparisons previously discussed and addresses directly the question of absolute efficiency standards and the uncertainty over whether the comparators used themselves embody some level of inefficiency. Secondly, it helps to identify more specific sources of inefficiency in particular cases, for example the scale of operation, managerial overheads, the use of capital assets, staffing levels and structures, and so forth. The approach is best illustrated through two examples.

Our first example concerns the use of cost-benefit analysis to examine the effectiveness of subsidies to public transport operations, particularly bus services (Glaister, 1984; Evans, 1985). Underlying such cost-benefit analyses are models of public transport operation which involve such variables as route network characteristics, population distribution and characteristics such as car ownership, service frequencies and fare levels. These models typically involve both supply-side relationships (i.e. cost functions) and demand-side relationships (i.e. functions predicting levels of patronage). These relationships may be quantified on the basis of past research (e.g. on the response of patronage to frequencies and fares), prior reasoning (e.g. on the relationship between population distribution and the time passengers spend walking to and waiting at bus stops), and statistical models (e.g. explaining variations in cost per bus-mile).

Such models may be used to derive the 'optimal' combination of service frequencies and fares for given levels of subsidy and service objectives (e.g. maximize patronage, maximize net economic benefit, etc.).

Our second example concerns the choice of 'service mode' for the dependent elderly and the search for the optimal 'balance of care' in the light of levels and types of need, available resources, costs of inputs, and existing availability of relatively expensive and fixed modes like geriatric hospital places (Department of Health and Social Security, 1981). Elderly people may be classified into categories according to both the severity of their need or dependency and particular dimensions of need (e.g. physical infirmity, mental disorder, social isolation, housing problems). While detailed surveys are needed to assign individuals to particular categories, predicted numbers in each category can be made for particular areas given some census-type information about the population on the basis of past research. On the basis of professional judgements, alternative packages of care can be identified for each category, giving ideal or adequate standards of life for the individuals concerned. For example, alternative packages might include a place in residential care or a combination of home help time, home nursing visits and meals on wheels. Combining such packages for different categories of need can allow alternative deployments of given total resources to be explored and the most cost-effective combination identified. An important element in this is the actual allocation of services to clients, and the methodology incorporates surveys of the dependency characteristics of existing service recipients.

To sum up, synthetic models of this kind are particularly useful in analysing complex situations where there are significant choices about the mode of service provision. They are not particularly concerned with the quality of management within particular modes. Their limitations chiefly revolve around the feasibility and cost of transition from the present situation to the preferred optimum. They also depend on reliable or robust forecasts of future levels of need or demand.

Explanations of inefficiency

The preceding sections have concerned themselves with the identification of inefficiencies or, to put it more positively, opportunities for improvement in performance. If we seek a better understanding of these problems and wish to recommend ways of improving performance, our next step is to try to explain how and why inefficiencies arise or persist. Such explanations are best seen as falling into two parts. The first follows closely from identification and measurement and concerns the 'how' more than the 'why'. We term this 'intermediate explanations', by which we mean attempts to account for poor performance in terms of detailed aspects of the production of services. The second goes more widely, and seeks to tackle the 'why' question in terms of political and organizational processes. Such explanations, we suggest, fall under two headings: (1) economic and organizational, and (2) political influences.

Intermediate explanations

It is generally possible, on the basis of detailed comparisons of the kind already discussed, to account for inefficiencies in terms of aspects of the production process. This step is essential for management of the service in question and is a useful contribution to explaining the emergence if not the persistence of the problem. We do no more here than list the kinds of factors which may be involved.

(1) inappropriate scale of service units;
(2) inappropriate choice of technique, i.e. combination of different kinds of input (e.g. buildings, different gradings of staff);
(3) operating below capacity;
(4) paying more per unit for inputs than is necessary;
(5) failure to employ new technology;
(6) inappropriate balance between alternative service modes;
(7) failure to monitor and control particular inputs (e.g. fuel, overtime);
(8) inappropriate geographical distribution of service (e.g. increasing travel costs);
(9) inappropriate rationing and allocation of services to clients.

Economic and organizational explanations

The discussion earlier in this chapter indicated some ways in which economic analysis may begin to explain inefficiencies in social services. Economies and diseconomies of scale, tendencies to monopoly, and information/uncertainty problems are important elements. These may be allied to the insights of the 'public choice' school (Niskanen, 1971; Jackson, 1982; Borcherding, 1977) which predict tendencies to oversupply and organizational slack, albeit on the basis of assumptions about motivation which may be questionable. The 'organizational failures' framework of Williamson (1975) is also an interesting source of ideas about the key roles of information and of 'contracts' between consumers and suppliers or between managers and workers. An organizational perspective would go on to highlight issues about the structure of organizations, particularly spans of managerial control and patterns of accountability. It would also pay attention to the 'competence' of managers and staff in service agencies, including their knowledge, skills, experience and personal resources, and to the significance of 'organizational culture' (attitudes, beliefs, values, norms of behaviour) with particular reference to the relative importance of service ethics versus instrumental attitudes to jobs. We discussed organizational issues in some depth in the previous chapter and do not pursue these further here.

Political explanations

The foregoing discussion suggests that political process and the exercise of power must be essential elements in the ultimate explanation of inefficiencies in the social services. Yet although much has been written on the politics of social policy (for example, the literature reviewed in chapters 2 and 8), there is relatively little which bears directly on this question. Why is this? In part it reflects the concern of political analysts with broad, macro-issues such as the size and scope of the public sector. In part it reflects the assumptive world of politics, which sees the political process as a zero-sum conflict over distribution of valued resources, and this is reinforced by the special concern of social administration with the distribution of welfare. It also reflects the difficulties of developing adequate, comprehensive measures of service outputs or benefits, which leads to an almost exclusive emphasis on the volume of resource inputs to competing programmes. Given a relative dearth of material on the politics of efficiency, we can do no more here than suggest tentatively some lines of enquiry which may be relevant.

As a first hypothesis we might suggest that there is a general tendency for producer interests to dominate over consumer interests. This is widely accepted as a general description of political systems, whether within a pluralist framework where producer interest groups (e.g. professions, business organizations, public agencies) are better organized and resourced than the fragmented issue-based pressure groups which operate in the social policy field, or in a corporatist framework which stresses the dominance of large-scale businesses, unions and government itself. This tendency is reinforced in the social policy field by the low social status of many consumers, by the importance of professionalism, and by the licensing of monopoly supplier roles to statutory agencies and professions.

A second hypothesis would be that the dominant political debate over social policy polarizes attitudes and allegiances in a way which drives out considerations of efficiency and effectiveness. Broadly speaking, the left favours 'more' social policy and measures its achievement by the volume of public expenditure (inputs) deployed in this direction. It derives substantial electoral support from public sector employees and financial and organizational support from their unions, who have a direct interest in maximizing public employment. To question the efficiency of modes of provision is easily portrayed as to favour 'cuts'. The right is more inclined to espouse efficiency slogans but may not in practice be particularly scrupulous in distinguishing cuts in 'waste' from cuts in service outputs, and may adopt a simplistic attitude to what types of resources are worthwhile (e.g. administrative support in the health service).

Thirdly, the dominant style of decision making in government is incremental (Lindblom, 1979; Ham and Hill, 1984; Wildavsky, 1964). Attempts at instituting more comprehensively rational decision making processes – PPBS or programme budgeting, the British 'Central Policy Review Staff' (CPRS) and 'Programme Analysis and Review' (PAR), corporate planning in local government – have typically enjoyed a short and chequered history. Incrementalism is variously seen as inevitable, realistic, or 'politically rational'. However, it is an approach which takes the vast bulk of existing practice and expenditure as given, tinkering at the margin and eschewing systematic evaluation techniques such as cost-benefit or cost-effectiveness analysis.

Our fourth hypothesis is that the economic climate conditions political attitudes in a way which is unhelpful to the pursuit of efficiency. In a period of prosperity (such as the 1960s) there is a supply of additional resources for social services. Needs and demands can be accommodated by allocating additional funds, so there is less incentive to seek more efficient means of provision. Management and politicians concentrate on getting the resources spent. With low unemployment labour is scarce and this may lead to an improvement in pay and working conditions to retain or attract staff. In a recession, such as that experienced in the late 1970s and early 1980s, different forces come into play. From a management perspective efficiency seems to acquire a greater priority. However, workers and unions, aware of the high level of unemployment, probably become more defensive about existing jobs. How successful this defence is will vary with the bargaining power of the group involved, professional groups appearing to have more success than low-status manual workers, particularly women working part-time. Pay levels may suffer, causing a decline in morale. The net effect of this defensiveness is to tend to freeze the existing pattern of employment and provision.

As a final political hypothesis we would suggest that the intensifying conflict between central control and local autonomy in the social services may create further barriers to the pursuit of efficiency. The development and scope of this conflict has been adequately documented elsewhere (see for example, Bramley, 1984; Boddy and Fudge, 1984). That central governments may seek to control local governments in the name of efficiency (or, at least, 'economy') is somewhat paradoxical, in so far as decentralized, responsive, accountable units such as local government have traditionally been defended on grounds of efficiency. It runs counter to contemporary management wisdom, which stresses decentralization, deconcentration, 'small is beautiful', and such-like, as well as to traditional and popular abhorrence of centralized bureaucracies. At the local level the defence of local autonomy may create a resistance to measures designed to identify opportunities for improved performance. Our previous section suggested that inter-agency comparisons were a key method of measuring relative efficiency; but in a political climate where the autonomy of local government is under threat, such comparisons may be resisted or ignored on the grounds that they represent an unwarrantable interference in local autonomy. Extreme localists may adopt the position that no such comparisons between localities are meaningful.

From explanation to solutions

We have concentrated in this chapter primarily on defining concepts of efficiency and exploring ways in which opportunities of improving efficiency in social programmes may be identified. We have also more briefly considered explanations of inefficiency. Lack of space prevents us from exploring the next step in the argument, which concerns solutions to these problems. Clearly, the particular solutions available depend heavily on the specific characteristics of the service in question. However, there is also an agenda of more general types of measure which may be propounded in part or wholly as ways of improving efficiency. We do no more here than list a few of these:

(1) privatization, as discussed in chapter 6; particular contract-
    ing arrangements;

(2) competing public or semi-public agencies;
(3) separation of 'client representative' and 'producer' roles within public agencies;
(4) decentralization of service delivery (Donnison, 1984);
(5) sponsoring self-help/mutual aid/community care modes of service provision;
(6) tighter resource controls (cash limits, manpower ceilings) with encouragement to managers to innovate within these;
(7) budgetary incentives, typically allowing sub-units a proportion of identified savings to fund new developments;
(8) more flexible pay structures to reward good performance;
(9) renegotiation of work contracts to create greater flexibility;
(10) devolve and clarify managerial responsibility (so-called 'cost' or 'responsibility centres');
(11) setting and monitoring performance targets for individual units;
(12) enhance the role of external auditors, as with the Audit Commission;
(13) increase resources for training and staff development.

The political economy of efficiency

We began this chapter by making certain observations on the way 'efficiency' has risen up the political agenda and on the nature of efficiency as a political issue. It seems appropriate to conclude with some broader comments on the politics of efficiency – points which cut across the detailed issues of definition, measurement, explanation and solutions upon which we have concentrated.

To say that efficiency is 'high on the agenda' is a bit like saying it is in fashion. This is too sweeping, of course, as it is not just coincidence that efficiency issues are in the forefront. However, there is a sense in which policy issues behave like fashions, with many actors in the system finding it expedient to concentrate on those issues when other key actors are doing the same. The work of Dunleavy (1981) provides an interesting model of the role of professional fashion in directing public policy; and there is more than an air of fashion about some of the policy and institutional initiatives mentioned in the previous section: privatization, decentralization, and responsibility centres could be viewed in this light, for example. The real challenge is to get the underlying theory beyond the level of fashion. In other words, we need more completely argued reasons and harder evidence that particular initiatives do have tangible and beneficial results.

It was pointed out at the outset that efficiency has the potential to be a positive-sum game and thereby a basis for consensus. In practice it is very difficult to achieve this. Instead we often find a quite spurious aura of consensus surrounding recommendations for efficiency from governments, auditors or management consultants. The consensus is spurious because the specific recommendations in the specific context in which they are set more often than not do involve uncompensated losers as well as gainers, and may involve values which are not universally subscribed to. Efficiency is often falsely equated with economy, and issues of effectiveness are often ignored.

Attitudes to efficiency are inextricably bound up with attitudes to the state and management of the economy as a whole. There is no consensus that there is a fiscal crisis which necessitates reductions in public expenditure. Nor is there a consensus that efficiency savings which involve a loss of jobs are an unmitigated blessing, since there is no agreement about what determines the level of unemployment, whether government policy is responsible for unemployment, and how serious the impact of unemployment is on individuals or communities. In addition, some efficiency initiatives involve a direct challenge to the power of organized labour, such as it is, in the workplace. These relationships are very starkly illustrated by what has been the most important political issue in Britain in 1984, the miners' strike.

While unemployment is perhaps the factor which most colours efficiency as a political issue at the time of writing, one may hope that this may not always remain the case. In the longer term, the underlying issue which will be seen to be most important will be the relationship between producer and consumer interests. The innovations we should be seeking are those which best align the interests of producers and consumers of social services.

11

Participation and Accountability

Introduction

Earlier chapters have discussed the relationship between the policy process and those forms of state activity concerned with social welfare. This chapter will explore the ways in which citizens who are affected by or benefit from social policies may strive to influence those policies, not so much by primary political interventions, but by more specific interactions with the policy delivery system. It will therefore look at issues about participation in the policy delivery process and about the use and limits of judicial or quasi-judicial devices to secure attention to specific grievances.

The concerns of this chapter must, however, be seen in the wider political context discussed earlier. In chapter 2 we explored various ways in which the evolution of welfare policy may be explained. For the purposes of this discussion we may put those explanations in three categories: those seeing welfare policies as essentially social control policies advanced by dominant elites reluctant to share economic or political power, those seeing them as the product of concern by elites about inequalities and human suffering, and those seeing them as responses to democratic political demands.

Clearly if our explanations of social policy growth are drawn from the first of these explanatory frameworks we will tend to see devices to extend participation and deal with grievances as essentially palliative. They will be concessions, often of a symbolic kind, designed to damp down conflict whilst not conceding power.

Explanations of policy growth set in the second framework tend to involve a very consensual model of society. Those with power and responsibility will be seen as exercising them responsively, and devices to enhance participation will be seen as largely unnecessary. This is the way in which traditional authoritarian modes of control over policy are defended; it is argued that those delivering benefits and services should be trusted to operate in the best interests of their clients. Devices to extend participation or judicial control are seen as getting in the way of the smooth operation of policy.

Explanations in our third group seem therefore to offer approaches which can most easily find a place for the participative devices with which this chapter is concerned. Forms of participation, particularly when organized through pressure groups, are seen as a significant political force, and disputes within the courts may equally be seen as part of an open political process.

Yet explanations of the policy process rooted in the idea of pluralist competition direct our attention to an important normative argument about the role of the participative devices to be discussed in this chapter. Just as they may be seen as a source of disruption for the consensual decision-making process implied by the second approach discussed above, so equally they are often perceived as illegitimate interventions in a democratic policy making process, which it is argued should be the responsibility of parliaments. Activities which seek to change policy by means of grass roots participation or by invoking judicial interventions may be regarded as distorting influences in the total system.

We suggest, therefore, that the two phenomena with which this chapter will be concerned both (a) tend to be ignored in many presentations of the policy process and (b) are often regarded as illegitimate intrusions into that process. However the issues about, and the attitudes to, participation on the one hand and the intervention of judicial or quasi-judicial processes on the other are rather different. Hence the two will be discussed separately within this chapter.

Participation: an overview

We have already referred to the way in which claims for forms of participation offer a challenge to older models of the way a democratic political system should operate. Modern arguments for participation rest upon a view that the right to vote is not enough, a view that in a complex society in which complex policies are formulated and implemented other modes of citizen intervention are necessary. There is an analytical problem, therefore, about what is implied by participation. A claim to participate is a claim to be given more power. The response to such a claim might be anything from, at one extreme, some slight extension of the voting process (for example, the organization of occasional referenda) to, at the other extreme, the extension of mass involvement in decision making of the kind embodied in the traditional New England town meeting or Swiss *Gemeindever-sammlung* (for discussion of these see Mansbridge, 1981; Steinberg, 1976).

In most cases participative devices involve not so much the explicit extension of opportunities for democratic participation to the whole of a relevant community as the intervention of some local and/or service-specific representative device below the level of the primary representative system (parliament). These devices are then themselves controversial because of the extent to which the degree of real participation they offer is of necessity limited. There are two particular respects in which a grant of participation will attract criticism as a less than complete form of power delegation. First, the body which extends participation will retain certain overriding powers. It will determine that certain policies and principles must continue to be upheld. It is also likely to retain considerable control over finance. Second, the composition of the new participating body will be determined by some kind of selection or election process. If selection is involved that will naturally be controversial, but even if an election process is adopted all the old questions which arise about representative democracy (that representatives differ in social characteristics from the electorate, once in power they lose touch with the electorate etc.), will again be relevant.

We have spelt these last points out at some length because the problem about analysing participation is that one is dealing with a political ideal, and that any actual form of participation at sub-nation state level is clearly going to fall short of that ideal. An often-quoted article speaks of a 'ladder of participation' extending up from manipulation, therapy, informing, consultation and placation – all seen as token forms of participation – by way of partnership and delegated power to an ideal at the top of the ladder of citizen control (Arnstein, 1971). However, that seems to impose too stringent a test of the extent to which an extension of participation is genuine. It is rather better to see participation as Richardson has expressed it as 'a bargaining mechanism' (Richardson, 1979; 1983). She sees extensions of participation, therefore, as processes of bringing new participants into political bargaining systems. It is inevitable that the outcomes of such processes are to some extent unpredictable.

Richardson also recognizes that where new participants are entering into a bargaining process the outcome for them may be both gains and losses. She argues:

> Both those who expect it to lead to an increase in power of the new participants and those who expect the reverse are in some ways correct. It is the nature of the bargaining process that the ability of particular groups to achieve their aims (and therefore to be powerful in practice) not only varies between issues and over time but also is not determined from the outset. The new participants may gain by some bargains and lose by others; such gains or losses may be with respect to different issues or over time or between different participation schemes. (Richardson, 1979, p. 242)

This perspective challenges the one-dimensional ladder approach to participation in Arnstein's article. It also needs to be related to the arguments rehearsed in chapter 2 about the social control perspective on social policy. It was suggested in that discussion that policy 'concessions' may both provide benefits and extend control, and Richardson is making a similar point about extensions of participation.

Richardson's book on participation (1983) similarly deals with the other issue in our general discussion above: the issue of the choice of participants. She distinguishes 'direct' and 'indirect' participation, but goes on to recognize that a variety of practical questions 'of time and space' (p. 15) inevitably limit the extent of the former. On the whole the direct forms of participation tend to be *ad hoc* meetings to consult on specific issues or open access for individuals to contribute to the consideration of decisions.

The indirect forms of participation raise, as suggested above, many of the standard issues about representative democracy. Yet in some respects they are more difficult to resolve with reference to individual services and/or areas than they are at nation state level. As far as representative democracy is concerned most theorists, other than a minority of 'corporatists', resolve the question of who should participate by arguing that the system should be open to 'everyone'. However, if we examine similar debates in respect of participation in the management of individual services we often find that the arguments are complex (see Packwood, 1984, for example, on school management). What, for example, are the respective rights of employees and consumers?, and how does one define the consumer group when the composition of this group varies over time and in the extent of their involvement with the service? Hence, for example, determining participation in hospital or school management involves reaching some means of resolving each of these issues. They have to be resolved if, for example, an election process is to be involved, in respect of the determination of who is eligible to vote, who is eligible to stand for election, and what should be the balance between the respective constituencies. From a consideration of these issues it should come as no surprise that selection rather than election devices are often adopted.

Participation and sub-national government

In the discussion above participation was seen as likely to have both a service-specific and an area-specific dimension. Clearly there is a need to consider to what extent sub-national state organs of government are more appropriately analysed in terms of the issues about participation rather than as separately distinguishable political systems. Clearly they offer opportunities for citizen involvement in the policy process below the level of the nation state, and many advocates of increased participation argue for the extension and development of local democracy rather than in favour of a variety of service-specific and/or *ad hoc* forms of citizen involvement (see Stewart, 1983; Jones and Stewart, 1983). Yet those advocates may feel that to discuss them in the context of a section on participation is somehow to belittle local democracy.

It is also a little rash to try to generalize about central-local relationships in a brief section within a discussion of participation. This is a subject on which it is important to be sensitive to differences, between nation states, which have deep historical roots. An important distinction must be made between federal and unitary states, since the former group generally have written constitutions which were established and have evolved through argument, and sometimes violent conflict, between some constituent sub-national governments, about the respective powers of the various tiers in the system; but even that dichotomy oversimplifies. There are federal states where the constituent parts are very different and fiercely protective of their autonomy (Switzerland, for example). There are others where federalism was to some degree imported from outside at the end of a period of colonial domination (Australia) or a war (West Germany). The issue is also very much affected by geographical distance, since many federal states are very large (United States, Australia). On the other side there are unitary states were local government reorganization at the behest of central government has proved very difficult (Italy), but others where the centre seems to be able to rearrange local government areas and powers with relative ease (Great Britain). Our picture is further complicated by the extent to which central-local relations involve in any case not two tiers but three or more. Again constitutional and historical arrangements differ, particularly in the extent to which the centre may enjoy direct relationships with lower tiers that bypass intervening ones. Here Britain is perhaps an extreme case, with a structure in which districts are in no way accountable to the counties which contain them. But the United States is interesting in the extent to which federal initiatives have been able to bypass the states to relate to lower-tier local government units in ways unanticipated by the constitution. At the time of writing, however, Reagan's 'new federalism' involves a closing of this 'bypass' system.

What this brief selection of examples suggests, then, is that we must be cautious about generalization. However there is a sense in which in some societies local government has an autonomy derived from a central/local compromise, often taking a federalist form, whilst in others its autonomy is very limited and in many it makes most sense to see it as providing opportunities for local participation in a nationally determined political process. Switzerland and Great Britain perhaps offer the extremes in this continuum, with France running Britain close in this respect though often perceived as more centralized (see Ashford, 1982) and the United States running Switzerland close.

Recent analyses of central-local relations have portrayed these, just as Richardson portrays participation, as a bargaining process (Rhodes, 1979); but the use of a bargaining model has been challenged as misleading where central government is the dominant party, as in Britain (Elliott, 1981). What is interesting about the argument on this issue that has developed in Britain is the extent to which the phenomena which enhance the bargaining aspect of the relationship are particularly associated with the growth of social policy and the dispersal of power within the social policy delivery system. Some aspects of this were discussed in chapter 9, particularly with reference to professional power.

We have noted elsewhere in this book the extent to which the growth of social policy and the growth of state activity and expenditure are closely related. A significant feature of that growth, in many countries, has been the increase in the use of centrally raised cash to fund services which depend upon local government for their delivery. Britain is perhaps unusual in the extent to which certain key services were taken out of the hands of local government early in this process (the Poor Law and the health service, in particular), yet nevertheless other locally controlled services (education and the personal services, in particular) have still contributed to a marked growth in the need for central subventions to local government. In the United States similar developments transformed the role of the federal government, between the 1930s and the 1970s, towards a positive involvement in local service delivery requiring engagement with both state and local governments. This gave the federal government a new importance relative to the states in American society which was quite out of line with that envisaged by the writers of the American constitution. Its legitimation requried therefore both constitutional amendments and some creative reinterpretation of the constitution by the Supreme Court.

What this growth created was an important interdependency between central governments who provided the cash in the hope that their newly emergent policy goals would be met and the local-level officials who had responsibility for policy delivery. In extending services distant central governments were inevitably granting power to local agencies and officials to provide professional or bureaucratic interpretations of complex issues such as 'need'. Inevitably central departments did not just dish out money to local agencies: they sought to develop rules to determine its distribution amongst clients and services, and ways to inspect and control local actions. However, they clearly faced a control problem, and hence they might be described as placed in a situation in which they had to bargain. They had money, they wanted to spend it, but they were dependent upon the co-operation of people nearer to the service delivery end of the system.

At the local delivery end this situation enhanced the powers of local professionals and officials, placing them in a good position to enforce their claims to participate in the policy process; but the recipients of this new expenditure remained relatively powerless. They witnessed growing public bureaucracies upon whose 'largesse' they depended. Hence they argued for new forms of participation. Their arguments secured a response from central politicians and officials, particularly where they felt that resources were being prevented from reaching those whom they really wanted them to reach. Hence, for example, in the United States in the 1960s the early stages of the 'War on Poverty' involved the setting up of new participative institutions to bypass existing local government to try to ensure that federal funds really reached deprived groups (see Marris and Rein, 1967; Moynihan, 1969). Again, of course, this situation may be interpreted from a social control perspective (see Piven and Cloward, 1972): the federal government fearful of urban unrest, particularly amongst blacks, set out, by evading lower tiers of government and enhancing participation, to 'co-opt' black leaders (see also Katznelson, 1973). Another version of this approach, particularly evident in Britain, was to see the problems of deprivation as remediable by greater efforts on the part of the poor to help themselves. Participation was in this respect seen as morale-raising. This was a view evident in some of the early thinking about the Community Development Programme (see Higgins et al., 1983) and in some versions of the 'cycle of deprivation' theory popularized at central government level by Sir Keith Joseph in the early 1970s.

It would be wrong, however, to suggest that extensions of participation did not secure support at the local level, and from some of those responsible for the delivery of services. For many in these groups the extension of participation provided new allies in battles to secure support for services. In Britain the development in the 1970s of new forms of participation through Community Health Councils and through new arrangements for school management, for example, offered new ways to involve patients and parents in struggles for more resources. Radical groups within professions saw in participation new ways to challenge vested interests, committed to old approaches and practices. In some cases the cause of participation itself implied the creation of new occupational groups – community workers, community planners and researchers – with responsibilities for the exploration of needs and the stimulation of consumer organizations.

Hence, paradoxically, the participation cause came to be seen as a threat to national government as well as an ally of it. It particularly became a threat once the concerns of national government turned towards the need to curb and cut back public expenditure. Once that happened then forms of participation concerned with the amplification of the voice of the consumer became a more significant political nuisance. However, there are other participants than consumers, and as the 'New Right' became more significant in political controversy in countries such as Britain and the United States, so the 'taxpayers' revolt' emerged as a significant form of participation. In the United States Proposition 13 in California and Proposition 2½ in Massachusetts, for example, represented effective taxpayers' movements against public expenditure (Goodenough, 1982). Once, with Ronald Reagan in the White House, the new Right was effectively in control of the federal government in the United States, the New Federalism movement involved a turning of responsibility for much social policy expenditure away from the centre and back to the states. No longer could states cheerfully accept the growth of social expenditure, knowing that the federal government would largely foot the bill.

In Britain Mrs Thatcher's economic policies took Britain down a similar path. As public expenditure was cut the local-government-controlled sector was required to bear the greater part of the burden; but in Britain the local authorities were not left alone to choose to replace national grants with the proceeds of local taxation (rates). In the interests of control over public expenditure as a whole, and to prevent an increased rates burden for both individuals and private enterprises, the government devised successive measures first to penalize local authorities who increased their rates (Burgess and Travers, 1980; Jones and Stewart, 1983), and later to prohibit rate rises by the high-spending authorities (Bramley, 1984; Boddy and Fudge, 1984). These devices were developed after the government had explored devices to increase the scope for direct ratepayer control over expenditure, and had presumably decided that they were bound to be ineffectual (Department of the Environment, 1983).

These central control devices had the effect of bringing to a head arguments about the case for local democracy. The notion that Britain had a participatory system of local democracy, operating with powers delegated by central government but essentially able to give local services a local character and able to bargain with the centre on many policy implementation issues, was confounded by a central government determined, at least as far as the fundamental issue of local expenditure was concerned, to enforce its dominance (Jones and Stewart, 1983).

This confrontation has forced local authorities opposed to the Thatcher government, which means of course very largely Labour Party-controlled ones, to argue more forcefully than ever before the case for local democracy. It will be interesting to see to what extent this localist ideology feeds through into central Labour Party thinking. In the past Labour governments have probably been more inclined than Conservative ones to force their will upon local authorities. It was a Labour government which nationalized many local-government-controlled public utilities and health services in the 1940s, and a later Labour government sought to impose comprehensive education systems on reluctant local authorities. Will the Labour Party now become a coherent exponent of local democracy in Britain, and play an active role in the development of decentralization, as the Socialists have in France?

It may also be suggested that the New Right provokes new

thinking on participation in another sense. It champions markets as the ideal means by which individuals may participate, by offering market choices instead of bureaucratically determined services. This is an issue discussed earlier in the book. It may be further argued, however, that it is forcing the advocates of state-controlled services to look again at the way public agencies relate to the consumer. This focuses their attention upon the problems of accountability to the consumer where services are professional dominated and/or bureaucratically run. One reaction to this attack has been to seek ways of *decentralizing* public services so that they may be more accessible, and of decentralizing their formal control so that they may be more accountable. These may involve the development of neighbourhood-based departments bringing together a wide range of local services, and offering scope for community and consumer control.

Hence local decentralization programmes have been adopted by some Labour Party-controlled local authorities in Britain. At the time of writing these are still being very slowly and painfully developed in the face of considerable suspicion from the staff likely to be involved. Professionals are concerned about the attack upon their discretion implied by the development of neighbourhood teams of workers in which different professions will have to work together, professional supervision devices will be weakened and lay political control will be strengthened. A particular problem for these Labour-controlled authorities is that the trade unions, upon whose support the Party counts, are suspicious of decentralization inasmuch as it appears to threaten agreements which distinguish and protect the specific charac-teristics of the different jobs and professions. Finally it is both laudable and ironic that this commitment to decentralization has emerged at a time when the grass roots organization of the Labour Party has become exceptionally weak. To what extent will the local Party activists be prepared to countenance the development of neighbourhood-level participatory bodies if they cannot be sure of dominating them?

So we conclude our discussion of participation by looking at one way in which issues about local democracy and issues about participation are coming together in Britain in the 1980s, and perhaps bringing to a head some of the issues about alternative models of participation – should they be essentially extensions of representative democracy, or specifically involve forms of con-sumer participation, and in either case what do they imply for 'producer' participation?

Judicial or quasi-judicial devices as instruments for securing public accountability

Just as the 1960s saw the development of an intense interest in new forms of participation, so too it saw the exploration of the ways in which judicial processes might be used to enforce or secure 'rights' to public social benefits and services.

The dominant tradition, where attempts are made to define rights, is that of Locke and the United States Constitution. They are seen as essentially devices to protect people from government. It is liberty that is at stake, and the rights are defined negatively in terms of the things the state *should not* or *must not* do.

When, in the nineteenth and twentieth centuries, egalitarian and socialist writers began to challenge the Lockean view of the state,' they tended to rest their arguments upon a notion of *equality* which they saw as in conflict with some of the principles upon which arguments for *liberty* were based. They saw the liberal argument for the latter, robustly expounded in the nineteenth century by Bentham and the Mills, at best as something which would have to be compromised in the general good and at worst as merely a defence of the *status quo*.

Just as the defence of liberty was built into constitutions like the American one, so too was it built into the assumptions of those who sought to develop legal principles to help determine the proper boundaries of state intervention. Legal philosophers such as Dicey (1905; see also the discussion of lawyers' perspectives in Harlow and Rawlings, 1984) saw the growth of the 'collectivist state' as a threat to liberty, and the practical interventions of judges largely reflected that perspective whenever state interests and individual property rights conflicted. The Supreme Court of the United States upheld until the 1930s an interpretation of the constitution which was deeply suspicious of state action. The British law lords were similarly inclined to support property against the state.

However, some inroads developed into this very negative approach to the prerogatives of the state largely as a pragmatic response to the needs of wartime government. Perhaps more importantly the United States Supreme Court began to recognize, in a series of decisions between the 1930s and the 1960s, that situations might arise in which state action in defence of deprived and discriminated-against individuals might be justified in terms of other liberties than simply the negative one of freedom to do as you please with what you own. The concept of liberty was given a slightly wider construction and the positive role of the state was granted grudging and cautious acceptance in both Britain and the United States.

However, simply to allow the state rather wider freedom of action did not satisfy some libertarian lawyers. In the United States, perhaps earlier than in Britain, it was recognized that to have a powerful state alongside a powerful private sector did not necessarily assist powerless individuals. Perhaps one of the blind spots of the Fabian Socialism, dominant on the British Left in the 1940s and 1950s, was a belief that a strengthening of the state and a weakening of capitalism would in its wake extend equality and thereby greater liberty for the dispossessed.

The alternative American liberal delusion was a belief that legal processes, through which some key victories were won in the battle against racial discrimination, could be developed and extended in the war against poverty and disadvantage. In an influential article Charles Reich argued that the courts had a duty to protect individual rights both against the powerful state and against powerful private interests. He argued:

> The concept of right is most urgently needed with respect to benefits like unemployment compensation, public assistance and old age insurance. . . . Only by making such benefits into rights can the welfare state achieve its goal of providing a secure minimum basis for individual well-being and dignity in a society where each man cannot be wholly the master of his own destiny. (Reich, 1964, p. 786)

Reich wrote of these social benefits as a 'new property' which could therefore be embraced within the Lockean argument for rights. Reich is one of a number of legal theorists who can thus be seen as 'founding fathers' of what has been described as the 'welfare rights movement'. That movement saw a potential for the use of litigation to do two things: to win explicit rights through contesting decisions in courts and tribunals and to exert political influence through the publicity those legal battles might gain. It is important, to be fair to the movement, to state their goals in terms of these two objectives since many who were sceptical about the scope for success with the former nevertheless felt the latter made their action worthwhile.

The limits of the law

While there is a variety of avenues open for citizens to pursue their dissatisfaction with public services, the enforcement of rights through complaints and appeal processes is subject to many limitations. The procedures available are often inaccessible, or at least deter their use by underprivileged citizens. The legal system is not really oriented towards providing assistance with the search for welfare rights; and the problems associated with discretion cannot readily be tackled by judicial processes. The CDP report *Limits of the Law* puts the problems bluntly:

> The substance of the law may change but it continues to play a key role in preserving dominant interests. We must conclude that within our society the law functions primarily to protect and promote the interests of capital. The law is one of the main ways in which the state ensures order and compliance in an unfair, unequal and exploitative economic system. The 'rights' of workers, tenants, or the unemployed must be seen in this context. They are not rights to challenge the real processes which rule their lives, but rather pressures to conform and wait for better times. (CDP, 1977, p. 52)

The report goes on to suggest, however, that within the state there is a tension between interests, and that through the conflict between interests adaptation to changing circumstances occurs. The legal system plays a central role in that adaptation process:

> as it balances its internal self-interest against the overall need for change. This produces friction with other parts of the state and can create the illusion that working class interests can be secured through using legal action against local authorities or other government agencies. We can find no evidence to suggest that this is true in the long run. On the contrary it is likely that increasing the powers of the courts over other parts of the state like, for example, a Bill of Rights, would reduce the possibility of change. (CDP, 1977, p. 52)

Clearly this conclusion about the role of the law is based upon a neo-marxist interpretation of power within the state. In a useful analysis of the role of law in the enforcement of rights Richard White (in P. Morris et al., 1973) has conceded that with such a view of the state procedures which assert, and endeavour to extend, rights are valueless. He suggests two other views of the state (providing, in all, a three-part typology rather like that we used at the beginning of this chapter). One of these is a consensus one in which, he argues, the assertion of rights is virtually unnecessary. The other corresponds with a social democratic view of society 'in a state of dichotomous power and conflict between those with power, wealth and authority and those without it'. In this type of society 'a strong concept of rights is essential . . . they are crucial means by which individuals and groups enter the arena'.

White then goes on to base his arguments for the establishment of rights by means of judicial processes upon an assumption that our society corresponds with this model. Even if this assumption is accepted, the argument that flows from it evades an important problem. White talks of 'a basic agreement that conflict resolution can be achieved within a framework of negotiation, arbitration, judicial decision and electoral battle', and argues therefore for the importance of the widespread availability of legal services. The problem is that his model sounds very like a football match between relatively equal sides, using an agreed framework of rules and with an impartial referee. However, the now widely accepted critique of the pluralist model of society suggests, even if one decides not to go as far as those marxist views which stress dichotomous conflict, that the sides are clearly unequal, that the referee is more easily influenced by one side than the other, and that the rules may be changed during the game by processes which one side is more easily able to influence than the other (see chapter 8). Of course, there are differences of view about the extent to which there is 'bias' in the social system, and the extent to which conflict is dichotomous or multi-faceted; but surely political conflict is both about operation within the rules and about the making of the rules. To put it more concretely, it is all very well for White to argue that the development of legal services for all will help people to make the allocation of social security benefits or local authority houses, and so on, operate more equitably, but the problem is that the very forces in our society which make them operate unfairly redistribute legal services inequitably too. A political system in which legislators are ready to reform the procedures by which disadvantaged individuals are able to claim rights will also be one in which they are ready to liberalize the processes which make the claiming of rights so difficult.

Hence some wider sociological questions about the relationship between rights enshrined in the administrative system and the structure of power in society, have practical implications for attempts to use or to reinforce the law in order to advance particular interests. While Lewis and Livock (1979) have done valuable work in exposing the secret, inefficient, inequitable and paternalistic nature of the processes by which council houses are allocated, they do seem to bring us up against some more fundamental problems about rationing, under the supervision of local political machines, in conditions of scarcity. For example, the Thatcher government has shown a concern to extend local authority tenants' rights; it has also, however, cut council house building to the bone, and the most important right established for tenants is the right to buy houses, thus worsening the housing prospects of the least privileged in future generations.

Assuredly Norman Lewis would be the first to agree about some of these problems. Indeed he has argued for new concepts of 'lawyering' which give more attention to political realities (Lewis, 1979). On the other hand there are still many academic lawyers who approach topics like this from a standpoint of considerable political naivety. For example, a lawyer, with considerable expertise in housing law, gave a paper at a Social Administration Association conference at which he pointed out the many weaknesses in the Housing (Homeless Persons) Act. He went on to suggest that these could have been avoided if the policy had been more carefully worked out and the law better drafted. This paid no attention to the complexities of the political situation in which this measure became law, and above all to the extensive efforts of its opponents to include clauses – on 'intentional homelessness' for example – which would provide loopholes for those local authorities who were unenthusiastic about it.

Prosser has shown that in the United States welfare rights campaigners have had similar experiences to the British one (Prosser, 1983). Stuart Scheingold's book *The Politics of Rights* (1974) provides an important perspective on this subject. He stresses the importance of 'legal symbols' in the context of American government. Thus he sees the 'myth of rights', the 'ideological manifestation of law' as serving as some sort of guide for political action. He suggests that despite the fact that 'research casts doubt on the descriptive validity' of the myth of rights, suggesting that laws are 'delivered to us' by the dominant political coalition, nevertheless this myth serves first to provide opportunities for political interventions by those with rights to claim or protect and second to provide a rallying ground for the under-privileged and thus to assist 'political mobilization'.

In Britain Lewis (1979) has argued in a rather similar way that law-skills should be seen as political resources. He argues that 'there is a depressing lack of lawyer-theory directed to the problems of urban stress and social-political deprivation'. He goes on 'The lamented Community Development Programme pointed the way.' Is the CDP pamphlet 'The Limits of Law' to be interpreted in this way? Was the experience of trying to make inadequate law work to the benefit of deprived communities a radicalizing experience in which legal issues served as a rallying ground, a basis for mobilization? Or is the pamphlet a demonstration of the irrelevance of the legal issues in the face of the wider political issues? In fact its conclusion suggests that its writers share Scheingold's view of the relationship between the assertion of rights through legal processes and political action. It reads as follows:

> Change, whether local or far reaching, is won through political action, by people organizing together to challenge the structures and decisions which oppress them. CDP evidence shows that groups that have borne this in mind whilst planning their use of administrative or legal tactics have been able to secure important victories. (CDP, 1977, p. 52)

Legal victories are essentially gains for individuals; they are most unlikely to shift the balance of rights for whole groups of people. The 'welfare rights' movement developed from the use of legal action by radicals in the United States; but such gains as the latter achieved needed to be seen in the context of a written constitution and an independent Supreme Court. Furthermore the Supreme Court was a 'liberal' force in American politics during only a brief phase in its history. As the 'liberals' died a reactionary President, Nixon, was able to change the bias of the Court with new appointees.

Traditional legal arguments about enforcing rights seem to imply a process of securing what is recognizably available, in which case the use of formal grievance procedures should be quite sufficient. But welfare rights are seldom unambiguously *rights*. Most welfare rights campaigners have come to recognize that action through courts and tribunals can only be a part of a wider political struggle.

Conclusion

This concluding chapter to our book has linked together some important over-riding issues about the relationship between the individual and the social policy delivery process. We dealt first with issues about the various forms of participation available to citizens, which may allow forms of input into the general policy process. Then, in the second half of the chapter we dealt with ways in which individuals may influence specific decisions which have an impact upon them. In the course of doing that we showed that there are severe limitations upon the extent to which rights to welfare can be established or enforced.

Does this represent in any sense a general conclusion to the book as a whole? In our first chapter we stressed the extent to which the chapters in this book should be seen as a series of essays; therefore there is no real sense in which either a concluding chapter or a brief concluding section can sum up the book as a whole. We see this book as an exploration of the contribution of policy analysis to the study of social policy. It has tried to explore in some depth the concepts and theories, drawn from a number of different disciplines, which need to be used in such an activity. We have tried to avoid specific value judgements whilst doing this, but undoubtedly from time to time our values and commitments show through. Above all our commitment *to* social policy must have been self-evident. However, we have sought to show that social policy goals are complex, are not readily distinguishable from other kinds of policy goals, and need to be explored in relation to broad social, economic and political factors in any society. We have repeatedly stressed that social policy is ultimately a political matter. As such, it will inevitably continue to be the subject of argument and of conflict.

References

Abel-Smith, B. and Townsend, P. (1965) *The Poor and the Poorest*. London: Bell.

Abrams, P. (edited by M. Bulmer) (1984) 'Realities of neighbourhood care', *Policy and Politics*, 12(4), 413-30.

Adler, M. and Asquith, S. (eds) (1981) *Discretion and Welfare*. London: Heinemann.

Aiken, M. and Depré, R. (1980) 'Policy and politics in Belgian cities', *Policy and Politics*, 8(1), 73-106.

Aiken, M. and Mott, P. E. (eds) (1970) *The Structure of Community Power*. New York: Random House.

Alford, R. (1972) 'The political economy of health care: dynamics without change', *Politics and Society*, Winter.

Alford, R. (1975) 'Paradigms of relations between state and society', in L. N. Lindberg, R. Alford, C. Crouch and C. Offe (eds), *Stress and Contradictions in Modern Capitalism*. Lexington, Mass.: Lexington Books.

Alt, J. E. (1971) 'Some social and political correlates of county borough expenditures', *British Journal of Political Science*, pp. 49-62.

Anderson, J. E. (1975) *Public Policy Making*. London: Nelson.

Andrews, G. and Stonham, P. (1984) 'Warning to bus company on cuts in services', *Guardian*, 2 April, p. 24.

Arnstein, S. R. (1971) 'Eight rungs on the ladder of citizen participation', in E. S. Cahn and B. A. Passett (eds), *Citizen Participation*. London: Praeger.

Ashby, E. and Anderson, M. (1981) *The Politics of Clean Air*. Oxford: Oxford University Press.

Ashford, D. E. (1982) *British Dogmatism and French Pragmatism*. London: Allen and Unwin.

Ashford, D. E. (1984) 'The structural comparison of social policy and intergovernmental politics', *Policy and Politics*, 12(4), 369-90.

Atkinson, A. B. (1971) 'Policies for poverty', *Lloyds Bank Review*, p. 100.

Audit Commission (1984) *Improving Economy, Efficiency and Effectiveness in Local Government in England and Wales: Draft Audit Commission Handbook*, Volume II. London: Audit Commission for Local Authorities in England and Wales.

Audit Inspectorate (1983) *Social Services: Provision of Care to the Elderly*. London: HMSO.

Austin, D. M. (1983) 'The political economy of human services', *Policy and Politics*, 11(3), 343-60.

Bachrach, P. and Baratz, M. S. (1970) *Power and Poverty*. New York: Oxford University Press.

Bacon, R. and Eltis, W. (1976) *Britain's Economic Problem: Too Few Producers*. London: Macmillan.

Bailey, R. and Brake, M. (1975) *Radical Social Work*. London: Edward Arnold.

Bailey, S. J. (1982) 'Central city decline and the provision of education services', *Urban Studies*, 19, 263-71.

Bailey, S. J. (1984) 'The costs of sixth form rationalisation', *Policy and Politics*, 12, 53-69.

Barclay Report (1982) National Institute for Social Work. *Social Workers: Their Roles and Tasks*. London: Bedford Square Press.

Barnett, J. (1982) *Inside the Treasury*. London: André Deutsch.

Barr, N. A. (1981) 'Empirical definitions of the poverty line', *Policy and Politics*, 9(1), 1-22.

Barrett, S. (1979) *Implementation of the Community Land Scheme*. Bristol: SAUS Occasional Paper.

Barrett, S. and Fudge, C. (eds) (1981) *Policy and Action*. London: Methuen.

Barrett, S. and Hill, M. (1984) 'Policy, bargaining and structure in implementation theory: toward an integrated perspective', *Policy and Politics*, 12(3), 219-40.

Barry, B. (1965) *Political Argument*. London: Routledge and Kegan Paul.

Baumol, W. J. and Oates, W. E. (1979) *Economics, Environmental Policy and the Quality of Life*. Englewood Cliffs, NJ: Prentice-Hall.

Bebbington, A. and Davies, B. (1980) 'Territorial needs indicators: a new approach', *Journal of Social Policy*, 9, 145-168, 433-462.

Bennett, R. J. (1980) *The Geography of Public Finance: Welfare under fiscal federalism and local government*. London: Methuen.

Bennett, R. J. (1982) *Central Grants to Local Governments: the political and economic impact of the Rate Support Grant in England and Wales*. Cambridge: Cambridge University Press.

Berthoud, R. and Ermisch, J. (1984) 'Evidence from the Policy Studies Institute', in P. Kemp and N. Raynsford (eds), *Housing Benefit: The Evidence*. London: Housing Centre Trust.

Beveridge, W. H. (1942) *Social Insurance and Allied Services*, Cmnd 6404. London: HMSO.

Blackaby, F. (ed.) (1979) *Deindustrialisation*. London: Heinemann and National Institute for Economic and Social Research.

Blades, D. (1982) 'The hidden economy and the national accounts', *OECD Economic Outlook*, Occasional Studies, June, pp. 28-45.

Blake, D. and Ormerod, P. (1980) *The Economics of Prosperity*. London: Grant MacIntyre.

Boaden, N. (1971) *Urban Policy Making*. Cambridge: Cambridge University Press.

Boddy, M. (1980) *The Building Societies*. London: Macmillan.

Boddy, M. and Fudge, C. (eds) (1984) *Local Socialism?* London: Macmillan.

Bonjean, C. M., Clark, T. N. and Lineberry, R. L. (1971) *Community Politics: A Behavioural Approach*. New York: Macmillan.

Borcherding, T. E. (ed.) (1977) *Budgets and Bureaucrats*. Durham, North Carolina: Duke University Press.

Bouden, R. (1973) *Education, Opportunity and Social Inequality*. New York: Wiley.

Boyson, R. (ed.) (1971) *Down with the Poor*. London: Churchill Press.

Bradshaw, J. (1972) 'The concept of social need', *New Society*, 30 March, pp. 640-3.

Bramley, G. (1984) 'Local government in crisis: a review article', *Policy and Politics*, 12, 311-24.

Bramley, G. (1985) *Grant-related Expenditure and Recreation*, SAUS Working Paper 51. Bristol: School for Advanced Urban Studies.

Bramley, G. and Evans, A. W. (1981) 'Block grant: some unresolved issues', *Policy and Politics*, 9, 173-204.

Bramley, G., Evans, A. W., Lambert, C. and Leather, P. (1983) *Grant-related Expenditure: A Review of the System*. SAUS Working Paper 29. Bristol: School for Advanced Urban Studies.

Bramley, G. and Stewart, M. (1981) 'Implementing public expenditure cuts', in S. Barrett and C. Fudge (eds), *Policy and Action*. London: Methuen.

Breton, A. (1974) *The Economic Theory of Representative Government*. Chicago: Aldine.

Briggs, A. (1967) 'The welfare state in historical perspective', in C. I. Schottland (ed.), *The Welfare State*. New York: Harper and Row, pp. 25-45.

Brittan, S. (1975) 'The economic contradictions of democracy', *British Journal of Political Science*, 5(1).

Brittan, S. (1977) *The Economic Consequences of Democracy*. London: Temple Smith.

Brown, C. V. (1983) *Taxation and the Incentive to Work*. London: Oxford University Press.

Brown, M. K. (1981) 'The allocation of justice and police-citizen encounters', in C. T. Goodsell (ed.), *The Public Encounter*. Bloomington: Indiana University Press.

Buchanan, J. and Tullock, G. (1962) *The Calculus of Consent*. Ann Arbor: University of Michigan Press.

Buchanan, J. and Wagner, R. E. (1977) *Democracy in Deficit: the political legacy of Lord Keynes*. New York: Academic Press.

Bull, D. (1980) *What Price 'Free' Education*, Poverty pamphlet 48. London: Child Poverty Action Group.

Bull, D. (1980) 'The anti-discretion movement in Britain: fact or phantom', *Journal of Social Welfare Law*.

Burgess, T. and Travers, T. (1980) *Ten Billion Pounds: Whitehall's Takeover of the Town Halls*. London: Grant McIntyre.

Carrier, J. and Kendall, I. (1977) 'The development of welfare states: the production of plausible accounts', *Journal of Social Policy*, 6(3), 271-90.

Cawson, A. (1982) *Corporatism and Welfare*. London: Heinemann.

Cawson, A. and Saunders, P. (1983) 'Corporatism, competitive politics and class struggle', in R. King (ed.), *Capital and Politics*. London: Routledge and Kegan Paul.

CDP (Community Development Project) (1977a) *Gilding the Ghetto*. London: Home Office.

CDP (1977b) *Limits of the Law*. London: CDP Inter-Project Editorial Team.

Challis, D. J. (1981) 'The measurement of outcome in social care of the elderly', *Journal of Social Policy*, 10, 179-208.

Challis, L. (1983) *Regulation in Welfare: Purposive Control and Non-Purposive Influences on Private and Voluntary Homes for the Elderly*. Bath: University of Bath, School of Humanities and Social Sciences: Centre for Analysis of Social Policy.

Cheetham, J. and Hill, M. (1973) 'Community work: social realities and ethical dilemmas', *British Journal of Social Work*, 3(3), 331-48.

Cherry, G. (1973) *Town Planning in its Social Context*, Aylesbury: Leonard Hill.

CIPFA (1974) Output Measurement Research Working Party, *Output Measurement Discussion Papers 1-6*. London: Chartered Institute of Public Finance and Accountancy.

Collard, D. (1972) *Prices, Markets and Welfare*. London: Faber and Faber.

Collard, D. (1978) *Altruism and Economy: A Study in Non-selfish Economics*. Oxford: Martin Robertson.

Coombs, R. W. (1981) 'Innovation, automation and the long wave theory', *Futures*, October, 360-70.

Cooper, M. H. (1975) *Rationing Health Care*. London: Croom Helm.

Cooper, M. H. (1979) 'The demand and need for dental care', *Social*

Policy and Administration, 13, 91-104.

Coopers and Lybrand Associates (1981) *Service Provision and Pricing in Local Government: Studies in Local Environmental Services*. London: HMSO.

Craig, J. (1984) 'Which local authorities were alike in 1981?', *Population Trends*, 36, 25-39.

Crozier, M. (1964) *The Bureaucratic Phenomenon*. Chicago: University of Chicago Press.

Culyer, A. J. (1976) *Need and the National Health Service*. Oxford: Martin Robertson.

Culyer, A. J. (1980) *The Political Economy of Social Policy*. Oxford: Martin Robertson.

Culyer, A. J. (1983) 'Economics without economic man', *Social Policy and Administration*, 17, 188-203.

Culyer, A. J., Lavers, R. J. and Williams, A. (1972) 'Health indicators', in A. Shonfield and S. Shaw (eds), *Social Indicators and Social Policy*. London: Heinemann, pp. 94-118.

Cunningham, G. (1963) 'Policy and practice', *Public Administration*, 41, 229-38.

Cuthbertson, K. (1979) *Macroeconomic Policy: the new Cambridge Keynesian and monetarist controversies*. London: Macmillan.

Dahl, R. A. (1961) *Who Governs?* New Haven: Yale University Press.

Daniels, N. (ed.) (1978) *Reading Rawls*. Oxford: Blackwell.

Davies, B. (1968) *Social Needs and Resources in Local Services*. London: Michael Joseph.

Davies, B. with Reddin, M. (1978) *Universality, Selectivity and Effectiveness in Social Policy*. London: Heinemann.

Davies, T. and Mason, C., with Davies, L. (1984) *Government and Local Labour Market Policy Implementation*. Aldershot: Gower.

Deacon, A. and Bradshaw, J. (1983) *Reserved for the Poor*. Oxford: Blackwell.

Deacon, B. (1983) *Social Policy and Socialism: the struggle for socialist relations of welfare*. London: Pluto Press.

Delbeke, J. (1981) 'Recent long-wave theories: a critical survey', *Futures*, August, 246-56.

Dennis, N. (1958) 'The popularity of the neighbourhood community idea', *Sociological Review*, 6(2).

Department of the Environment (1976) *Transport Policy: A Consultation Document*. London: HMSO.

Department of the Environment (1977) *Housing Policy: a consultative document* (the 'Housing Policy Review'). Cmnd 6851. London: HMSO.

Department of the Environment (1983) *Rates: proposals for rate limitation and reform of the rating system*. Cmnd 9008. London: HMSO.

Department of Health and Social Security (1981) *A User's Guide to the Balance of Care Report*. London: HMSO.

Department of Transport (1984) *Buses*. Cmnd 9300. London: HMSO.

Deutscher, I. and Thompson, E. J. (eds) (1968) *Among the People: encounters with the poor*. New York: Basic Books.

Dicey, A. V. (1905) *Lectures on the Relation between Law and Public Opinion in England*. London: Macmillan.

Dilnot, A. W. and Morris, C. N. (1981) 'What do we know about the black economy?', *Fiscal Studies*, 2, 58-73.

Dilnot, A. W., Kay, J. A. and Morris, C. N. (1984) *The Reform of Social Security*. Oxford: Clarendon Press.

Djilas, M. (1957) *The New Class*. London: Thames and Hudson.

Donnison, D. (1979) 'Social policy since Titmuss', *Journal of Social Policy*, 8(2), 145-56.

Donnison, D. (1982) *The Politics of Poverty*. Oxford: Martin Robertson.

Donnison, D. (1984) 'The progressive potential of privatisation', in J. Le Grand and R. Robinson (eds), *Privatisation and the Welfare State*. London: George Allen and Unwin.

Downs, A. (1957) *An Economic Theory of Democracy*. New York: Harper and Row.

Downs, A. (1967) *Inside Bureaucracy*. Boston: Little Brown.

Doyal, L. and Gough, I. (1984) 'A theory of human needs', *Critical Social Policy*, 10 (Summer), 6-33.

Dunleavy, P. (1980) *Urban Political Analysis*. London: Macmillan.

Dunleavy, P. (1981) 'Professions and policy change: notes towards a model of ideological corporatism', *Public Administration Bulletin*, 36, 3-16.

Dunsire, A. (1978a) *Implementation in a Bureaucracy*. Oxford: Martin Robertson.

Dunsire, A. (1978b) *Control in a Bureaucracy*. Oxford: Martin Robertson.

Dye, T. (1976) *Policy Analysis*. Alabama: University of Alabama Press.

Easton, D. (1965) *A Systems Analysis of Political Life*. New York: John Wiley.

Economist (1982) 'Thatcher's think-tank takes aim at the welfare state', *Economist*, 18 September, pp. 25-6.

Edelman, M. (1971) *Politics as Symbolic Action*. Chicago: Markham.

Elliott, M. (1981) *The Role of Law in Central-Local Relations*. London: Social Science Research Council.

Elmore, R. (1980) 'Backward mapping: implementation research and policy decisions', *Political Science Quarterly*, 601-16.

Etzioni, A. (1969) *The Semi Professions and their Organization*. New York: Free Press.

Evans, A. W. (1985) 'Equalising grants for public transport subsidy', *Journal of Transport Economics and Policy*, May.

Eversley, D. (1973) *The Planner in Society*. London: Faber.

Family Policy Studies Centre (1984) *Fact Sheet – The Family Today: continuity and change*. London: Family Policy Studies Centre.

Feldstein, M. (1975) 'Wealth neutrality and local choice in public education', *American Economic Review*, 65, 75-89.

Finch, J. and Groves, D. (1980) 'Community care and the family: a case for equal opportunities', *Journal of Social Policy*, 9(4), 487-512.

Forrest, R. and Murie, A. (1983) *Right to Buy? Issues of need, equity and polarisation in the sale of council houses*. SAUS Working Paper 40. Bristol: School for Advanced Urban Studies.

Foster, C., Jackman, R. and Perlman, M. (1980) *Local Government Finance in a Unitary State*. London: George Allen and Unwin.

Foster, P. (1983) *Access to Welfare: An Introduction to Welfare Rationing*. London: Macmillan.

Fox, A. (1974) *Beyond Contract: Work, Power and Trust Relations*. London: Faber.

Frankenburg, R. (1971) *Communities in Britain*. Harmondsworth: Penguin Books.

Freeman, C., Clark, J. and Soete, L. (1982) *Unemployment and Technical Innovation: a study of long waves and economic development*. London: Frances Pinter.

Freidson, E. (1970) *Professional Dominance*. New York: Atherton.

Friend, J. K., Power, J. M. and Yewlett, C. J. L. (1974) *Public Planning: the Inter-Corporate Dimension*. London: Tavistock.

Furniss, N. and Tilton, T. (1977) *The Case for the Welfare State*. Bloomington, Indiana: University Press.

Galbraith, J. K. (1958) *The Affluent Society*. Harmondsworth: Penguin.

Galbraith, J. K. (1984) *The Anatomy of Power*. London: Hamish Hamilton.

George, V. and Wilding, P. (1984) *The Impact of Social Policy*. London: Routledge and Kegan Paul.

Gershuny, J. I. (1982) 'Social innovation: change in the mode of provision of services', *Futures*, December, 496-516.

Gershuny, J. I. (1983) *Social Innovation and the Division of Labour*. London: Oxford University Press.

Gershuny, J. I. and Pahl, R. E. (1980) 'Britain in the decade of the three economies', *New Society*, 51, 7-9.

Gilbert, B. B. (1966) *The Origins of National Insurance*. London: Michael Joseph.

Gilbert, B. B. (1970) *British Social Policy 1914-1939*. London: Batsford.

Glaister, S. (1984) 'The allocation of urban public transport subsidy', in J. Le Grand and R. Robinson (eds), *Privatisation and the Welfare State*. London: George Allen and Unwin.

Glennerster, H. (ed.) (1983) *The Future of the Welfare State*. London: Heinemann.

Goodenough, R. (1982) 'Proposition 13 and its impact on local government programmes in California', *Policy and Politics*, 10(4), 439-58.

Gordon, A. (1982) *Economics and Social Policy*. Oxford: Martin Robertson.

Gordon, I., Lewis, J. and Young, K. (1977) 'Perspectives on policy analysis', *Public Administration Bulletin*, 25 (December).

Gough, I. (1979) *The Political Economy of the Welfare State*. London: Macmillan.

Gould, A. (1981) 'The salaried middle class in the corporatist welfare state', *Policy and Politics*, 9(4), 401-18.

Greenwood, E. (1957) 'Attributes of a profession', *Social Work*, 2.

Gunn, L. (1978) 'Why is implementation so difficult?', *Management Services in Government*.

Hadley, R. and Hatch, S. (1981) *Social Welfare and the Failure of the State*. London: George Allen and Unwin.

Hall, A. S. (1974) *The Point of Entry*. London: George Allen and Unwin.

Hall, P., Land, H., Parker, R. and Webb, A. (1975) *Change, Choice and Conflict in Social Policy*. London: Heinemann.

Halsey, A. H. (1969) 'Government against poverty'. Unpublished paper presented to the Anglo-American conference on the Evaluation of Social Action Programmes.

Halsey, A. H., Heath, A. F. and Ridge, J. M. (1980) *Origins and Destinations*. Oxford: Oxford University Press.

Ham, A. (1981) *Treasury Rules: Recurrent Themes in British Economic Policy*. London: Quartet.

Ham, C. J. (1982) *Health Policy in Britain*. London: Macmillan.

Ham, C. and Hill, M. (1984) *The Policy Process in the Modern Capitalist State*. Brighton: Wheatsheaf.

Harlow, C. and Rawlings, R. (1984) *Law and Administration*. London: Weidenfeld and Nicolson.

Harris, J. (1977) *William Beveridge*. London: Oxford University Press.

Head, J. G. (1974) *Public Goods and the Public Sector*. Durham, N. Carolina: Duke University Press.

Heald, D. (1983) *Public Expenditure: Its Defence and Reform*. Oxford: Martin Robertson.

Heclo, H. (1972) 'Review article: policy analysis', *British Journal of Political Science*, 2.

Heclo, H, (1974) *Modern Social Politics in Britain and Sweden*. New Haven: Yale University Press.

Heclo, H. and Wildavsky, A. (1981) *The Private Government of Public Money*, 2nd edn. London: Macmillan.

Heidenheimer, A. J., Heclo, H. and Adams, C. T. (1983) *Comparative Public Policy: The Politics of Social Choice in Europe and America*,

2nd edn. New York: St. Martins Press.

Heinze, R. G. and Olk, T. (1982) 'Development of the informal economy: a strategy for resolving the crisis of the welfare state', *Futures*, June, pp. 189-203.

Heller, A. (1976) *The Theory of Need in Marx*. London: Allison and Busby.

Hendry, D. F. and Ericsson, N. R. (1983) 'Assertion without empirical basis: an econometric appraisal of Friedman and Schrantz's "Monetary trends in . . . the United Kingdom" ', in Bank of England, *Monetary Trends in the United Kingdom*. London: Bank of England.

Higgins, J. (1981) *States of Welfare: Comparative Analysis in Social Policy*. Oxford: Basil Blackwell and Martin Robertson.

Higgins, J., Deakin, N. and Edwards, J. (1983) *Government and Urban Poverty*. Oxford: Blackwell.

Hill, M. (1969) 'The exercise of discretion in the National Assistance Board', *Public Administration*, 47, 75-90.

Hill, M. (1983) *Understanding Social Policy*, 2nd edn. Oxford: Basil Blackwell and Martin Robertson.

Hill, M. (1984) 'The implementation of housing benefit', *Journal of Social Policy*, 13(3), 297-320.

Hill, M. J. and Issacharoff, R. (1971) *Community Action and Race Relations*. London: Oxford University Press.

Hillery, G. (1955) 'Definitions of community', *Rural Sociology*, 20.

Hirsch, F. and Goldthorpe, J. H. (1978) *The Political Economy of Inflation*. London: Martin Robertson.

Hjern, B. and Porter, D. O. (1981) 'Implementation structures: a new unit of administrative analysis', *Organisational Studies*, 2.

HMSO (1978) *Royal Commission on the Distribution of Income and Wealth: Sixth Report*. London: HMSO.

HM Treasury (1972) *Public Expenditure White Papers: Handbook on Methodology*. London: HMSO.

HM Treasury (1982) *The Government's Expenditure Plans 1982-3 to 1984-5*. Cmnd 8494. London: HMSO.

HM Treasury (1983) *The Government's Expenditure Plans 1983-4 to 1985-6*. Cmnd 8789. London: HMSO.

HM Treasury (1984) *The Next Ten Years: Public Expenditure and Taxation into the 1990s*. Cmnd 9189. London: HMSO.

Hochman, H. M. and Rogers, J. D. (1969) 'Pareto-optimal redistribution', *American Economic Review*, 59, 542-57.

Holme, A. and Maizels, J. (1978) *Social Workers and Volunteers*. London: George Allen and Unwin.

Hood, C. C. (1976) *The Limits of Administration*. London: Wiley.

House of Commons (1976) *First Report of the Expenditure Committee 1975-6 Session: The Financing of Public Expenditure, HC69-V*. London: HMSO.

House of Commons (1980) *Treasury and Civil Service Committee, Session 1979-80. Memoranda on Monetary Policy, HC720.* London: HMSO.

House of Commons (1981) *Treasury and Civil Service Committee, Third Report Session, 1980-1: Monetary Policy, HC163.* London: HMSO.

House of Commons (1982) *Sixth Report of Treasury and Civil Service Committee, Session 1981-2, Budgetary Reform, HC137.* London: HMSO.

IEA (Institute of Economic Affairs) (1978) *The Economics of Politics.* IEA Readings 18. London: IEA.

Illich, I. (1975) *Medical Nemesis.* London: Boyars.

Illich, I. (1978) *Towards an History of Needs.* New York: Pantheon.

Imber, V. (1977) *A Classification of the English Personal Social Services Authorities.* DHSS Statistical and Research Report Series 16. London: HMSO.

Jackman, R. and Sellars, M. (1978) 'Local expenditure and local discretion', *CES Review*, 3, 13-21.

Jackson, P. M. (1982) *The Political Economy of Bureaucracy.* London: Phillip Allan.

Jenkins, W. I. (1978) *Policy Analysis: A political and organisational perspective.* London: Martin Robertson.

Jenks, C. (1979) *Who Gets Ahead?* New York: Basic Books.

Johnson, M. (1983a) 'Private lives', *Health and Social Service Journal*, 28 July, pp. 901-3.

Johnson, M. (1983b) 'A sharper eye on private homes', *Health and Social Services Journal*, 4 August, pp. 930-32.

Johnson, T. J. (1972) *Professions and Power.* London: Macmillan.

Jones, C. (1983) *State Social Work and the Working Class.* London: Macmillan.

Jones, D. and Mayo, M. (eds) (1974) *Community Work: One.* London: Routledge and Kegan Paul.

Jones, G. and Stewart, J. (1983) *The Case for Local Government.* London: George Allen and Unwin.

Jordan, B. (1974) *Poor Parents.* London: Routledge and Kegan Paul.

Jowell, J. (1973) 'The legal control of administrative discretion', *Public Law*.

Jowell, R. and Airey, C. (1984) *British Social Attitudes: the 1984 Report.* Aldershot: Gower.

Judge, K. (1978) *Rationing Social Services: a study of resource allocation and the personal social services.* London: Heinemann.

Judge, K. (ed.) (1981a) *Pricing the Social Services.* London: Macmillan.

Judge, K. (1981b) *The Mixed Economy of Welfare: purchase of service contracting in the personal social services.* Discussion Paper 195. Canterbury, Kent: University of Kent, Personal Social Services Research Unit.

Judge, K. and Matthews, J. (1980) *Charging for Social Care*. London: George Allen and Unwin.

Judge, K., Smith, J. and Taylor-Gooby, P. (1983) 'Public opinion and the privatisation of welfare: some theoretical implications', *Journal of Social Policy*, 12, 469-90.

Kaldor, N. (1982) *The Scourge of Monetarism*. London: Oxford University Press.

Katznelson, I. (1973) *Black Men, White Cities*. London: Oxford University Press.

Kay, J. and King, M. A. (1983) *The British Tax System*, 3rd edn. London: Oxford University Press.

Keefe, A. (1971) 'Is the customer never right?' *Social Work Today*, 1, 23-8; reprinted in E. Butterworth and R. Holman (eds), *Social Welfare in Modern Britain*. London: Fontana (1975).

Kennedy, I. (1983) *Unmasking Medicine*. London: Granada.

King, A. (1975) 'Overload: problems of governing in the 1970s', *Political Studies*, 23 (2 and 3).

Kingsley, J. D. (1944) *Representative Bureaucracy*. Yellow Springs, Ohio: Antioch Press.

Klein, R. (1973) *Complaints against Doctors*. London: Knight.

Klein, R. and Lewis, J. (1976) *The Politics of Community Representation*. London: Centre for Studies in Social Policy.

Knapp, M. (1984) *The Economics of Social Care*. Oxford: Martin Robertson.

Knapp, M. and Missiakoulis, S. (1982) 'Inter-sectorial cost comparisons: day care for the elderly', *Journal of Social Policy*, 11, 335-54.

Knoepfel, P. and Larrue, C. (1984) *Les Politiques Publiques Comparees: Tourisme Intelligent ou vrai Progres*. Lausanne: Cahiers de l'Idheap, University of Lausanne.

Knoepfel, P. and Weidner, H. (1982) 'Formulation and implementation of air quality control programmes: patterns of interest consideration', *Policy and Politics*, 10(1), 85-109.

Krausz, E. (1971) *Ethnic Minorities in Britain*. London: McGibbon and Kee.

Laffer, A. B. and Seymour, J. P. (eds) (1979) *The Economics of the Tax Revolt*. New York: Harcourt Brace Jovanovitch.

Lambert, R. J. (1962) 'A Victorian national health service', *Historical Journal*, V.

Land, H. (1978) 'Who cares for the family', *Journal of Social Policy*, 7(3), 257-84.

Laver, M. (1979) *The Politics of Private Desires*. Harmondsworth: Penguin.

Layard, R. (ed.) (1972) *Cost Benefit Analysis: Selected Readings*. Harmondsworth: Penguin.

de Leeuw, F. (1971) 'The demand for housing: a review of cross-section evidence', *Review of Economics and Statistics*, 53.

Lees, R. and Smith, G. (eds) (1975) *Action Research in Community Development*. London: Routledge and Kegan Paul.

Le Grand, J. (1982) *The Strategy of Equality*. London: George Allen and Unwin.

Le Grand, J. and Robinson, R. (1976) *The Economics of Social Problems: the market versus the state*. London: Macmillan.

Le Grand, J. and Robinson, R. (eds) (1984) *Privatisation and the Welfare State*. London: George Allen and Unwin.

Leibenstein, H. (1976) *Beyond Economic Man: a new foundation for microeconomics*. Cambridge, Mass.: Harvard University Press.

Leiss, W. (1976) *The Limits of Satisfaction: An essay on the problem of needs and commodities*. Toronto: University of Toronto Press.

Lessnoff, M. H. (1974) *The Structure of Social Science: a philosophical introduction*. London: George Allen and Unwin.

Levitt, R. (1980) *The People's Voice: CHCs after Five Years*. London: Kings Fund.

Lewin, K. (1947) 'Frontiers in group dynamics. II: Channels in group social planning and action research', *Human Relations*, 1.

Lewis, N. (1979) *Towards a Sociology of Lawyering in Public Administration*. Unpublished paper given at Social Administration Association Conference.

Lewis, N. and Livock, R. (1979) 'Council house allocation procedures: some problems of discretion and control', *Urban Law and Policy*, 2, 133-74.

Leys, C. (1983) *Politics in Britain*. London: Heinemann.

Liebow, E. (1970) 'No man can live with the terrible knowledge that he is not needed', *New York Times Magazine*, 5 April.

Liesner, T. and King, M. (eds) (1975) *Indexing for Inflation*. London: Heinemann (for the Institute for Fiscal Studies).

Lind, G. and Wiseman, C. (1978) 'Settling health priorities: a review of concepts and approaches', *Journal of Social Policy*, 7, 411-40.

Lindberg, L. N., Alford, R., Crouch, C. and Offe, C. (eds) (1975) *Stress and Contradictions in Modern Capitalism*. Lexington, Mass.: Lexington Books.

Lindblom, C. (1979) 'Still muddling, not yet through', *Public Administration Review*, 517-25.

Lipset, S. M. (1950) *Agrarian Socialism*. Berkeley: University of California Press.

Lipset, S. M. (1960) *Political Man*. London: Heinemann.

Lipsky, M. (1980) *Street-level Bureaucracy*. New York: Russell Sage.

Lister, R. (1975) *Social Security: the case for reform*. London: Child Poverty Action Group.

Lord, R. (1983) *Value for Money in Education*. London: Public Money.

Lowi, T. A. (1972) 'Four systems of policy, politics and choice', *Public*

Administration Review, 32.

Lukes, S. (1974) *Power: A Radical View*. London: Macmillan.

Mack, J. and Lansley, S. (1985) *Poor Britain*. London: Allen and Unwin.

Mansbridge, J. J. (1981) *Beyond Adversary Democracy*. New York: Basic Books.

Marcuse, H. (1964) *One-dimensional Man*. London: Routledge and Kegan Paul.

Marris, P. and Rein, M. (1967) *Dilemmas of Social Reform*. London: Routledge and Kegan Paul.

Marshall, T. H. (1973) 'The philosophy and history of need', in R. W. Canvin and N. G. Pearson (eds), *Needs of the Elderly*. Exeter: University of Exeter.

Marshall, T. H. (1975) *Social Policy*, rev. edn. London: Hutchinson.

Marx, K. and Engels, F. (1848/1967) *The Communist Manifesto*. Harmondsworth: Penguin Books.

Maslow, A. H. (1943) 'A theory of human motivation', *Psychological Review*, 50, 370-96.

Matthew, G. K. (1971) 'Measuring need and evaluating services', in G. McLachlan (ed.), *Portfolio for Health*. London: Oxford University Press.

McLennan, G., Held, D. and Hall, S. (1984) *State and Society in Contemporary Britain*. Cambridge: Polity Press.

Meacher Committee (1983) Report of the Treasury and Civil Service Committee. *The Structure of Personal Income Taxation and Income Support*, HC386. London: HMSO.

Middlemas, K. (1979) *Politics in Industrial Society*. London: André Deutsch.

Miller, D. (1976) *Social Justice*. Oxford: Clarendon Press.

Mill, J. S. (1975) *Considerations on Representative Government*. London: Oxford University Press.

Mills, C. W. (1956) *The Power Elite*. New York: Oxford University Press.

Mishra, R. (1977) *Society and Social Policy*. London: Macmillan.

Morris, P. *et al.* (1973) *Social Needs and Legal Action*. London: Martin Robertson.

Mosley, P. (1984) *The Making of Economic Policy*. Brighton: Wheatsheaf.

Moynihan, D. P. (1969) *Maximum Feasible Misunderstanding*. New York: Free Press.

Mueller, D. C. (1976) 'Public choice: a survey', *Journal of Economic Literature*, 14(2) (June), 395-433.

Mulley, C. and Glaister, S. (1983) *Public Control of the British Bus Industry*. Aldershot: Gower.

Murray, N. (1984) 'Privates on parade', *Community Care*, 8 March.

Musgrave, R. A. and Musgrave, P. (1975) *Public Finance in Theory and Practice*, 3rd edn. New York: McGraw-Hill.

National Consumer Council (1984) *Of Benefit to All*. London: National Consumer Council.

Nevitt, A. A. (1977) 'Demand and need', in H. Heisler (ed.), *Foundations of Social Administration*. London: Macmillan.

Newton, K. and Sharpe, L. J. (1977) 'Local outputs: some reflections and proposals', *Policy and Politics*, March.

Niskanen, W. A. (1971) *Bureaucracy and Representative Government*. New York: Aldine- Atherton.

Nordlinger, E. A. (1981) *On the Autonomy of the Democratic State*. Cambridge, Mass.: Harvard University Press.

Nozick, R. (1974) *Anarchy, State and Utopia*. Oxford: Basil Blackwell.

O'Connor, J. (1973) *The Fiscal Crisis of the State*. New York: St Martins Press.

OECD (1981) *The Welfare State in Crisis* (an account of the Conference on Social Policies in the 1980s). Paris: Organisation for Economic Co-operation and Development.

Offe, C. (1984) *Contradictions of the Welfare State*. London: Hutchinson.

Olson, M. Jr. (1965) *The Logic of Collection Action: Public Goods and the Theory of Groups*. Cambridge, Mass.: Harvard University Press.

Orshansky, M. (1969) 'How poverty is measured', *Monthly Labour Review*, February.

Packwood, T. (1984) 'School governing bodies: a case of uncertainty', *Policy and Politics*, 12(3), 269-80.

Parry, N. and Parry, J. (1976) *The Rise of the Medical Profession*. London: Croom Helm.

Piachaud, D. (1981) 'Peter Townsend and the Holy Grail', *New Society*, 57, 419-21.

Piven, F. F. and Cloward, R. A. (1972) *Regulating the Poor*. London: Tavistock.

Plant, R., Lesser, H. and Taylor-Gooby, P. (1980) *Political Philosophy and Social Welfare Essays on the Normative Basis of Welfare Provision*. London: Routledge and Kegan Paul.

Pliatzky, L. (1982) *Getting and Spending: Public expenditure, employment and inflation*. Oxford: Blackwell.

Poulantzas, N. (1969) 'The problem of the capitalist state', *New Left Review*, 58.

Poulantzas, N. (1973) *Political Power and Social Classes*. London: New Left Books.

Pratt, V. (1978) *The Philosophy of the Social Sciences*. London: Methuen.

Pressman, J. and Wildavsky, A. (1973) *Implementation*. Berkeley: University of California Press.

3

Prosser, T. (1981) 'The politics of discretion: aspects of discretionary power in the supplementary benefits scheme', in M. Adler and S. Asquith (eds), *Discretion and Welfare*. London: Heinemann.

Prottas, J. M. (1979) *People-Processing*. Lexington, Mass.: Lexington Books.

Rawls, J. (1972) *A Theory of Justice*. Oxford: Clarendon Press.

Reich, C. (1964) 'The new property', *Yale Law Journal*, 73, 733 ff.

Reidy, A. (1984) 'Social justice and social policy', *Social Policy and Administration*, 18, 27-40.

Reisman, D. A. (1977) *Richard Titmuss: Welfare and Society*. London: Heinemann.

Rex, J. and Moore, R. (1967) *Race, Community and Conflict*. London: Oxford University Press.

Rex, J. and Tomlinson, S. (1979) *Colonial Immigrants in a British City*. London: Routledge and Kegan Paul.

Rhodes, R. A. W. (1979) 'Research into central-local relations in Britain: a framework for analysis', in *Report of the Social Science Research Council's Panel on Research on Central-Local Relations*. London: SSRC.

Richardson, A. (1979) 'Thinking about participation', *Policy and Politics*, 7(3), 227-44.

Richardson, A. (1983) *Participation*. London: Routledge and Kegan Paul.

Richardson, J. J. and Jordan, A. G. (1979) *Governing under Pressure*. Oxford: Martin Robertson.

Rimmer, L. (1981) *Families in Focus*. London: Study Commission on the Family.

Roberts, D. (1968) *Victorian Origins of the British Welfare State*. New Haven: Yale University Press.

Roberts, G. K. (1971) *A Dictionary of Political Analysis*. London: Longman.

Room, G. (1979) *The Sociology of Welfare*. Oxford: Blackwell.

Rowntree, B. S. (1901) *Poverty: A Study of Town Life*. London: Macmillan.

Rowntree, B. S. (1941) *Poverty and Progress*. London: Longman.

Rowntree, B. S. and Lavers, G. R. (1951) *Poverty and the Welfare State*. London: Longmans.

Ryan, A. (1970) *The Philosophy of the Social Sciences*. London: Macmillan.

Sabatier, P. and Mazmanian, D. (1979) 'The conditions of effective implementation: a guide to accomplishing policy objectives', *Policy Analysis*, 481-504.

Satyamurti, C. (1981) *Occupational Survival*. Oxford: Blackwell.

Saunders, P. (1981) *Social Theory and the Urban Question*. London: Hutchinson.

Saunders, P. and Dearlove, J. (1984) *An Introduction to British Politics: Analysing a Capitalist Democracy*. Cambridge: Polity Press.

Savas, E. S. (1980) 'Comparative costs of public and private enterprise in a municipal service', in W. J. Baumol (ed.), *Public and Private Enterprise in a Mixed Economy*. London: Macmillan.

Scheingold, S. (1974) *The Politics of Rights*. New Haven: Yale University Press.

Schumpeter, J. (1947) *Capitalism, Socialism and Democracy*, 2nd rev. edn. London: George Allen and Unwin.

Schumpeter, J. (1964) *Business Cycles*. New York: McGraw-Hill (1964 edition).

SDP (Social Democratic Party) (1982) *A New Deal for Britain: Attacking Poverty.* London: SDP.

Segal, L. (ed.) (1984) *What is to be done about the Family?* Harmondsworth: Penguin.

Seldon, A. (1977) *Charge!* London: Temple Smith.

Semmel, B. (1960) *Imperialism and Social Reform*. Cambridge, Mass.: Harvard University Press.

Shankland, G. (1980) *Our Secret Economy*. London/Bonn: Anglo-German Foundation.

Shankland, G., Willmott, P. and Jordan, D. (1977) *Inner London: Policies for Dispersal and Balance: Final Report of the Lambeth Inner Area Study*. London: HMSO.

Sharpe, L. J. and Newton, K. (1984) *Does Politics Matter?* Oxford: Clarendon Press.

Shaw, G. B. (1947) *The Doctor's Dilemma*. London: Constable.

Shonfield, A. and Shaw, S. (1972) *Social Indicators and Social Policy*. London: Heinemann.

Showler, B. and Sinfield, A. (eds) (1981) *The Workless State*. Oxford: Martin Robertson.

Simey, T. S. and Simey, M. B. (1960) *Charles Booth: Social Scientist*. Oxford: Oxford University Press.

Simmie, J. M. (1974) *Citizens in Conflict*. London: Hutchinson.

Simon, H. A. (1945) *Administrative Behaviour*. Glencoe, Ill.: Free Press.

Sinfield, A. (1978) 'Analyses in the social division of welfare', *Journal of Social Policy*, 7(2), 129-56.

Sinfield, A. (1981) *What Unemployment Means*. Oxford: Martin Robertson.

Sleeman, J. F. (1979) *Resources for the Welfare State: an economic introduction*. London: Longman.

Smith, G. (1980) *Social Need: Policy, Practice and Research*. London: Routledge and Kegan Paul.

Smith, K. (1984) *The British Economic Crisis*. Harmondsworth: Penguin Books.

Soper, K. (1981) *On Human Need*. Sussex: Harvester Press.

Spicker, P. (1984) *Stigma and Social Welfare*. Beckenham, Kent: Croom Helm.

Springborg, P. (1981) *The Problem of Human Needs and the Critique of Civilisation*. London: George Allen and Unwin.

Steinberg, J. (1976) *Why Switzerland?* Cambridge: Cambridge University Press.

Stewart, J. (1983) *Local Government: the conditions of local choice*. London: George Allen and Unwin.

Sugden, R. (1981) *The Political Economy of Public Choice*. Oxford: Martin Robertson.

Sugden, R. and Williams, A. (1978) *The Principles of Practical Cost-Benefit Analysis*. Oxford: Oxford University Press.

Taylor, P. (1959) ' "Need" statements', *Analysis*, 19, 106-11.

Thomas, D. N. (1983) *The Making of Community Work*. London: George Allen and Unwin.

Titmuss, R. M. (1963) *Essays on 'The Welfare State'*, 2nd edn. London: George Allen and Unwin.

Titmuss, R. M. (1968) *Commitment to Welfare*. London: Allen and Unwin.

Titmuss, R. M. (1973) *The Gift Relationship*. Harmondsworth: Penguin Books.

Tobin, J. (1970) 'On limiting the domain of inequality', *Journal of Law and Economics*, 13.

De Tocqueville, A. (1954) *Democracy in America* (trans H. Reeve and P. Bradley). New York: Vintage Books.

Townsend, P. (1975) 'The scope and limitations of means-tested social services in Britain', in *Sociology and Social Policy*. London: Allen Lane.

Townsend, P. (1979) *Poverty in the United Kingdom*. Harmondsworth: Penguin Books.

Townsend, P. (1984) *Why are the Many Poor?* Fabian Tract 500. London: Fabian Society.

Townsend, P. and Davidson, N. (eds) (1982) *Inequalities in Health: The Black Report*. Harmondsworth: Penguin Books.

Tullock, G. (1967) *The Politics of Bureaucracy*. New York: Public Affairs Press.

Tullock, G. (1976) *The Vote Motive*. London: Institute of Economic Affairs.

Walker, A. (ed.) (1982) *Community Care*. Oxford: Blackwell.

Walker, A. (1984) 'The political economy of privatisation', in J. Le Grand and R. Robinson (eds), *Privatisation and the Welfare State*. London: George Allen and Unwin.

Ward, T. S. and Neild, R. R. (1978) *The Measurement and Reform of Budgetary Policy*. London: Heinemann, for the Institute for Fiscal Studies.

236   *References*

Watson, D. (1980) *Caring for Strangers: an introduction to practical philosophy for students of social administration*. London: Routledge and Kegan Paul.

Weale, A. (1978) *Equality and Social Policy*. London: Routledge and Kegan Paul.

Weale, A. (1983) *Political Theory and Social Policy*. London: Macmillan.

Weatherley, R. (1979) *Reforming Special Education: Policy Implementation from State Level to Street Level*. Cambridge, Mass.: MIT Press.

Webb, A. and Wistow, G. (1982) *Whither State Welfare?* London: RIPA.

Webb, N. and Wybrow, R. (1981) *The Gallup Report*. London: Sphere.

Webber, R. and Craig, J. (1976) 'Which local authorities are alike?', *Population Trends*, 5, 13-19.

Weber, M. (1947) *The Theory of Social and Economic Organisation* (trans. A. M. Henderson and T. Parsons). Glencoe, Ill.: Free Press.

Webster, D. (1981) 'A social market in housing', *New Society*, 12 November.

Whiteley, P. (ed.) (1980) *Models of Political Economy*. London: Sage.

Whiteley, P. (1981) 'Public opinion and the demand for social welfare in Britain', *Journal of Social Policy*, 10, 453-76.

Whitmore, R. (1984) 'Modelling the policy/implementation distinction: the case of child abuse', *Policy and Politics*, 12, 241-66.

Wildavsky, A. (1964) *The Politics of the Budgetary Process*. Boston, Mass.: Little Brown.

Wildavsky, A. (1979) *The Art and Craft of Policy Analysis*. London: Macmillan.

Wilding, P. (1982) *Professional Power and Social Welfare*. London: Routledge and Kegan Paul.

Wilding, P. (ed.) (1983) *Thatcherism and the Poor*. London: Child Poverty Action Group.

Wilensky, H. (1975) *The Welfare State and Equality*. Berkeley, Calif.: University of California Press.

Williams, A. (1974) ' "Need" as a demand concept (with special reference to health)', in A. J. Culyer (ed.), *Economic Problems and Social Goals*. London: Martin Robertson, pp. 60-76.

Williams, A. and Anderson, R. (1975) *Efficiency in the Social Services*. Oxford: Basil Blackwell and Martin Robertson.

Williams, W. (1971) *Social Policy Research and Analysis*. New York: Elsevier.

Williamson, O. (1975) *Markets and Hierarchies: Analysis and Antitrust Implications*. New York: Free Press.

Wilson, E. (1977) *Women and the Welfare State*. London: Tavistock.

Winkler, J. (1976) 'Corporatism', in *Archives Européennes de Sociologie*, XVII(1).

Wolfe, A. (1977) *The Limits of Legitimacy*. New York: Free Press.

Wolff, R. P. (1977) *Understanding Rawls*. Princeton, NJ: Princeton University Press.

Woodroffe, K. (1962) *From Charity to Social Work in England and the United States*. London: Routledge and Kegan Paul.

Wright, M. (1977) 'Public expenditure in Britain: the crisis of control', *Public Administration*, 55, 143-70.

Young, M. and Willmott, P. (1957) *Family and Kinship in East London*. London: Routledge and Kegan Paul.

Index

market failure, 10, 108-9, 114
markets, 5, 65, 102-17, 123, 125, 176
Marx, K., 29-30, 151
marxian, marxist theories, 14-17, 27, 29-35, 75, 95-7, 150-3, 214
Maslow, A., 61, 64
means tests, 47-50
merit goods, 10
Mills, C. W., 150-1
mixed economy of welfare, 136; *see also* markets; privatization; voluntary sector
monetarism, monetarists, 12, 86-7, 99
Musgrave, R., 9-12, 141

National Health Service, 4, 121-2
need, concept of, 56-76
negative income tax, 49-50

O'Connor, J., 14-15, 31-2, 77, 95-7, 144-6
Offe, C., 35, 77, 145-6
opportunity cost, 186
organization failures, 197; *see also* implementation deficit
Organisation for Economic Co-operation and Development (OECD), 77, 88-95
outcomes, 74, 153
outputs, 153, 181, 187

'Pareto optimality', 58
participation, 202-11
pensions, 45-6, 48-50
performance comparisons, 187-95
personal social services, 4, 54, 122, 172
Piven, F. F. and Cloward, R. A., 31-2, 143
Plant, R. et al., 60-1
pluralism, pluralist theory, 107, 137, 149-51, 152-3, 197-8, 215
policy analysis, 1-2, 18-20, 218
policy implementation, 18-19, 137, 139-40, 147, 156-9, 160-76, 210
policy making, 18-20, 137-59
policy, meaning of, 2-3, 138-40

political business cycle, 98-9
political economy, 14-17, 95-101
'post-parliamentary democracy', 152-3
poverty, 39-54
poverty, definition of, 39-44, 63
poverty trap, 49-50
Pressman, J. and Wildavsky, A., 162
privatization, 103-7, 111-12, 116, 193
production models of social services, 194-5
productivity, 188-9; *see also* 'relative price effect'
professionalism, professionals, 35-6, 61-2, 107, 123, 131, 145, 153, 160-76, 207-9, 211
Prosser, T., 167, 216
public accountability, 175, 212-18
public choice theory, 98-101
public employees, 34-6, 99, 107, 112, 198-9, 205, 208
public expenditure, 5, 34, 51-4, 78-82, 88-95
public opinion surveys, 62
'public sector borrowing requirement' (PSBR), 85-6

rationing, 76, 103-4, 169, 171-2, 215-16
Rawls, J., 58-9, 74
redistribution, 11, 17-18, 38-9, 50-5, 141-4
regulation, 5, 13, 79, 105, 112-14, 141-4
Reich, C., 213
relative deprivation, 41-3
'relative price effect' (RPE), 81-2
residual role for state welfare, 104, 110, 112
Richardson, A., 204-5
Rowntree, S., 40-7

Scheingold, S., 216-17
self-help, 119
semi-professions, 170
Simon, H. A., 161, 164
Smith, G., 61